THE
SIX-YEAR
OFFENSIVE

THE SIX-YEAR OFFENSIVE

Bomber Command in World War Two

KEN DELVE AND PETER JACOBS

ARMS AND
ARMOUR

Arms and Armour Press
A Cassell Imprint
Villiers House, 41–47 Strand, London WC2N 5JE.

Distributed in Australia by Capricorn Link (Australia) Pty. Ltd, P.O.
Box 665, Lane Cove, New South Wales 2066.

British Library Cataloguing-in-Publication Data: a catalogue record for
this book is available from the British Library

ISBN 1-85409-142-5

Jacket illustration: *The Augsburg Raid* by Chris Stothard, depicting the
attack by Nos 44 and 97 Squadron Lancasters on the MAN factory at
Augsburg on 17 April 1942. The publishers gratefully acknowledge the
permission of No 44 (Rhodesia) Squadron to reproduce the painting,
which is currently on loan to RAF Waddington.

Printed in Great Britain by The Bath Press, Avon

CONTENTS

'There are no words with which I can do justice to the aircrew under my command. There is no parallel in warfare to such courage and determination in the face of danger over so prolonged a period.'
—Arthur T. Harris

FOREWORD

Albert Speer was from 1942 to 1945 the undisputed 'Master' of the German war machine in terms of raw materials, supply and manpower. While he was in Spandau Prison in 1959, a book on the Army Air Forces in Europe was smuggled into his cell. He felt that this book, like all the other accounts of the bombing he had read, missed the main point. The importance of the air war consisted in the fact that it opened up a second front, long before the invasion of Europe.

The Six Year Offensive excellently emphasizes that this front was the skies over Germany and occupied territories. The unpredictability of the attack made this front gigantic: every square metre of territory controlled by the Germans was a kind of front line. The book shows how Bomber Command took the war to Germany, demonstrating to the Germans, even when defeat followed defeat in other theatres of war, that the British people would not give up easily; and every bomb that fell on German soil was seen as a victory and a just reply for those that were falling on the UK.

The British public were certainly behind the Offensive, and the air crews had relatives who were proud that they were taking the war to Germany. If the German homeland had not been attacked, the enemy's resources and capability would have increased even more— and it is far better to fight over the enemy's territory, for then he has to defend it.

This book is fully illustrated and covers all aspects for the Bomber Command enthusiast and historian, from the top level to the air crew and ground crew on day-to-day operations. I would certainly recommend it to anyone who has an interest in what went on within Bomber Command during the Six-Year Offensive.

Flight Lieutenant William Reid, VC, BSc
Nos 61 and 617 Squadrons RAFVR
Syerston and Woodhall Spa

TO THE AIRCREW AND GROUNDCREW OF BOMBER COMMAND
1939–1945

AUTHORS' PREFACE

ON 3 SEPTEMBER 1939 the world entered the second of the devastating wars of the 20th century. It was a war that was to last almost six years and cost millions of lives; such was the upheaval that the world would never be the same again. Only one force on the Allied side was continuously involved with active operations against the German homeland—Royal Air Force Bomber Command. The day that war started a Blenheim of No 139 Squadron flew a reconnaissance sortie to locate German shipping. For the next six years Bomber Command took the war to the enemy, at first with limited effect but from 1942 with increasing resources and greater accuracy, and with an ever greater impact.

Bomber Command played a critical role at many stages of the conflict; some would argue that it was a war-winning part, although in many instances this was either misunderstood or misrepresented (both at the time and since). As with all military and military/ political relationships the problems of 'vested interest' arose to complicate the issues, sometimes with almost tragic consequences. Certainly, Bomber Command paid a heavy price for its non-stop participation: with forces of well over 5,000 aircrew involved night after night against strong and well organized defences, losses were bound to be high. The overall average loss rate was 4 per cent of aircraft dispatched, which translates into a human cost of 47,268 aircrew killed on operations, with a further 8,090 being lost on non-operational sorties (Air Ministry figures).

As Bomber Command's great wartime leader, Air Chief Marshal Sir Arthur Harris, so aptly said: '... an extraordinary lack of sense of proportion affects outside appreciation of the meaning, extent and results of Bomber Command operations. What shouts of victory would arise if a Commando wrecked the entire Renault factory in a night, with the loss of seven men! What credible assumptions of an early end to the war would follow upon the destruction of one-third of Cologne in an hour and a half by some swift mechanized force which with but 200 casualties withdrew and was ready to repeat the operation 24 hours later. What acclaim would greet the virtual destruction of Rostock and the Heinkel main and subsidiary factories by a naval bombardment. Yet there are many who still avert their gaze, pass on the other side, and question whether 30 squadrons of night bombers make any worthwhile contribution to the war.' After the war another of the great air leaders, Tedder, pointed out that 'the air war was being fought out over Germany not over Britain'. The initiative rested with those conducting offensive operations.

During this period of the 50th anniversary of the Second World War, and especially in view of the fact that 50 years ago, February 1942, Air Marshal Harris took command of Bomber Command, it seems appropriate to publish a new analysis. The 'Six-Year Offensive' is unique in the annals of military aviation; the story of Bomber Command is a central part of air power history. It is hoped that this book will go some way towards setting the record straight.

ACKNOWLEDGMENTS

The authors would like to thank all those ex-Bomber Command personnel, aircrew and groundcrew, who have given so freely of their time with questionnaires and interviews. Without your memories this story could not truly be told: Kenneth Pincott, Harry Parsons, Ron Tettenborn, Harry Hull, Lawrence Stow, Dennis Merry, Neil Scott, Peter Rowland, Cryil Kelly, James Major-Dunkley, Tom Wingham, George Dove, Les Bartlett, Arthur Simmonds, Arthur Tindall, David Oliver, Ken Sockett, Robert Roberts, T. Williamson, Ian Anderson, Ossie Stewart, Stan Bradford, John Gee, Les Webber, Les Mims, Nick Knilans, Jack Dixon, John Carson, Bill Seymour, C. Spalding, James Stark, Jack Dixon, Cambell Muirhead, F. Slater, Reg Thackeray, Tom Treadwell and Robert Hart—and many others (our apologies for not listing you all!).

As usual, the staff of the Air Historical Branch, London, have been of enormous help with source material. The authors have spent much time going through a wide range of such material; too often 'old' attitudes and views and have been re-treaded from one published work to another. The photographic collection has come largely from squadron records, individuals, and the Peter Green Collection. Thanks to you all.

Bomber Command raid statistics are based on those given in *Bomber Command War Diaries*, by Martin Middlebrook and Chris Everitt. We thank them for permission to use their data.

The authors appreciate that a history of a topic such as this will generate interest—perhaps controversy—and would welcome correspondence from those who feel that they can add to the story in words or pictures. Aviation history is an on-going subject!

Ken Delve and Peter Jacobs

CHAPTER ONE

The Development of British Strategic Bombing Theory

IN THE YEARS following the First World War, and particularly in the 1920s, a great deal was written about the future application of air power, theories based upon the experiences gained in the latter years of the 'war to end all wars'. It was the belief of many that the future lay with the bomber and that a co-ordinated bombing offensive would be the deciding factor in any future conflict. However, by the late 1920s and early 1930s the doctrine for the application of air power was changing in certain European countries, notably Germany, and strategic doctrine was not as clear-cut as once it had seemed. To achieve an understanding of Bomber Command as it existed in 1939, it is essential to examine the origins and development of British strategic bombing theory.

THE GENESIS OF BOMBER COMMAND

On 19 January 1915 two German naval airships bombed targets in East Anglia, the greatest damage being done in King's Lynn. It was a severe shock to a nation used to being immune from attack. A few months later, on 31 May, the first attack on London took place, again causing little damage and few casualties but having enormous pyschological impact. The effects of the German Zeppelin raids on London and, more significantly, the heavy bomber raids of 1918, were vastly overrated by both sides. In Germany the early raids were hailed with headlines such as 'England No Longer an Island—a statement that was not lost on the British public who had been used to the security which the Channel had for centuries given them. Public reaction and press over-reaction brought intense pressure on the authorities to create an effective defence. The establishment of an aeroplane defence system around London took place in the spring of 1916 with the formation of No 39 (Home Defence) Squadron RFC. On the night of 2/3 September 1916, 2nd Lieutenant William Leefe Robinson, flying a B.E.2c, shot down the airship SL11—to the great delight of the watching Londoners. A grateful nation awarded him the Victoria Cross, a reflection of the relief that the previously untouchable threat had been countered. In the space of four weeks the squadron destroyed a further three airships. The second round of the strategic bombing campaign had been won by the defences. However, as post-war analysis showed, as soon as the defences were able to cope with a particular threat then a new one developed—with the 'bomber' always seeming to have the upper hand.

As early as September 1916 Trenchard had outlined a possible doctrine for the Royal Flying Corps: 'Even with an unlimited number of machines for defensive purposes, it would still be impossible to prevent hostile machines from crossing the line if they were determined to do so, simply because the sky is too large to defend.' He went on to suggest that the only solution was to go onto the offensive behind the enemy lines: in this way the enemy would be compelled to divert his own aircraft from offence to defence—but would fail to achieve any real result. Other voices cried from a different perspective, including that of Field Marshal Haig: 'Long-distance bombing as a means of defeating the enemy is entirely secondary to the requirements of the army; its success is far more doubtful and, even when successful, both theory and practice go to show that usually the results are comparatively unimportant.' Nevertheless, a number of successful, albeit small-scale, strategic raids were carried out by the Royal Naval Air Service, and these showed what could be achieved. The RNAS had in fact been the pioneers in strategic bombing, and to meet their requirements the Handley Page O/100 and O/400 had been developed—Britain's first long-range heavy bombers.

The British heavy bombing offensive had not really begun by the end of the war (when less than 5 per cent of British aircraft strength comprised true 'bombers'), other than operations by the Independent Force. In October 1918 the Independent Force consisted of 125 bombers, including many of poor performance and bomb load, and their early operations had brought little success but many problems. There was insufficient intelligence on which to base target planning, although a French plan of 1917 had highlighted the Ruhr as a prime target area. Trenchard decreed that attacks should concentrate on as many of the large industrial centres as were within reach, in order to affect German morale and tie down resources.

Despite the lack of conclusive answers to many vital questions, it was nevertheless a widely held belief that the future lay with the bomber. In the inter-service wranglings over the post-war composition of the British Armed Forces, when the Navy and Army tried as hard as they could to kill off the young Royal Air Force and absorb those parts of air power which they considered

Handley Page O/400 of No 100 Squadron, 1919. Inherited from the RNAS, this type was the RAF's first heavy bomber. [100 Sqn records]

power strategists on both sides of the Channel, and in America, with claims that the bomber would always be decisive and unbeatable—'the bomber will always get through'. Perhaps the greatest of these strategic thinkers was the Italian, General Douhet, and his writings provided the basis of many of the air plans being laid in the capitals of Europe. The British Air Staff needed no convincing; it was their theory that 'The strategic air offensive is a means of direct attack on the enemy state with the object of depriving it of the means or will to continue the war. It may in itself be the instrument of victory or it may be the means by which victory can be won by other forces. It differs from all previous kinds of armed attack in that it alone can be brought to bear immediately, directly and destructively against the heartland of the enemy.'

The 'proof' of this philosophy appeared in every exercise held in the UK; waves of 'heavily armed' bombers attacked targets defended by fighters whose performance hardly bettered that of their opponents. While some of the bombers were 'shot down', enough got through to the targets to create 'massive' destruction. Despite the conviction that here was the war-winner, it was not until the early 1930s that the RAF began to replace its outdated biplane bombers, and even then performance specifications were very low. The period from 1922 to 1932 was very difficult for the

important, the need for an independent control of this war-winning weapon, the bomber, was one of the factors used by Trenchard to secure the future of his service. It was inevitable, therefore, that when he was successful the 'Trenchard Doctrine' should become firmly established and enhanced: '... the nation that would stand being bombed longest would win in the end ... to win it will be necessary to pursue a relentless offensive by bombing the enemy's country, destroying his sources of supply of aircraft and engines, and breaking the morale of his people.'

Bomber theory was enhanced in the 1920s by air

Standard day bomber of the 1920s was the D.H.9A—here from No 39 Squadron.

planners; the politicians had little interest in things military, working on the 'no major war for at least ten years' principle, and the world economic situation left little flexibility for any alternative policy.

During this period there were some, almost lone, voices seeking changes in the way the bomber force was organized and employed. Among them was the Officer Commanding No 58 Squadron, Arthur Harris, who suggested that, 'flying in formation, night bombers would be better able to defend themselves when returning in daylight or twilight from long raids, and would navigate more accurately in war since the lowering of navigation standards might be offset by the few really good navigators being able to guide the rest of the squadron to the target.'

A significant memo was put forward in May 1928 by Trenchard. It opened in an attacking style: 'An un-willingness on the part of the other services to accept the contention of the Air Staff that in future wars air attacks would most certainly be carried out against the vital centres of commerce and of the manufacture of munitions of war of every sort no matter where these centres were situated.' He went on to declare that the RAF doctrine was 'to break down the enemy means of resistance by attacks on objectives selected as most likely to achieve this end'. It was better, he believed, to attack military targets at 'source' (the factories) rather than in the field; it would have greater effect for less effort, and would include 'persuading' workers to stop working; further, 'The Hague Commission allows for military targets, including production centres. What is illegitimate, as being contrary to the dictates of humanity, is the indiscriminate bombing of a city for the sole purpose of terrorizing the civilian population'. The heads of the other services replied in kind, the Chief of the Imperial General Staff commenting that 'It is ridiculous to contend that the dropping of bombs has reached such a stage of accuracy as to ensure that the bombs would hit only the so-called military targets'. The Chief of the Naval Staff replied in similar fashion, and both stressed the problems of being bombed in return.

A variety of expansion schemes had been proposed from the mid-1920s onwards but there was little impetus to see them come to fruition. It needed a major political change to bring action. This change came in the early 1930s with the rapid collapse of the international security system, the first major break being Japan's seizure of Manchuria in 1931. Throughout the 1920s there had been real moral, as well as economic, pressure to restrict military expansion and political adventuring. A genuine desire for peace led to comprehensive armaments treaties and humanitarian agreements such as the 1923 Hague Commission on the restriction of bombing. With the Nazi party's rise to power, Hitler becoming Chancellor in 1933, the stage was set for future conflict.

EXPANSION SCHEMES

While the RAF saw the bomber as a strategic weapon, operating primarily independently of ground and naval forces, in the rapidly rearming Germany of the 1930s the doctrine of air power application had switched more towards co-operation with other arms—i.e., a tactical application. This, however, is a somewhat contentious point; in the early years the reborn Luftwaffe was controlled by non-aviation general officers, who under-standably were inclined to look to their previous experience. Nevertheless, there were strong elements in the Luftwaffe and Nazi party who saw a more devasta-ting role for air power—fleets of aircraft laying waste enemy territory, much more in keeping with the general concept of strategic air power! Eventually, it was needs must with regard to limited resources and the strategic bombers under development were put on hold, a mistake which some have seen as central to the overall failure of German strategy.

By the mid-1930s it was obvious even to the ostrich-like British politicians that Europe was not as peaceful as it had appeared to be and at long last, and perhaps too late, major rearmament plans were given greater impetus. It was not before time. In March 1933 the RAF's fully operational home bomber force comprised a mere five night bomber squadrons and six day bomber squadrons. The state of the equipment itself gave no

D.H.9As of No 47 Squadron over Mesopotamia. [47 Sqn records]

Above: The heavy bombers progress towards their target, fighting off enemy aircraft. Vickers Virginias of No 58 Squadron during an exercise. [58 Sqn records]

Below: Many of the future bomber commanders developed their ideas during 'policing' actions in Mesopotamia and India. Hawker Harts of No 39 Squadron over the North-West Frontier Province.

Above right: Hendon 1932, a display of the latest types entering RAF service, included only one operational monoplane, the Fairey Hendon (right foreground).

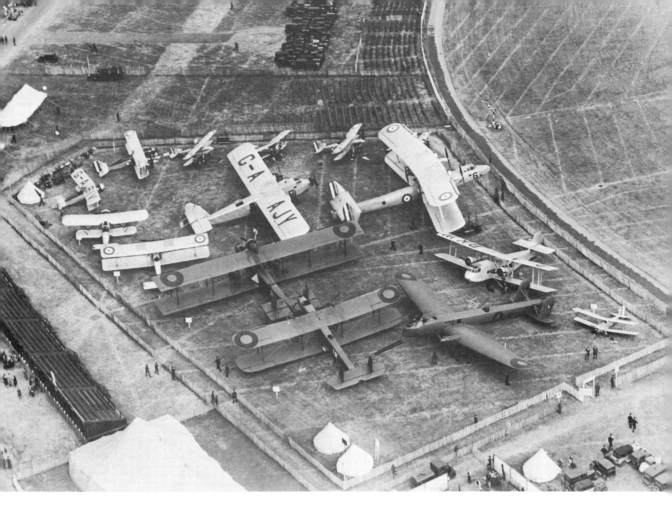

grounds for confidence either. The Westland Wapiti and Hawker Hart day bombers, both excellent machines in their time, were out of place in the early 1930s. The Vickers Virginia heavy bombers of the night squadrons were little better, having a top speed of only 108mph at 5,000ft and a bomb load of just over 3,000lb. Training and tactics were unrealistic; the bombers were expected to win in exercises—and so they did. Without ciné guns in the bombers it was difficult to assess their success against the fighter interceptions. Bombing on the ranges was—as peacetime bombing always is—too easy, against a fixed, well-known target, and with no struggles against the weather, decoys and defences. The theoretical accuracy, even at night, looked good on paper, against the smallest of targets. Bombsights and bombs had changed little since the First World War—both were inadequate. As for bombs, the Air Staff had ruled in 1932 that there would be no requirement for a bomb heavier than 500lb and that the 250lb bomb would be the standard weapon. In almost all other areas of military development the situation was the same—stagnation.

In October 1932 the Air Ministry had issued Specification B.9/32 for a twin-engined medium bomber of good performance and long range; the actual figures of 1,000lb bomb load and 720 miles' range do not appear as progressive as the introduction might suggest. One problem was that the aircraft's all-up weight was limited to 6,300lb in accordance with international agreements. However, this specification led in due course to two aircraft that were to become the mainstays of Bomber Command's strategic bomber force for the first three years of the war—the Vickers Wellington and the Handley Page Hampden.

A Foreign Office appraisal of 1933 stated that Germany, '. . . controlled by a frenzied nationalism and resolved to assert her rights to full equality, will proceed to the building of formidable armaments on land and especially in the air'. A Chiefs of Staff review in October the same year agreed, but saw the danger as longer term; apart from which there was a need for Britain to rearm all aspects of her forces to ensure the security of her world-wide commitments. The 'one-power' standard, aimed for many years at France, now looked inappropriate. The Government suggested that the military draw up their expansion plans and present them for consideration. The Defence Requirements Committee sat from November to February. Its report gave priority to the establishment by the RAF of a Home Defence force strong enough to counter any attack (it is im-

HANDLEY PAGE HEYFORD

A few months before the outbreak of war the RAF phased out of front-line service the last of the ungainly Heyford biplane bombers. The type had been operational for six years, having entered service with No 99 Squadron in November 1933 at Upper Heyford. It was the culmination of a series of large biplane bombers from the Handley Page stable which could be traced back to the RNAS's O/400 of the latter years of World War One—the aircraft with which the RAF developed its theories of strategic bombing.

Developed from the HP.38, the Heyford was designed to Specification 23/32 and the prototype (K3489) first flew in June 1933. With the unusual arrangement of the fuselage being attached to the upper rather than lower wing, large spats on the wheels and a rather square fuselage, it was not a very attractive aircraft. One of its few advanced features was the arrangement for internal bomb carriage, in cells in the centre-section of the lower wing. Having been given 'all round' protection with Lewis guns in three positions, the Heyford was considered to be well able to fight its way through to the target—where it would cruise around in daylight at around 10,000 feet until able to drop its bombs.

Heyfords at Finningley, late 1936. The airfield is in the process of being built.

HEYFORD IA DATA
Crew: Four
Engines: Two 575hp Rolls-Royce Kestrel IIIS
Span: 75ft
Length: 58ft
Height: 17ft 6in
Weight empty: 9,200lb
Weight loaded: 16,900lb

Max. speed: 142mph at 13,000ft
Ceiling: 21,000ft
Range: 920 miles with 1,600lb bomb load
Armament: Up to three Lewis guns in nose, dorsal and ventral (dustbin) positions. 3,500lb max. bomb load

Squadrons (Bomber Command): Nos 7, 9, 10, 38, 78, 97, 99, 102, 148, 149, 166

portant to appreciate here that Home Defence included an offensive bombing force as a central element). The failure of Chamberlain's Air Pact, whereby the states of Europe would promise not to drop bombs on each other's territory, gave further impetus to expansion plans. July 1934 brought Expansion Scheme A, under which the RAF would be ready for war in eight years' time. It provided the basis for a deterrent force plus the foundation of a training establishment as the basis for further expansion; this was probably the single most important decision taken during this period, and one that was to prove critical to success.

With Germany identified as the most likely opponent, there was a need to develop aircraft with the range and performance to attack targets in the Ruhr and Rhineland. Acceptance of the requirement was one thing, funding the re-equipment quite another; there simply was not enough money available for the preferred solutions to be put into effect. The net result of this was a policy of numbers not quality, the idea being that the latter would follow in due course as more funding became available and superior aircraft types were in production. The problem was illustrated by comparing the cost of twelve Hart light bombers (£245,000 to acquire and £83,000 a year to run) with that of ten Virginia heavy bombers (£375,000 to acquire and £139,000 a year to run). With a revised estimate of the German expansion and capability, the RAF scheme was re-examined and in May 1935 Expansion Scheme C gave a 'programme of requirements in which financial considerations were to be secondary to the attainment

of the earliest possible security'. Two months later the Air Staff outlined a strategic doctrine: 'Provided a sufficient weight of air attack could be brought to bear on the Rhineland–Ruhr–Saar area, Germany's armament industry would be paralysed, which would in turn preclude her from maintaining an army in the field'— thus maintaining the doctrine of attack to defend.

In 1935 the major elements of the offensive bombing force comprised squadrons of Handley Page Heyfords and Virginias. Even the latest 'hot ship', the Fairey Hendon night bomber, which was notable as being the first all-metal low-wing monoplane bomber to enter RAF squadron service (in November 1936), had a top speed of only 155mph and a bomb load of only 1,660lb. Of the 350 aircraft on show at the King's Jubilee Review in July 1935, *all* were obsolete biplanes and the fastest of them, the Gloster Gauntlet fighter at 231mph, had not yet reached the squadrons. However, 1935 was to prove the watershed year as aircraft manufacturers came to grips with new technology and presented a variety of advanced types for consideration.

The political will was slowly changing and, whereas two years previously little progress could have been made, there was now a realization that the situation had become serious. Rearmament was behind schedule, although revised Expansion Schemes appeared at regular intervals, including Scheme F which saw the bomber element as an offensive rather than counter-offensive (part of Home Defence) weapon, 'to make it a principal weapon for winning the war on the continent of Europe'. Dated February 1936, this scheme included provision for 68 bomber squadrons, with 990 aircraft, scheduled for completion by March 1939.

In July the same year came a major change of structure with the formation of new Commands, including Bomber Command which came into existence on 14 July. Bomber Command's first commander was Sir John Steel and his HQ was established at Uxbridge, although this was moved to High Wycombe in September 1937. It was also a year of great change in Europe as the Germans marched back into the Rhineland, with hardly a murmur from the Western powers; the threat of German arms served to keep the other European states in check while their own military expansion took place.

In Britain this brought another rash of expansion schemes, during 1937 the most important being Scheme H; this was the highpoint of suggested bomber strength, proposing 90 squadrons with a strength of 1,659 aircraft—but not due for completion unti 1943. However, continued problems of translating paper plans into reality caused a re-think. The aircraft were simply not available. For years the aircraft manufacturers had struggled against official indifference and a paucity of orders for aircraft, and no impetus for new ideas and types. This situation could not be reversed overnight; it would take time for new designs to come to fruition, and even longer for them to be produced in quantity.

There had also been a gradual conversion amongst the Air Staff towards the concept of fewer but more powerful bombers, the genesis of the 'all heavy bomber' philosophy which was to become central to Bomber Command planning. Figures supporting this conclusion showed that a squadron of twelve light bombers could deliver 6,000lb of bombs whereas a squadron of ten of the new heavy bombers (to Specification B.1/35) could deliver 20,000lb. The death-knell of the light bomber had been sounded by Sir John Ellington (Chief of the Air Staff) at the end of 1935, when it was decided that the medium bomber would in future be the backbone of the bomber force. The question of even larger and more powerful bombers caused much discussion at Air Ministry and Cabinet level. However, the go-ahead was given and Specification B.12/36 was issued for a four-engined aircraft of 100ft wingspan (a maximum figure, dictated by existing RAF hangar door size), 47,000lb all-up weight and 230mph cruising speed and with a range of 1,500 miles. The aircraft was also to have the latest navigation equipment, and three power-operated gun turrets including a four-gun tail turret. It was a huge advance on anything previously proposed, but it would be some years before it was ready. In the meantime the expansion had to go ahead with whatever was available. The 90-squadron plan was questioned by Sir Thomas Inskip on the grounds of cost and also from a conviction

No 76 Squadron in the late 1930s with one of the RAF's most advanced bombers, the Vickers Wellesley. [RAF Finningley records]

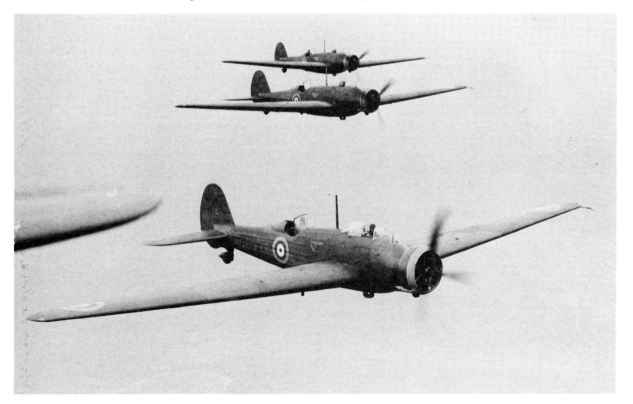

BRISTOL BLENHEIM

Developed from a private-venture design, the Blenheim was intended to enter RAF service as a light bomber. When it first flew in June 1936 it outperformed most of the RAF's current fighters. The design appeared at a time when the need for rearmament and modernization of the RAF had finally been realized; hence it was ordered into production straight off the drawing-board with an order for 150 being placed in August 1935. Just less than one year later, 25 June 1936, the prototype (K7033) took to the air.

Development was rapid and in March 1937 No 114 Squadron at Wyton became the first RAF squadron to operate this advanced aircraft. A total of 1,134 Blenheim Mk Is were built and despite the severe limitations which became clear as more modern fighter aircraft appeared, the Blenheim was a vital link in bringing the RAF bomber forces into a position from which they could move forward to more advanced types. By the outbreak of war the Blenheim Is had been replaced in Bomber Command by the more definitive Blenheim Mk IV with superior crew arrangement although, unfortunately, not greatly improved performance.

Blenheim IV 'OM-J' of No 107 Squadron.

Nevertheless, Bomber Command's Blenheim squadrons had to shoulder the daylight operational burden during the first two years of war. Attempts were made to improve survivability by adding extra armament and even armour plate, but losses on the daylight raids remained high. There were notable successes, such as the daring low-level attack against Bremen on 4 July 1941. Almost from the outbreak of war it was recognized that the limitations of the Blenheim would require its replacement in Bomber Command's inventory. With the advent of the American light/medium bombers purchased by the RAF and as the new four-engined bombers were delivered in increasing numbers, so the numbers of Blenheims declined, the type flying its last Bomber Command mission on 18 August 1942.

In other theatres of the war both the Blenheim I and IV saw extensive operational service, often in the face of enormous odds. The type also served in a variety of other roles, including those of day and night fighter.

BLENHEIM IV DATA
Crew: Three
Engines: Two 905hp Bristol Mercury XV
Span: 56ft 4in
Length: 42ft 7in
Height: 9ft 10in
Weight empty: 9,790lb
Weight loaded: 14,400lb
Max. speed: 266mph at 11,800ft
Ceiling: 22,000ft
Armament: One fixed forward 0.303in gun, dorsal turret and under-nose blister with twin 0.303in guns. Max. bomb load 1,000lb internal plus 320lb external

Squadrons (Bomber Command): Nos 15, 18, 21, 34, 35, 40, 44, 57, 61, 62, 82, 88, 90, 101, 104, 105, 107, 108, 110, 114, 139, 144, 218, 226

---

that the strategic concept was wrong; he thought that the RAF should adopt a more defensive doctrine and have a greater percentage of fighters, balanced only by light bombers and medium bombers. The Air Staff were dismayed; they held to the offensive doctrine but had to accept a cut in the proposed size of the bomber force (Scheme K coming into effect in 1938 with provision for 77 bomber squadrons, and a larger percentage of fighters in the overall total).

On view in the New Types Park at the 1936 Hendon RAF Display were such revelations as the Supermarine Spitfire, Hawker Hurricane, Fairey Battle, Bristol Blenheim and Vickers Wellington, and although they were all some way from entry into squadron service, it was a marked contrast to the situation in 1935 at the Mildenhall review. What was needed now was time, time to get sufficient numbers of the new types into squadron service, and time for enough aircrew to be trained.

Private ventures such as the Hurricane and Blenheim (derived from the Bristol 142 'Britain First') showed what the manufacturers could do if given support. When the Bristol 142, a high-speed, twin-engined monoplane, was first shown to the Air Staff they were immediately impressed and sought its adoption as a light/medium bomber. In mid-1936 the Blenheim could outperform the RAF's current front-line fighters and bomber theory

looked sound; however, the fighters then under development (Spitfire and Hurricane) would not have been outshone so easily had they been available. The Blenheim was therefore acquired under a somewhat outdated concept; in operational service three years later the crews were to pay a heavy price for this unfounded optimism. The same was true of the Fairey Battle, also making its appearance in 1936. It appeared to be an excellent prospect as a light bomber, but in view of contemporary fighter development was anything but.

Doctrine had to be turned into plans and 1937 brought great advances in this area, although much remained to be done. The starting point for the planners was the doctrine of independent bombing of Germany to achieve victory, or at the very least to prevent German ability to support a field army. It was a tall order. The original assumptions made by the Joint Planning Committee (Harris was the Air Ministry representative)—and which proved to be remarkably accurate—suggested a three-phase campaign:

1. Countering the all-out German air offensive, by attacking Luftwaffe installations.

2. Countering the German land offensive, by attacking ground forces.

3. A war-winning air offensive against German industry and transport.

The need to attack the Luftwaffe, especially its bomber formations, was stressed in view of the degree of destruction this 'German air menace' could inflict. This general outline was taken up by the Joint Planning Committee in October 1936: 'The offensive employment of our own and allied bombers is the only measure which could affect the issue during the first weeks of the war. The three classes of objectives are:

'1. Demoralize the German people, by methods similar to those we foresee the Germans themselves using against us, [so that] their Government might be forced to desist from this type of attack.

'2. Discover and attack some target, the security of which was regarded by Germany as vital to her survival during the limited period within which she hoped to gain a decision over us, [so that] she would be forced to divert her air attacks on to our own aerodromes and maintenance organization.

'3. Inflict direct casualties upon the German bombing aircraft, either in the air or the ground, or upon their maintenance organization; the intensity of German attacks would [then] be directly and quickly affected.'

Unfortunately, the paper went on to explain, none of these categories was particularly suitable for attack by the British bomber force, mainly because of the German superior air striking power and the vulnerability of Britain to air attack. Britain would therefore have to adopt a defensive air strategy to reduce the scale of the German air attack to survivable limits.

The second class of objective is interesting: the thought that a single target, or more accurately target system (a group of installations of one particular type), could be vital enough to provide the decisive element—destroy this and the war would be won! The philosophy of these so-called 'panacea' targets (so called by those not in support of the theory) was to rear its head throughout the war, and has formed the basis of many a good argument since.

THE WESTERN AIR PLANS

By 1937 this general philosophy had been translated into 'Planning for a War with Germany', the blueprint for the war. The Air Targets Intelligence sub-committee, formed in 1936, was now issuing appreciations on certain industrial and military targets, although the data on which they based their assessments were very limited. There was also an oversimplification of the effect of aerial bombardment, a failing that was to persist for many years in some circles. Towards the end of the year these initial summaries were being issued as definite plans, the Western Air (WA) Plans.

On 13 December 1937 Bomber Command was instructed to commence detailed planning for WA 1, WA 4 and WA 5, planning to be complete by 1 April 1938. The time-scale was extended because of the sheer amount of work to be done, and the reorganization of Bomber Command that took place in the first half of 1938. Ludlow-Hewitt had ordered the reorganization in order to reflect the requirements of these offensive plans—to put aircraft in the right locations to suit their part in the overall strategy, plus a desire to combine aircraft of the same type within a single Group.

Blenheim I K7059 of No 90 Squadron with pre-war code on fuselage. Wheels-up landings after hydraulic failure were typical of the accidents in the early days of aircraft with advanced systems such as retractable undercarriages.

During the early part of 1938 these plans were modified many times, but by mid-1938 the list of Western Air Plans was the basis of Bomber Command strategy. At that time the list was:

WA 1—German Air Force organization and associated industries.

WA 2—Reconnaissance of home waters and East Atlantic, in co-operation with the Royal Navy.

WA 3—Convoy protection in home waters and East Atlantic.

WA 4—German Army concentration areas and lines of communication.

WA 5—Manufacturing Resources:

WA 5(a)—Ruhr.

WA 5(b)—Inland waterways. Ruhr/Baltic/North Sea ports.

WA 5(c)—Outside of Ruhr.

WA 6—Stores, especially oil.

WA 7—Counter-offensive in co-operation with the Navy in defence of seaborne trade.

WA 8—Night attacks.

WA 9—Kiel Canal and associated waterways.

WA 10—Shipping and facilities, especially the Baltic.

WA 11—Forest and crops.

WA 12—German fleet in harbour or at sea.

WA 13—Adminstrative centres, especially Berlin.

As one post-war study put it, 'Completion of these plans and appreciations marked an important stage in the crystallization of both Air Staff and Bomber Command opinion upon the character and objectives of the bomber offensive'. This statement was particularly apt following an internal Bomber Command appraisal of the three detailed plans. In essence, this concluded that of all the three target systems the only one in which Bomber Command was likely to be truly successful was WA 5, both of the others comprising targets of an inappropriate nature for offensive strategic bombers.

Thus they were left with Bomber Command as an independent strategic weapon undertaking an offensive to paralyse the Ruhr, and especially the coking plants and power stations, which would 'prevent Germany waging war on a large scale in less than three months'. They estimated that in 3,000 sorties, with 176 aircraft losses, the Command could knock out 26 coking plans and nineteen power stations, the effect of which would be to bring total disruption to the industries of the Ruhr. Thus for little effort the bombers would have a decisive effect on the war.

FAIREY BATTLE

'It was a responsive aeroplane and it had some agreeable qualities, but not as an operational machine. It could only carry four 250lb bombs and it was far too slow if there were any fighters around.'

In May 1937 the Fairey Battle entered service with No 63 Squadron at Upwood, a few months after the RAF's other new light bomber, the Blenheim. Both replaced the obsolete biplane Harts and Hinds which had formed the backbone of the RAF's light bomber force. By the time Specification P.27/32 was issued the Air Staff had already more or less agreed that the light bomber was of limited use in the future inventory of the bomber force, and yet the Battle, and Blenheim, were designated 'LB' and at the outbreak of war formed the major part of Bomber Command's front-line strength.

The prototype Battle (K4303) first flew on 10 March 1936, its sleek lines and stressed-skin construction giving it an advanced appearance. However, within two years it was realized that the aircraft would not be viable in the face of rapidly advancing fighter technology. Nevertheless, there was no option but to increase production of 'proven' types such as the Battle to replace even more obsolete types and provide equipment for the now rapidly expanding RAF. If war had come a year or two later, the Battle would probably have gone down in RAF history as an excellent interim type from which to convert to more modern aircraft. As it was, war came earlier and the Battle, despite the resilience and courage of its crews, suffered enormous losses.

In the role of tactical bomber these aircraft were sent into battle as part of the British forces deployed to France. Their vulnerability was soon all too obvious as German fighters took their toll of the (usually) unescorted Battles. Worse was to follow. The German offensive of May 1940 sliced through the Allied defences and the Battles were thrown in to try to stem the flood by attacking bridges and troop concentrations. In just one day over half of the available aircraft were lost.

The remnants of the Battle squadrons were withdrawn to Britain to be rested and built back up to full strength; re-equipment was still not possible as other types were not yet available and every operational aircraft was needed. Battles continued to operate against the Channel ports, playing an important part in the destruction of concentrations of invasion barges.

By the end of 1940 the Battle's operational life in Europe was over, but it continued to provide worthwhile service in a variety of training roles.

BATTLE I DATA
Crew: Three
Engine: 1,030hp Rolls-Royce Merlin
Span: 54ft
Length: 42ft 1¾in
Height: 15ft 6in
Weight empty: 6,647lb
Weight loaded: 10,792lb
Max. speed: 241mph at 13,000ft
Ceiling: 23,500ft
Range: 1,050 miles
Armament: Fixed 0.303in in starboard wing, single Vickers 'K' gun rear of canopy; 1,000lb bomb load

Squadrons (Bomber Command): Nos 12, 15, 35, 40, 52, 63, 88, 98, 103, 105, 106, 142, 150, 185, 207, 218, 226, 300, 301, 304, 305

No 218 Squadron Fairey Battles. [218 Sqn records]

DEAD RECKONING NAVIGATION

In the absence of sophisticated navigation systems, the primary navigational technique is that of DR (Dead, or Deduced, Reckoning), the principle being that of carrying out a plot of where the aircraft has flown since it took off from a known point.

If the aircraft starts off from Point 'A' and flies a certain course at a certain speed then it should, in theory, be possible to work out where it will be at any given time by simply plotting the distance flown along the course. These two elements are the heading and airspeed of the aircraft, taken from the compass and the airspeed indicator respectively. However, there are problems with this since the compass is not always very accurate (certainly true of compasses in 1939) and the pilot might not be flying a steady course—especially if being engaged by enemy defences! Any change in the heading flown will alter the position of the 'air plot' at the rate of 1 mile for every 60 miles flown per degree of error—i.e., if the heading is in error by 3 degrees there will be 3 miles of error in position for every 60 miles flown.

Similar problems arise with the speed. Instruments are not always accurate and they do not show the True Air Speed (TAS) of the aircraft as this depends on the a number of factors related to height and temperature; this IAS (Indicated Air Speed) to TAS relationship is calculated before take-off but has to be modified according to the actual height/temperature. Even if both these elements are accurate and achievable, the resultant position is still not where the aircraft truly is; it is only an air position and not a ground position.

The other major factor is the wind. If an aircraft heads off in a particular direction it is affected by the wind, thus altering both where it is going and at what speed. As it is essential to know where the aircraft is in relationship to the ground, then the wind must be taken into account. At the planning stage the navigator will apply the forecast wind to his route planning and derive the expected drift (the directional effect of the wind) and groundspeed (the speed effect of the wind) to apply to his intended tracks. This enables an accurate plan to be calculated which will, if the forecast wind is accurate, keep the aircraft on planned track and on time—subject to the compass errors mentioned above.

As usual, it is never quite as simple as that and for various reasons, including instrument problems and errors in the 'met' forecast, the planning figures are not enough to ensure success. The navigator flies his plan and keeps his air plot updated, using planned winds to obtain ground positions, but he must also update that information by fixing the position of the aircraft and calculating actual winds and temperatures. The best fix is a visual one—to see the aircraft flying over an identifiable point. This can then be compared with the plot position and the error calculated—leading to the calculation of a new wind, which is then used for the next stage of the flight. Other fixing methods are also used but the basic principle remains the same. Without a fix the error in the air plot can be enormous if the forecast wind is grossly in error; this happened all too often in the early years of the war.

German rearmament was continuing at a fast pace, albeit along different lines, and Hitler was confident enough, and sure enough of the political weakness of France and Britain, to continue his territorial claims in Europe. Czechoslovakia was his next target—a gamble that brought the world to the brink of war in 1938. When the Munich Crisis broke in September 1938 Bomber Command mobilized a total of 42 squadrons, only ten of which were of 'heavies' (Whitley/Harrow), and with only a 10 per cent reserve capability (compared with the plan for a 225 per cent war reserve). Not only was this a weak force in numbers, it was also of low capability, especially bearing in mind the targets it was theoretically scheduled to attack. The rapid expansion had proved difficult, squadrons splitting to form new squadrons and thus reducing the overall levels of experience and efficiency. The training organization was still in its infancy, especially the advanced elements, and with no Operational Training Units the majority of this work was carried out by designated squadrons, on the front-line units. A Bomber Command Operational Training Instruction of 1937 stated that 'During the process of expansion and re-arming, and pending the completion of the new scheme in the Flying Training Schools, it will be necessary for squadrons not only to convert their new pilots to service types, but also to consolidate and complete the flying and ground training given to pilots and air observers that form part of the Training School Syllabus.' The net effect of this was that the experienced crews on the squadrons spent much of their time teaching the new crews, and there was little time left to develop tactics or improve standards. At the end of 1937 Ludlow-Hewitt, who had been appointed C-in-C Bomber Command in September, said that

Bomber Command was 'entirely unprepared for war, unable to operate except in fair weather, and extremely vulnerable in the air and on the ground.'

This short comment covered many of the problems that had been faced by the Command in the late 1930s. At last the required numbers of aircraft were being made available, and most of them were great improvements over their predecessors, but this presented fresh difficulties that only time and experience could overcome. In the event, Bomber Command was to be given too little of either; it would have to learn as it went along—and it paid the price. At a time when aircraft were becoming more complex and in most cases harder to fly (with retractable undercarriages, higher performance and so on), the overall experience level of the pilots was dropping. The training units were turning out numbers but they could not turn out experience.

Navigation and bombing training had changed little since the 1920s. The former was still the responsibility of one of the pilots in the aircraft, although in 1938 it was recognized that 'navigation must in war be in the hands of an observer devoted mainly to that subject'—although he was still to be trained in bomb-aiming and gunnery. While the whole question of navigation had received some attention, it had not progressed significantly. What little work had been done had tended to deal with how to destroy the target, not how to *find* the target.

The primary navigation technique was 'DR' (Dead, or Deduced, Reckoning), a system that relied on accurate flying and the ability to obtain positional information with which to update the navigational plot. The latter element could be obtained from one of three sources: visual pinpoints, astro, or radio aids. Map-reading was the most common technique, although it required a great deal of practice to become proficient, even when flying in peace-time conditions over England; it was harder at night, although quite possible in even small amounts of moonlight. Astro was an excellent technique but required even more expertise and practice; it was not, however, very accurate, mainly because of the lack of suitable sextants. The last method, radio aids, was still in its infancy and was confined mainly to Direction Finding (DF) whereby a bearing from a ground station could be obtained. A combination of bearings from several stations could be put together to form a 'fix' of the aircraft's position. Once again, it was a complex procedure and not terribly accurate, except as a means of homing back to base. More in optimism than certainty, Bomber Command continued its standard training pattern and held to the doctrine of being able to bomb small targets at night. In May 1938 it was suggested that using DR alone the bombers could only guarantee to get within 50 miles of the target area.

However, new aids such as the improved astro sextants and astro calculation tables would, it was hoped, provide the solution—and so the problem was glossed over.

The Munich Crisis of September 1938 was resolved when the French and British Governments withdrew their support from Czechoslovakia and applied pressure on that country's leader, Beneš, to agree to the German plan for a divided Czechoslovakia. Hitler had won again. Western leaders, such as Chamberlain with his 'Peace in our time' statement, have often received much criticism; true, it was a shameful political sell-out—but it did gain precious time. The RAF that would go to war in late 1939 was far more prepared than that of the Munich Crisis. This final year of peace was used by all parties to acquire more armaments and prepare for the inevitable conflict.

The RAF still had major problems and serious doubts were raised from 1938 onwards. If the targets could not be hit by night because of navigational problems, then

BOMBER AIRFIELDS

One of the most immediate problems of the late 1930s expansion period was the lack of airfields. A programme to provide more airfields, especially in the north and east of the country to combat the direction of the threat from Germany, began in 1935 and over the next ten years airfields sprang up around Britain at an incredible rate. The requirements of the bombers of 1935 were little changed from those of the late 1920s—an adequate stretch of compacted grass for take-off and landing. Most airfields were planned with a surface area 'in which a circle of 1,100 yards could be inscribed'. Other facilities, especially hangars, were placed on the outer edge of the circle. Survey teams toured the country selecting sites, which were then purchased from the landowners or taken into long-term lease, and construction work commenced. All sites required a degree of levelling, draining and resurfacing.

Even as the programme was getting under way the requirements were changing: the latest specifications for heavy bombers would mean that all the existing layouts would be unsuitable. The Wellington weighed in at around 32,000lb and required a take-off run of 520 yards (landing 490 yards); the Lancaster needed almost twice as much with 850 yards for take-off at a gross weight of 65,000lb. The grass-surfaced airfields rapidly deteriorated and became unusable in bad weather.

All-weather airfields were essential and the standard pattern for a bomber airfield in 1940 was for three runways at 60 degrees to each other, each of 1,000 yards but with capacity for expansion to 1,400 yards for the main runway and 1,100 yards for the secondaries. Dimensions and requirements changed frequently and the Class A airfield became the standard for heavy bombers; this had a main runway of 2,000 yards plus two secondary runways of 1,400 yards, all to be of concrete/tarmac construction, plus extensive trackways and hardstands. In the latter years of the war Marham was typical of the 'very-heavy bomber airfields', having a main runway of 3,000 yards plus two of 2,000 yards, of high-grade concrete laid on a stabilized foundation. In all, 1,035,000 square yards of runway, hardstand and perimeter track were laid, taking a work force of 1,035 some 18 months to complete—at a cost of almost £2m! With the number of aircraft to launch and recover it was essential that the airfields were well equipped—although it was not until the latter years of the war that this was truly the case. The FIDO-equipped airfields certainly worked and enabled aircraft to recover in even the thickest fog; but the heat generated by the burners meant that an aircraft was reluctant to land, requiring a concerted push-down on the controls to overcome the uplift.

The C-type hangar remained the most common, although other types were employed, especially on airfields built during the war when time and materials were in short supply. Operational, administrative and domestic facilities varied greatly from station to station, the pre-war permanent stations being by far the best, while some of the 'war' airfields were very primitive. It was quite a shock for crews to move from a well-established and comfortable airfield to one of the new constructions, where wooden huts, or even tents, were the order of the day.

The classic 1942/43 bomber airfield pattern as displayed by Elsham Wolds. This photograph shows the camouflage technique employed in the early years of the war—'paint' fields and boundaries to disrupt the pattern of the airfield and make it blend with the countryside. [Author]

surely, it was argued, they could be hit by day when the bombers could map-read their way to the target—an extension of the 1920s policy, planning and training. This raised the question of how to cope with enemy fighters. The advent of high-performance monoplane fighters in the mid-1930s had called into question bomber survivability through performance alone; it was now obvious that the bomber would have to fight. Throughout the 1930s small-scale trials had been undertaken into a wide range of tactical problems, one of which related to the question of armament. For various

Above: Vickers Wellington crews walk out to their aircraft.

Below: Bombing up a Bristol Blenheim IV. Note under-nose gun blister.

reasons the RAF decided to put its faith in the 0.303in machine-gun for both defensive and offensive situations. The one innovation that went with this was the development of power-operated turrets to take multiple gun settings. The idea developed that the bomber with its heavy turret armament would be able to look after

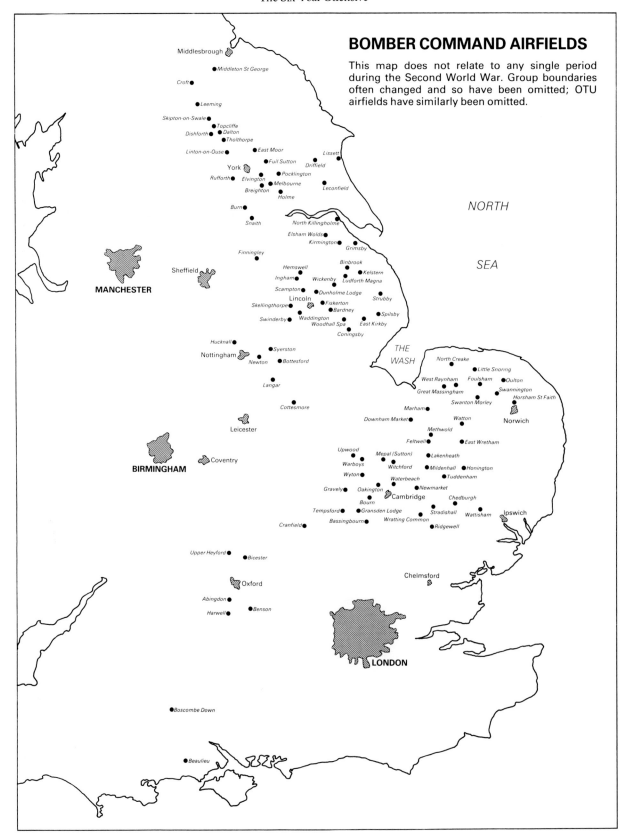

BOMBER COMMAND AIRFIELDS

This map does not relate to any single period during the Second World War. Group boundaries often changed and so have been omitted; OTU airfields have similarly been omitted.

itself. Little thought was given to the provision of a training programme to go with it. On the question of armour plate and self-sealing fuel tanks, the Air Ministry reserved judgment, but for the moment did nothing.

Regarding methods of attacking the target, there were two alternatives: high-level bombing, but with consequent loss of accuracy, and low-level bombing, with better accuracy but greater exposure to ground defences. A third alternative, shallow dive-bombing, was considered as a compromise. The primary training consideration was that 'all pilots should be trained in high-level precision bombing'. Other elements, such as the use of flares to illuminate the target at night, were discussed, but in the absence of an effective trials and development unit little solid work could be carried out. There was simply too much to be done and too many calls on resources. Bomber Command was by no means alone in the myriad problems it faced.

As the years of peace drained away towards the late 1930s, the British advocates of strategic bombing could pride themselves that they held firm to the doctrine of an independent bombing force, but in practical terms Bomber Command was not equipped for the role it was assigned.

At the outbreak of war Bomber Command had five operational Groups (Nos 1, 2, 3, 4 and 5) plus No 6 (Training) Group. Its 55 squadrons were equipped with Battles, Blenheims, Whitleys, Hampdens and Wellingtons—a huge improvement on the position of late 1938. Nevertheless, most of these types (with the exception of the Wellington when it was switched to night bombing) were soon found to be lacking in a modern air scenario.

The twelve months since Munich had been put to good use and the RAF was a much stronger, more organized force than it had been—but would it stand the test of war?

CHAPTER TWO

The Difficult Years

BOMBER COMMAND was involved in active operations from day one of the war, with Wellingtons and Blenheims tasked against enemy naval installations and shipping. At the outbreak of war the Command tried to implement its pre-war plans, the 'Western Air' (WA) Plans, but found itself constrained by the politicians, who decreed that no land target could be attacked. All the pre-war planning was put to one side as the only 'acceptable' target was the German Fleet.

THE OPENING MOVES

Statistics for September 1939 show the daily serviceability (averaged for the month) of aircraft at 494, with 653 crews available. By Groups this was divided into: No 1 Group/AASF—145; No 2 Group—140; No 3 Group—77; No 4 Group—61; and No 5 Group—71. On paper it looked a powerful force. The problem now was how best to employ it. There was a reluctance to commit this strategic force (in concept if not capability) to combined tactical operations, although No 1 Group, with ten Battle squadrons, was detached to France in September 1939 to become part of the Advanced Air Striking Force (AASF); even then the initial intention was simply to put the bombers within range of targets inside Germany. For this detached force the high state of readiness and expectation of immediate action drifted into the period known as the 'Phoney War'. There were

A dramatic photograph of a Blenheim anti-shipping attack.

two main problems facing those in Bomber Command who favoured a stategic bombing offensive: first, a lack of the right aircraft, in type or quantity, to pursue such a strategy; and second, a reluctance in certain quarters to start a 'total war' against an enemy who appeared to have great potential to hit back hard!

Thus, in the early months of the war, and except for the daylight operations conducted by No 2 Group and the force committed to France, the main aspects of the Command's operations were confined to:

1. Leaflet-dropping over Germany at night, primarily by the Whitleys of No 4 Group.

2. Daylight attacks on German shipping, primarily by the Wellingtons of No 3 Group.

The opening move, on 3 September, was made by a lone Blenheim IV (N6215 crewed by Flying Officer A. McPherson, Commander Thompson, RN, and Corporal V. Arrowsmith) of No 139 Squadron from Wyton which crossed the German coast to photograph shipping at Wilhelmshaven. The crew had been on standby since the General Mobilization ordered on 1 September, the remainder of the squadron being 'warned to stand by for operations against the German fleet'. After a second day of waiting, the order to go came at midday on the 3rd. The aircraft landed a 1650 after 'Duty successfully carried out, 75 photographs taken of the German fleet, no anti-aircraft fire seen, no aircraft seen, flown at 22,000ft, fleet juśt leaving Wilhelmshaven'. McPherson flew a similar reconnaissance sortie the following day, plus others later in the month, and on 10 October was awarded the Distinguished Flying Cross (DFC) for this work.

Also on 3 September a small force of Wellingtons and Hampdens went in search of German shipping, but in the prevailing poor weather conditions, and with the strict rules about what and where to bomb, found nothing. That night ten Whitleys from Nos 51 and 58 Squadrons flew over the Ruhr, Bremen and Hamburg to drop leaflets, no fewer than 5.4 million being distributed. For No 51 Squadron this involved instructions to carry out Operation Order No 3, sending three aircraft (Whitley IIIs K8982, K8938 and K8941) to fly the northern route towards Hamburg. The first aircraft was airborne at 2030. All three had an uneventful trip, meeting no opposition, seeing a few searchlights, but finding the target covered in cloud. The last aircraft (K8938—Flying Officer Milne and crew) landed at 0615;

PROPAGANDA LEAFLETS

On 31 August 1939 the Whitleys of No 51 Squadron at Linton-on-Ouse were put on standby to execute Operational Order No 3: 'to Nickel Germany, dropping 8½in × 5in leaflets in bundles of 1,500, each pack containing 12 bundles'. On the first two nights of the war the Whitleys dropped Nickel No 273, a 'Warning Message from Great Britain' stating that the war was brought about by the policies of the Nazis and was not in the interest of the German people. During September leaflet-dropping sorties were flown on eleven nights (65 sorties), with a total of 20,683,000 leaflets being dropped. Most of this early series of propaganda leaflets concentrated on stating that the war should not be fought and that the German people were being let down by the Nazis, who were making vast fortunes at the expense of the people.

During the next six months the leaflet-dropping sorties continued, with an average of only 20 sorties a month; in March 1940, however, the total was 142 sorties on nineteen nights. With the packs of leaflets stacked inside the Whitley, there was not much room to manoeuvre and the task of cutting the retaining string on each bundle and then shoving it down the flare chute was quite tiring. The idea then was that the rubber band would be removed by the slipstream and the leaflets would float down to earth. The propaganda was not very sophisticated and at a time when the German military was scoring success after success it was bound to have little effect. Many of the crews were not convinced of the value of their task. However, it must be remembered that Bomber Command was prohibited from attacking targets in Germany until May 1940, so these nightly ventures over Europe provided invaluable training, and highlighted the difficulties of night operation.

Right: Leaflet No 67: 'The French and English know why they are fighting to the end—for Freedom! And the Germans? For [Himmler] and an annexation policy!'

Below: Leaflet-dropping from a Whitley.

Die **Franzosen und Engländer** wissen wofür sie kämpfen bis zum Ende für die

Freiheit!

und die Deutschen ?

für und

Annektionswahn!

The style of leaflets gradually changed, concentrating more on the achievements of the Allies and the failures of the Nazi regime. Other types, such as fake clothing cards and ration cards, were intended to de-stabilize the German economy. Perhaps the most successful of all were the news-sheets aimed at the inhabitants of the Occupied Countries, such as *Whirlwind* (Dutch) and *Courier de l'Air* (French)—'In Occupied Countries leaflets serve to maintain the belief in Allied victory and increase the ever-growing spirit of resistance.'

As the bombing offensive built up so 'Nickelling' became a secondary activity, bombers dropping bundles of leaflets as part of their normal attack pattern. The OTUs continued to mount leaflet-dropping sorties as part of the crew preparation syllabus; it was a policy that had many opponents. No target over Europe was an easy one, so why risk a partly trained crew? The task of pushing leaflets out of the flare chutes gave way to automatic dispensers, usually modified SBCs, attached to the bomb beam—a far more satisfactory system.

as this had also been the first aircraft airborne, the sortie had lasted nearly 10 hours.

The following day the first real encounter took place. Twenty-nine Blenheims and Wellingtons were tasked to attack German warships. The Operation Order stated that 'The greatest care is to be taken not to injure the civilian population. The intention is to destroy the German fleet. There is no alternative target'. The weather was again poor and one-third of each formation failed to make contact with the enemy. The remaining Blenheims swept in at low level to attack warships in Wilhelmshaven harbour: 'The leader skimmed over a tender and pulled up just high enough to clear the mast

of the *Admiral Scheer*. His observer saw men leaning against the rails of the ship and a line of washing out to dry. The attack was a complete surprise. One moment the German crew were taking their ease on deck, the next they were doubling to their action stations.' It seems that at least three bombs hit *Admiral Scheer*, but no damage was caused since none of the bombs exploded, no doubt partly due to the ultra-low release height; one of the major problems Bomber Command was to suffer for many months was the inadequacy of its bombs. The defences were soon awake and lively; five of the Blenheims were lost, probably to flak although at least one crashed into the cruiser

Emden. Meanwhile the Wellingtons appear to have attacked shipping near Brunsbüttel, causing no damage but losing two of their number.

Towards the end of the month Bomber Command squadrons commenced anti-shipping searches off the coast of Germany, the idea being to attack any warships that were found. It was a policy that started badly when two formations of Hampdens found two destroyers in the Heligoland Bight on 29 September. The first section of six attacked and withdrew without damage, but the formation of five aircraft of No 144 Squadron which arrived next was 'bounced' by German fighters. All five aircraft were shot down. The destroyers were un-damaged.

A number of similar sweeps were carried out in October and November but no contacts were made. During the same period routine reconnaissance flights were made by Blenheims to monitor German ports and

Left: Blenheims flew vital reconnaissance sorties—and suffered heavy losses.

Below left: Wellington crews after operations over Heligoland.

Below: The Wellington was able to take great damage. On a raid over Duisburg, flak tore the fabric away from the fuselage of this aircraft, exposing the geodetic structure.

to carry out photo-recce of north-west Germany. These lone aircraft battled against bad weather, and non-existent navigation equipment, and suffered heavy losses. In many cases the exact cause of the losses remained a mystery: some must have fallen to German fighters, others may have strayed low and been hit by flak, and some may simply have become lost in the bad weather and run out of fuel. The overall result was a loss rate of almost 20 per cent. The reconnaissance flights were halted on 25 November, the benefits having been outweighed by the losses.

As yet there had been no real test of the medium bomber's (i.e., Wellington's) ability to face fighter attack; this 'trial' came during December. On 3 December 24 Wellingtons were tasked to attack warships in the North Sea near Heligoland; the bombers claimed hits on at least one vessel. Fighters, no doubt summoned by the ships, arrived on the scene and the first running fights developed. There appeared to be a reluctance on the part of the Messerschmitt Bf 109s and Bf 110s to close in on the bombers. In the various combats none of the bombers was shot down, although some were damaged, whereas the gunners claimed one Bf 109. Among the 44 aircraft operating on 14 December was a force of twelve Wellingtons which attacked shipping 12 miles south-west of Heligoland. The weather was very poor and the bombers had to go down to sea-level to

attack from below cloud. Some 20 enemy fighters appeared and in the ensuing combats five of the Wellingtons were shot down, although some sources suggest that part of these losses may have been caused by flak from the ships. The gunners in the bombers claimed to have shot down five fighters (German figures concede the loss of one aircraft) and, according to the reports, 'The crews of the Wellingtons were very well satisfied with the mutual fire-power developed by the power-operated turrets. They had inflicted losses heavier than those they had themselves sustained.' With no definite proof either way as to the viability of bombers for daylight attacks, the trial continued. Four days later, on 18 December, an even stronger force of Wellingtons set out for the Wilhelmshaven area. Detected by the German 'Freya' early-warning radar, the Wellingtons flew into a veritable hornets' nest of waiting fighters from II/JG 77 and I/ZG 76. Although instructed to bomb from above 10,000 feet so as to avoid the worst of the flak, the formations were forced to open out to reduce the risk from the intense flak over the port. Of the 22 Wellingtons which reached the target area twelve were shot down, most falling to the fighters.

Even this disastrous outcome did not convince all in Bomber Command that the concept of mutual defence in daylight was invalid; some argued that poor formation-keeping had allowed the fighters to get between the mutual defence zones. If they could have seen contemporary German reports they would have read that the German fighter pilots considered that the close formation made their job easier! Thus, the first four months of war had brought little tactical change as far as the planners were concerned. Losses had been high on some sorties, but overall the position remained promising and there was no reason why the hoped-for daylight attack on the Ruhr should not prove decisive. No such attack was possible until the politicans gave the go-ahead, and that they were not about to do.

During this period other smaller-scale, and less significant, shipping searches were made by Hampdens, Wellingtons, Whitleys and Blenheims. Most of the sorties involved hours of fruitless searching, a battle against the elements, and a return to base for a welcome meal and a rest.

Likewise the leaflet-dropping raids were a regular feature of the operational plan. The night defences over Germany were almost non-existent at this stage of the war. German policy at the outbreak of the war had been to rely heavily on flak defences in Air Defence Zone West, an element of the Siegfried Line system, whereby aircraft would be exposed to a barrage of flak that would take 2–4 minutes to cross—'The enemy over the zone will suffer continual losses and have his effectiveness steadily drained away, particularly as he must pass through it twice. If he wants to get out of range he will have to ascend to a vast height—at which accurate bombing will be hampered by poor visibility.' By autumn 1939 this zone contained 197 heavy batteries (averaging four guns per battery) and 48 light batteries. The flak element of the Luftwaffe comprised almost 1 million personnel and it was responsible both for Home Defence and for field support of the Army. In the area of medium and light anti-aircraft guns the Luftwaffe had developed superb weapons, as low-flying RAF aircraft were soon to discover, and air defence was included as an essential, and integrated, element of any ground force.

The fighter element of Home Defence was organized primarily around day defence, comprising single-engined fighters. A system was developed for using these aircraft, mainly Bf 109s, at night in conjunction with searchlights, but it proved totally inadequate. Flak caused few losses and the roving 'night fighters' even fewer; but it has already been shown how effective the fighters had been in countering the RAF's 'experimental' daylight raids. To improve the night defences Junkers Ju 88 and Bf 110 twin-engined fighters were later brought in to form the first true nightfighter Group, eventually forming part of the Nightfighter Division under General Kammhuber. This was further developed into the so-called Kammhuber Line, using the 'Himmelbett' ('Four-poster bed') tactic.

The autumn weather was proving to be a major problem, not only from the point of view of finding the targets, but also from that of simply getting there; getting back was often even more difficult, the struggle against the bad weather having eaten into precious fuel reserves.

RAF aircraft were not designed for comfort, and the Whitley was certainly not designed to give its crew a comfortable journey into the freezing night air over Germany. The temperature inside the aircraft often fell to –20°C. The flying clothing (Sidcot suits and sheepskin flying boots, electric Irvin suit and boots for the gunner), mainly from the era of the open cockpit, was bulky and uncomfortable, and after a period of time became even worse. Crews had to endure hour after hour of freezing cold, with no heating and no way of alleviating the problem other than 'bashing' the extremities of the body to try to create a bit of heat. The poor old tail gunner suffered more than most: stuck in his cramped turret, almost open to the elements, it was both freezing and numbing—'Whenever a Whitley landed it was easy to spot the tail gunner. He was the bow-legged one frantically massaging his numb bum!' The introduction of the Mk V version of the Whitley eased the situation a little, the new and better enclosed tail turret stopping the dreaded icy draught that used to whistle through.

George Dove was a gunner with No 10 Squadron: 'The Whitley was ungainly but built like a tank, and never once let us down. I had great confidence in it. The

The cramped and uncomfortable rear turret of the Whitley.

trouble was that in the winter the tail turret was no place to be, no heating to speak of and no electric-heated clothing. I wonder how we were able to sit there for as long as 9–10 hours without moving. I was glad when I was finally able to move into the cockpit as first WOP—which we did after half a tour.'

Towards the end of October the Whitleys operated out of advanced bases in France, such as Villeneuve, to try to overcome some of the difficulties being caused by the weather.

During the first three months of the war Bomber Command had attempted a mixture of daylight and night operations, there being few days or nights when no operations took place. Overall the missions were small-scale, being in the nature of experimental thrusts to determine capability and tactics. The pre-war notion of the invincible bomber survived a few early disasters but by the end of December had (almost) been laid to rest. The medium bombers had failed to achieve any major success when engaged in daylight operations but had taken heavy losses. At night, however, the Whitleys had flown 123 'Nickel' (leaflet-dropping) sorties for the loss of only four aircraft, and this included far-ranging missions into the heart of Germany; on the occasion they were included in the anti-shipping task losses had risen dramatically. The Hampden squadrons seemed to have fared much better, although their rate of tasking was particularly low. Their greatest loss was on 21

December when two aircraft were misidentified and shot down by Spitfires. For the Blenheim squadrons it had been a mixture of reconnaissance sorties and anti-shipping searches, again at a fairly low tasking rate. Most of the anti-shipping searches were abortive in that the targets could not be found.

During January 1940 the Wellingtons and Hampdens joined in the leaflet-dropping task; this was mainly to allow the crews to gain experience in night operations, rather than because of any desire to increase the amount of paper being spread over Europe. While bombing of the mainland remained prohibited there was little else that could be done to give crews this invaluable experience. A second element was added with the tasking of aircraft, at first only the Whitleys, with reconnaissance sorties over Germany, especially the Ruhr. The idea behind this was to investigate how conditions such as weather, searchlights and moonlight affected the visibility of particular types of target. This was not only good navigational practice but it also provided an excellent source of data on what type of targets crews *should* be able to find, and in what conditions. The Hampdens and Wellingtons joined this routine in March 1940.

It was estimated that a crew should be able to get to

THE GERMAN DEFENCES

There were four elements in the active German defence organization: Early Warning and Ground Controlled Interception, searchlights, anti-aircraft artillery ('flak') and fighters. All were interconnected at various levels and, from 1942, formed an effective system that caused heavy casualties among the Allied bombers.

EARLY WARNING AND GCI

As with the British EW system, the Germans had old-fashioned sound locators, which were not very efficient, and radar (still called RDF—Radio Direction Finding—by the British at this stage of the war). The standard German radar was the 'Freya' with a maximum detection range of 180 miles. It was an excellent radar and at 60 miles' range had an accuracy of one degree in bearing (equating to one mile error) and 1,000 yards in range. Like most other early radars, it had no true height-finding capability. Two long-range radars were developed, 'Chimney' and 'Mammut', both with maximum detection ranges of about 250 miles; long-range detection, of course, depended on the height of the target—e.g. for 'Mammut' the maximum range was 187 miles for a target at 26,000ft.

The other ground radar elements were those connected with the control of fighters and guns. The 'Freya' system had many variants, some of which were used for GCI. The other GCI radar was the 'Giant Würzburg'; with its 24ft aerial this radar was very accurate—bearing accuracy of one-tenth of a degree at 25 miles' range, and height information to within 200ft. The primary purpose of the original 'Würzburg' radar was the control of heavy flak batteries.

SEARCHLIGHTS

The primary role of the searchlights was to assist the guns and fighters in the destruction of enemy aircraft. Many of the major targets in Germany had extensive searchlight defences, dozens of beams lighting up the sky and turning day into night. In a co-ordinated system, tied in with sound locators, optical devices and radar, the master beam (usually distinguishable by its blue/mauve tinge) would latch onto a target, to be followed by many others forming a cone of light which then became the focus for the flak barrage. Three main searchlight types were in use: 60cm for light flak, 150cm and 200cm for heavy batteries and general use.

'At that moment, the first searchlight flicked on, and absolutely smack on us without any searching around. It had a mauve tinge to it and was obviously a master beam controlled by radar which had nailed us so accurately; the second it found us, every single searchlight in the whole area was switched on immediately and fastened on us, some 80 beams counted by the rear gunner, and of course we all knew that the flak would start coming up at us at any second.'

It was essential to get out of the beam as soon as possible, twisting and turning, diving and climbing. One of the accepted techniques was to dive down the beam, making prediction for tracking and gun-laying more difficult, and then breaking away to one side. If it looked as if a beam was going to pass through the aircraft, the best technique was to turn into it so that it crossed the aircraft as rapidly as possible. Unfortunately, the target had still to be bombed—straight and level to give the bomb-aimer a chance.

The total number of searchlights in Germany doubled between 1941 and late 1944, with almost 5,000 in position by early 1945.

FLAK

Anti-aircraft (AA) guns, or Flak (from Fliegerabwehrkanonen), were an important part of the Luftwaffe; they also proved to be a heavy drain on German resources. Divided into light and heavy types, the former were used both as mobile defence for the Army and as point defence of important targets, to counter low-level attack. For the heavy guns, usually in batteries of four or six guns, the standard tactics were either aimed fire, relying on data fed into a predictor, or unaimed box barrage. The main heavy weapons were:

Calibre (mm)	Max. range (yd)	Max. ceiling (ft)	Rounds/ min
88	1,620	32,500	15
Mod 88	22,000	40,000	20
105	19,100	37,000	10
128	19,600	40,000	8

The combined effect of flak and searchlights over Bremen on 2/3 July 1943, photographed by a Lancaster of No 97 Squadron. [97 Sqn records]

'If exploding flak could be heard above the continuous dull roar of the engines then it was too near for safety.' The sight of a flak barrage was enough to terrify the first-timer; the entire sky seemed to be covered in black and white puffs—thick enough to walk on was a frequent comment. It was soon realized that it looked much worse that it was; the chances of a direct hit were very low (but devastating) and to cause serious damage to the bomber, the shell had to explode within a few yards. The bigger danger was injury, or death, from fragments, the fragile skin of the bomber offering little resistance to high-speed jagged chunks of metal. In a heavy barrage the flak splinters could be heard hitting the aircraft; those without penetrative power simply bounced off like hailstones. Many aircraft came back looking like a pepperpot with holes all over various parts of the structure. Casualties were not particularly high but were nevertheless significant; some aircrew sat on their parachutes in order to protect certain parts of their anatomy. There were numerous instances of somebody leaning forward just at the right moment—as a flak splinter imbeded itself where they would otherwise have been. Such incidents helped create superstitions and the use of lucky mascots.

The heavy flak batteries were only one part of the system. The light flak weapons were far more numerous—and deadly to low-flying aircraft (although some of the weapons were effective to over 10,000ft). They were all optically-laid rapid-fire weapons, relying for their effect on the sheer quantity of shells being thrown into an area. The three main weapons were:

Type	Calibre (mm)	Max. range (yd)	Max. ceiling (ft)	Rounds/ min
Flak 38	20	5,230	7,200	220
Flak 36	37	7,085	13,800	60
Flak 41	50		17,000	

'Light flak tracer which seemed to be sprayed up all over the place, in all directions in prodigious quantities. Multi-coloured strings of orange, red, or even green were hosed upwards, sometimes with a sort of "S"-bend in them, white and yellow blobs of fairy lights creeping up almost lazily at first, then gradually increasing velocity to zip past the wings at terrific speed.'

The combined defences could be quite extensive. The Ruhr, or 'Happy Valley' as it was called by Bomber Command aircrew, was very heavily defended by searchlights and guns. By late 1943 typical figures were:

Berlin: 350 heavy and 250 light flak guns, 200 searchlights
Bremen: 230 heavy and 350 light flak guns, 100 searchlights
Munich: 130 heavy and 90 light flak guns, 60 searchlights
Ostend: 28 heavy and 60 light flak guns, 20 searchlights

By January 1944 the overall figures, in Germany only, stood at 6,716 heavy guns and 8,484 medium/light guns.

NIGHT FIGHTERS

The German night fighter defences grew from a not very effective collection of single-engined fighters, mainly Bf 109s, to a complex organization that reacted well to the tactical changes made by the bombers and remained potent up to the last weeks of the war. The early single-engined fighter tactics, working with searchlights, made very few kills.

With the RAF's general move to a night bombing offensive, and the increased numbers and quality of EW/GCI radars, the Luftwaffe night defences expanded. By mid-1941 the basic tactic was based around the zones (boxes) of the Kammhuber Line, and any bomber penetrating the box would be dealt with by the night fighter patrol in that box. The increased use of radar meant that the bombers were picked up at long range and as they entered a box they were 'handed off' to a controller. Both target and fighter were tracked on 'Giant Würzburg' radars and the interception was set up to allow the fighter to pick up the bomber. Following Bomber Command's adoption of stream tactics to swamp a limited number of boxes (from mid-1942), the defensive belt was deepened so that the stream would have to penetrate more boxes.

With the advent of 'Lichtenstein' AI radar, the German two-seat night fighters had an excellent interception system although the GCI unit still positioned the fighter in the approximate area. Each of the boxes was based on a beacon; the fighters would orbit the beacon until sent off on an interception, and would return to the beacon once the combat was over. With minor modifications the system worked well until the advent of 'Window'; this device, and the later RCM techniques, made the German GCI task much more difficult and led to many variations of tactic. In essence the system devolved into two main types: 'Wilde Sau' (Wild Boar) and 'Zahme Sau' (Tame Boar). The 'Zahme Sau' was an extension of the existing controlled tactic, the fighter orbiting a beacon and being given control towards the bombers, the variations being those required to counter the use of 'Window' and communications jamming. 'Wilde Sau' was a reintroduction of the single-engined fighter to the night fighting role, under the system proposed by Major Hans-Joachim Hermann; the specialist unit JG 300, in the Bonn area, became the initial exponents of this tactic. It proved successful and so further units were formed at Munich (JG 301) and Berlin (JG 302). These two basic tactical concepts remained valid until the end of the war, with minor changes to incorporate new equipment or modify tactics to suit changing bomber tactics.

The potent AI-equipped Junkers Ju 88 night fighter.

Improved radars, such as the SN-2 (FuG 220) version of 'Lichtenstein', and the use of homers such as 'Flensburg' (to home onto 'Monica') and 'Naxos' (to home onto H2S), helped counter the use of RCM by Bomber Command. New weapons were introduced in an attempt to bring down the bombers with fewer hits and thus give a greater chance of a 'first-pass' kill. Certain pilots had exceptional records of multiple kills; Heinz Schnaufer destroyed nine bombers on the night of 7 March 1945, two during the first sortie and seven on the second (his total eventually rose to 121).

Despite the increased fighter threat the basic bomber tactic remained that of avoiding contact, or if an interception took place 'to finish the combat without being seriously damaged, and this can only be achieved by manoeuvring so that the fighter's fire goes wide, and making up for the lighter armament of the turret by firing accurately at the fighter'. The advised technique was that of the 'corkscrew' (see accompanying diagram), a stomach-churning manoeuvre but one that saved the lives of many Bomber Command aircrew. During the corkscrew the pilot was meant to call the next part of the manoeuvre so that the gunners could allow for it . . . 'going down port . . . going up starboard . . . rolling . . .'.

It was a constant battle of wits—new tactics, new counters, revised tactics . . .

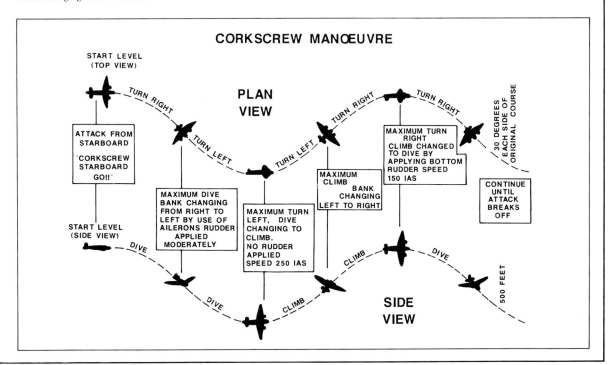

CORKSCREW MANOEUVRE

PLAN VIEW

START LEVEL (TOP VIEW)

TURN RIGHT

TURN LEFT

TURN LEFT

TURN RIGHT

TURN RIGHT

30 DEGREES EACH SIDE OF ORIGINAL COURSE

ATTACK FROM STARBOARD
"CORKSCREW STARBOARD GO!!"

MAXIMUM DIVE BANK CHANGING FROM RIGHT TO LEFT BY USE OF AILERONS RUDDER APPLIED MODERATELY

MAXIMUM TURN LEFT, DIVE CHANGING TO CLIMB. NO RUDDER APPLIED SPEED 250 IAS

MAXIMUM CLIMB BANK CHANGING LEFT TO RIGHT

MAXIMUM TURN RIGHT CLIMB CHANGED TO DIVE BY APPLYING BOTTOM RUDDER SPEED 150 IAS

CONTINUE UNTIL ATTACK BREAKS OFF

START LEVEL (SIDE VIEW)

DIVE

DIVE

CLIMB

CLIMB

DIVE

SIDE VIEW

500 FEET

Wellingtons of No 300 (Polish) Squadron, formed in July 1940 (with Battles) as the first of the Polish bomber squadrons.

within 10 miles of the target using DR navigation; once within this 'box' they would have to identify features on the ground from which to locate the target. However, one analysis at the time concluded: 'Our general opinion is that under war conditions the average crew of a night bomber could not be relied upon to identify and attack targets at night except under the very best conditions of visiblity, even when the target is on the coast or on a very large river like the Rhine . . . very few inexperienced crews would be likely to find it under any conditions.' Yet, at the same time, official Bomber Command policy was that crews could attack small pinpoint targets at night!

Using forward bases in France the Whitleys extended their leaflet-dropping flights to Prague and Vienna in late January, although the majority of the millions of leaflets still went to areas of Germany, where they had absolutely no effect. When two Whitleys flew to Warsaw on 15/16 March it was the longest operational flight to date by Bomber Command, and '. . . all for the sake of bits of paper'. On return one of the aircraft landed in France, the other landed thinking it was in France; the crew were greeted by a number of locals who made it clear that they had landed in Germany and that France was a few miles 'over there'! They climbed back into the aircraft just as German troops appeared; safely airborne, they made it to France and safety.

Leaflet raids comprised the largest element of Bomber Command's effort during the first months of 1940, with Whitleys, Wellingtons and Hampdens spreading their cargo of 'bumph' across Europe. Daylight anti-shipping searches continued, although from February onwards they were primarily confined to the Blenheims of No 2 Group. Most were remarkable only for their monotony and lack of targets, one rare exception being the sinking on 11 March of the submarine *U-31* by a No 82 Squadron Blenheim—although the U-boat was subsequently salved. Since the middle of December there had also been the task of mounting standing patrols over German seaplane bases, the idea being to bomb the base, or rather the flare-path (still no bombing of land targets), when there was sign of activity.

On 16 March Air Marshal Sir Charles Portal took over as AOC Bomber Command, some seeing the removal of Ludlow-Hewitt as a shameful trick by the Air Staff to dispose of a commander who did not meet with their favour. It is true that Ludlow-Hewitt had made many comments as to the inadequacies of his force, predicting the heavy losses, and in January had suggested a move to night attacks. He was also upset by the Air Staff's reluctance to agree to Bomber Command's opening a strategic offensive and, like many others, he had the feeling that Newall, as Chief of the Air Staff, was giving too much ground to the politicians.

A few days after Portal took control, Bomber Command was authorized to make its first attack on a land target in Germany, a reprisal for a German bombing raid on Scapa Flow in the Orkneys during which bombs had

HANDLEY PAGE HAMPDEN

'It was a near perfect, if mildly eccentric, flying machine. It handled in tight turns and other off-beat manoeuvres like a fighter; the single-seat cockpit, cramped and cluttered though it was, provided a view from wing-tip to wing-tip, and it was as viceless as made no matter.'

Designed to the same twin-engined bomber specification as the Wellington, B.9/32, the sleek all-metal stressed-skin HP.52, which first flew on 21 June 1936 (K4240), looked promising. With a higher speed than the Wellington and better range/load capability than the Blenheim, the Hampden was set to become one of the mainstays of the Bomber Command re-equipment programme. In August 1936 an initial order was placed for 180 aircraft.

Entry to service came two years later, August 1938, with deliveries to No 49 Squadron at Scampton and by the outbreak of war the Command had ten squadrons in service. As with the Blenheim, the Hampden was really overtaken by the developments in fighter aircraft, its performance, despite its good manoeuvrability, being inadequate to guarantee its protection. The original manually operated gun armament was increased but it was still to prove insufficient, and in the early daylight raids the Hampden squadrons suffered heavy losses.

An additional problem was that of aircraft recognition; the long thin fuselage of the Hampden (which gave it its nickname of 'Flying Panhandle') led to frequent confusion with the Dornier Do 17 and there were numerous instances of aircraft being attacked in error by fighters and ground defences. Nevertheless, in the first years of the war the Hampdens played an integral part in the full range of Bomber Command operations, with daylight and night bombing, including Berlin, leaflet-dropping, and minelaying. It was in this last role that the Hampdens of No 5 Group became specialists, being the first Command aircraft to carry out this duty, and shouldering the responsibility for over two years.

For two years the squadrons of No 5 Group carried out operations with their Hampdens but it was inevitable from almost the opening months of the war that the type had severe limitations. A raid on Wilhelmshaven on 14/15 September 1942 brought its operational career with Bomber Command to an end.

HAMPDEN I DATA
Crew: Four
Engines: Two 1,000hp Bristol Pegasus XVIII
Span: 69ft 2in
Length: 53ft 7in
Height: 14ft 11in
Weight empty: 11,780lb
Weight loaded: 18,756lb
Max. speed: 254mph at 13,800ft
Ceiling: 19,000ft
Range: 1,885 miles (2000lb bomb load)
Armament: One fixed and one movable 0.303in gun forward, upper and ventral twin 0.303in guns; max. bomb load 4,000lb

Handley Page Hampdens of No 49 Squadron, whose 'EA' code is faintly visible on the nearest aircraft. [49 Sqn records]

Squadrons (Bomber Command): Nos 7, 44, 49, 50, 61, 76, 83, 106, 144, 185, 207, 408, 420, 455

Above: German seaplane base on the island of Sylt.

Opposite top: Hampden crews after the attack on shipping at Bergen on 9 April 1940.

Opposite bottom: Hampdens played a major part in all aspects of the bomber offensive and pioneered the minelaying role.

partly a reflection of the difficulty of assessing damage. As a bomb explodes it creates an impression of devastation, throwing debris into the air and covering the area in smoke and dust; when the debris settles the actual damage might be very light.

Statistics from the various types of sortie flown between September 1939 and March 1940 were frequently reviewed. The amount of data was small as Bomber Command had not been heavily tasked, but the comparison between day and night operations was particularly interesting. Daylight losses amongst the Wellingtons had been high, as much as 50 per cent in some instances—a totally unsupportable loss rate. The losses amongst the night-flying Whitleys were far lower, a statistic used by some (Ludlow-Hewitt included) to prove that the only prospects for the future lay with night bombing. Although the statistics vary, the general average up to March 1940 appeared to be around 13 per cent losses for daylight missions as against only 2 per cent for the night missions. The former loss rate could not be accepted over a period of greater than a few months; the latter was less than had been predicted and therefore held great promise. As was to be shown, however, it was not as simple as that—although the general principle was to hold good until 1945 and the final collapse of an effective day air defence system over Germany. Although Bomber Command never abandoned daylight operations, it is true that from the spring of 1940 onwards the emphasis, especially with the strategic campaign, moved towards night operations. Unfortunately Bomber Command was ill-equipped to carry out its task at night; neither the equipment nor the training was orientated towards a night campaign.

THE GERMAN INVASION OF SCANDINAVIA

The German invasion of Scandinavia, launched on 9 April, caused much discussion among stategists in the British Government and Military. As soon as the first German moves were made, with the mobilizing of shipping during the first week of April, Bomber Command was instructed to undertake anti-shipping operations. On 9 April 24 Hampdens flew anti-shipping searches off Bergen in Norway; half the force was recalled and of the remainder only two aircraft managed to put in attacks, which were unsuccessful, on enemy shipping. Two days later a force of six Wellingtons from No 115 Squadron carried out the first (intentional) bombing raid on a target in mainland Europe when they attacked the German-held airfield at Stavanger/Sola in Norway. The raid was led by Squadron Leader du Boulay in Wellington P9230/R, the task being to 'bomb runways, aircraft and aerodrome installations'. Take-off was at 1810 and the aircraft were loaded with 500lb SAP bombs to be dropped from 1,000 feet. The first section of three aircraft attacked the target with little difficulty, but the second section found the defences ready and

fallen on land. A force of 30 Whitleys and 20 Hampdens took off on the evening of 19 March and had little difficulty in locating their target on the southern tip of the island of Sylt. The seaplane base at Hornum had been chosen for this significant raid because it was well away from civilian areas. In this first substantial bombing raid the attackers dropped forty 500lb bombs, eighty-four 250lb bombs and approximately 1,200 incendiaries. Some weeks were to elapse before further 'real' bombing targets were cleared for attack.

A photographic sortie on 6 April showed no visible damage at the seaplane base. It seemed unlikely that any significant amount of damage could have been repaired or concealed and so the raid, and the optimistic reports of the crews, was called into question. Crews genuinely thought that they had attacked the right place, but some would appear to have been miles away. Of those that did attack the right place, the optimistic reports were

waiting. The leader, Pilot Officer Barber in P9284, was shot down by flak and both of the other aircraft were damaged—P9271 (Flight Sergeant Powell) was hit three times and had the hydraulics damaged, leading to a wheels-up landing for which the pilot received the DFM (one of the crew had been wounded); P9235 (Flying Officer Scott) was hit by flak which wounded the navigator. None of this section dropped its bombs.

In similar fashion, the bombers were called upon to make frequent anti-shipping searches. On 12 April a force of 80-plus Hampdens, Wellingtons and Blenheims was tasked to attack shipping near Stavanger. As soon as the bombers appeared in the area they were met by heavy flak—and swarms of fighters from the nearby airfield. The Bf 110s and Bf 109s pursued the bomber formations out to sea, as far as 200 miles in some cases,

---

MINELAYING

'It is not unusual for the minelaying aircraft to fly round and round for a considerable time in order to make quite sure that the mine is laid exactly in the correct place. It calls for great skill and resolution. Moreover, the crew do not have the satisfaction of seeing even the partial results of their work. There is no coloured explosion, no burgeoning of fire to report on their return home. At best all they see is a splash on the surface of a darkened and inhospitable sea.' In these words, a Bomber Command summary of 1941 described minelaying. On the night of 13/14 April 1940 a number of Hampdens flew to the Danish coast to lay the first mines in what was to develop into a major Bomber Command offensive.

Minelaying, or 'Gardening' as it was code-named, involved the aircraft laying a mine ('planting a vegetable') in a specific location. All these locations were given suitable agricultural names (flowers and vegetables) in line with the general terminology implied by 'gardening', although some had the names of sea creatures. (Among the most frequented areas were 'Eglantine' (approach to Heligoland), 'Nectarines' (Frisian Islands), 'Artichokes' (Lorient) and 'Forget-me-nots' (Kiel Canal); there were just under 130 code-names in total.

In the first months of the operation it was the Hampdens that carried the major responsibility for this type of attack, there being between three and six squadrons allocated to the task. Each aircraft could carry only a single 1,500lb A Mk I mine. As with so many other aspects of Bomber Command's operations in the first half of the war, the major problem was one of navigation—how to get to the target area and then 'plant the vegetable' in exactly the right spot. Navigation relied on DR and whatever fixes, astro or visual, were available; the actual drop itself was usually carried out by timed run from a visual fixpoint in the area of the target.

At first Bomber Command was given five general areas for its minelaying operations, part of a co-ordinated campaign being run by the Admiralty through Coastal Command; the areas were Norwegian waters, Danish waters, Baltic, Kiel Canal and Elbe estuary, and the Bay of Biscay. As the campaign progressed, and especially following Harris's offer to drop 1,000 mines a month, the areas were

Loading mines into a Stirling, March 1944.

extended so that in effect Bomber Command was 'Gardening' from the extreme north of Norway right down to the Spanish border. The overall mining campaign was under the control of the Admiralty Directorate of Minelaying Operations. Within the constraints of the broad directives the Admiralty issued, the Air Ministry and Bomber Command had a large degree of flexibility regarding the actual targets and percentage of effort in a given period (Harris when he put forward his 1,000 a month plan specified that this must not interfere with the main strategic offensive). In consultation with naval advisers, and with consideration of the prevailing strategic situation (for example, U-boat waters became a key target area during the period of anti-U-boat operations), tasking took place and the Groups were notified of their effort. The planning procedure then followed that for a normal bombing mission.

The intensity of the campaign is brought home by such statistics as the 227 aircraft which laid 600 mines on the night of 28/29 April 1943—an enormous effort! In the period 1 February 1942 to 8 May 1945, Bomber Command flew 16,240 mining sorties, dropping a total of 45,428 mines. Statistics as to the losses of enemy shipping are hard to determine, and often show great variance; one post-war Bomber Command analysis claimed 491 ships sunk and 410 damaged—an average of one ship per 50 mines dropped. The total effort by the Command from April 1940 onwards was 47,152 mines, for a loss of 467 aircraft.

The mines were robust and reliable devices, fitted with a drogue parachute to slow them down for water entry. Up to 1943 all delivery was at low level, but in that year the Stirlings carried out trials dropping mines from 12,000ft. This caused no problems and became the standard technique. When the Wellingtons joined in the campaign they doubled the capability as they could carry two mines; later the Manchester and Halifax were equipped to carry four mines, and the Lancaster could take six. Throughout the war improvements were made in the mines, including the use of acoustic mines from September 1942. A variety of mines of between 1,000lb and 2,000lb were used during the period. The primary weapons were:

1. 1,500lb A Mk I with about 750lb high-explosive. Modifications led to others up to Mk IV. Acoustic or combination mine.
2. 1,000lb A Mk V with about 650lb HE. Magnetic mine.
3. 2,000lb A Mk VI, more HE and greater sophistication of fusing.
4. 1,000lb A Mk VII with greater sophistication all round.
(There were sub-variants and variations on the above.)

There was always a degree of argument as to what effect this campaign was having and whether the effort expended was worth the result. Although the actual sinkings do not always look particularly impressive it is essential to remember other equally important factors. A great quantity of shipping was damaged and this had a direct impact on the construction yards; effort, including resources and manpower, had to be expended on repairing these vessels. In order to reduce the danger the Germans conducted an intensive minesweeping programme, again involving resources and manpower that would have been employed elsewhere. Every ship sunk or damaged caused disruption in the communications of military and civil, often industrial, material. Losses, or the threat of losses, eventually became so severe that neutral countries, the most important being Sweden with the supply of raw materials such as iron ore, were reluctant to ship goods to Germany. Any one of these elements was important; taken together they were very significant. Harris was convinced that the minelaying 'put a large part of the German navy on the work of minesweeping, and many workers on to the repair of ships'.

and during the running fights nine bombers (six Hampdens and three Wellingtons) were shot down; the gunners had, however, claimed five of the attacking fighters in return. This raid had been the largest yet mounted by Bomber Command; it was also the last major daylight raid by the Wellingtons and Hampdens.

The four-week period from the start of this 'campaign' saw Bomber Command operating almost every day, and night, in an effort to counter the German invasion and give time for an Allied intervention to support Norwegian resistance. For the first week anti-shipping operations were the main task, formations of bombers trying to get through fighter and flak defences to reach their targets. A major problem was the rapid build-up of Stavangar/Sola as a major German fighter airfield. Although the airfield was attacked day and night, it was only by small numbers of bombers and little damage was caused, but bomber losses were high.

In mid-April a new form of anti-shipping operation began. When fifteen Hampdens took off on 13 April on a 'Gardening' sortie to 'plant vegetables' off the coast of Denmark it was the opening move in what was to become a key element of Bomber Command's operations. Throughout 1940 these minelaying sorties remained a standing task carried out by the Hampdens of No 5 Group. The number of squadrons allocated depended on negotiations between the Air Staff and the Admiralty, but usually was between three and six. On this first sortie, fourteen of the aircraft put their single mines in the target areas, but the remaining Hampden did not return to base. As was so often the case with this type of sortie, the reason for the loss remained a mystery. A typical minelaying sortie was that by Hampden L4038 on No 49 Squadron (F/O Burnett, P/O Gower, Sgt Bunting, AC Cartwright) on the night of 21/22 April:

'On 21 April we were detailed to carry out Gardening operations in "Daffodil" area. We took off at 1930 hours and set course for coast, climbing at 135mph to 5,000 feet. At 1952 hours we set course 083 degrees for Sylt. We proceeded uneventfully at 5,000 feet above 8/10 to 10/10 cloud until we saw Sylt through a break in the cloud at 2150 hours. We continued on the same course and at 2205 hours observed a green light on our port bow which we mistook for a sea navigation light. It was however the navigation lights of another aircraft which we identified as an enemy aircraft. We descended through the cloud at 2230 hours and at the ETA determined our position to be south of the target so set North and fifteen minutes later recognized the target area. We ascertained our target and dropped "melon" according to plan at 2315 hours. We set course of 255 degrees Magnetic for base and began climbing through cloud to 6,000 feet. At 0030 hours we crossed the German coast at Yarding. At 0136 hours we obtained fix from Heston and altered course at 267 degrees for base. Coast crossed at 0250. We received several homing bearings from base and landed at 0310.'

For the Hampden squadrons minelaying became their principal task, operations taking place on fourteen nights between 14 April and 9 May. The largest single effort was that of 21/22 April when 36 aircraft were employed, one of which was lost. Meanwhile the other squadrons, and a number of Hampdens, were engaged on anti-shipping and anti-airfield work, the larger-scale raids taking place at night in recognition of the growing German defensive capability by day. After heavy involvement in the daylight ops, the Blenheims flew their last Norwegian mission on 2 May—to Stavanger and Rye airfields—and were then withdrawn from the

Arming a No 49 Squadron Hampden. [49 Sqn records]

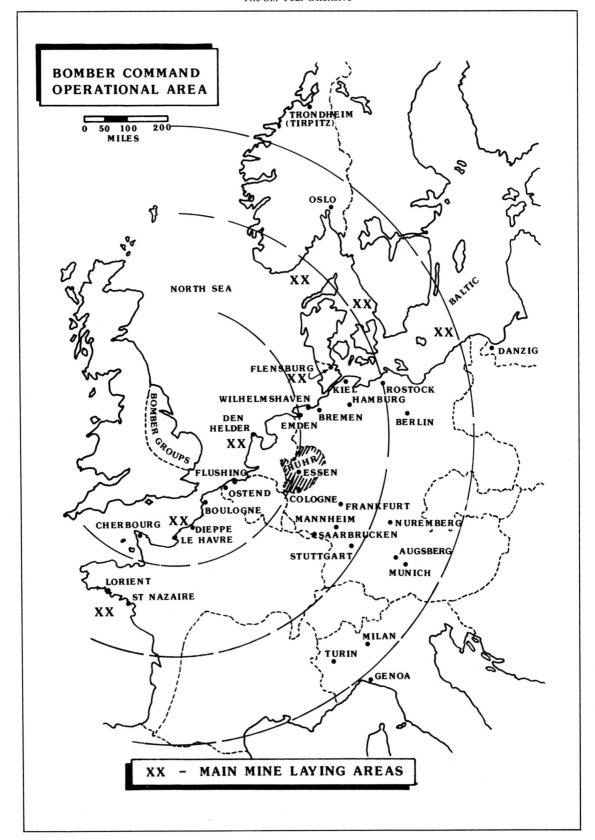

France, May 1940, and a No 114 Squadron Blenheim that will take no further part in the war. The Blenheim squadrons undertook operations far in excess of their capability; losses were severe but there was simply nothing else to send. [Gordon Hampton]

campaign to prepare for employment against the antici-pated German offensive into France.

Anti-shipping, minelaying and airfield attacks in connection with the Norwegian campaign continued until 9 May, at which point another crisis broke upon the British leadership—the German invasion in the West. A Bomber Command summary of the Norwegian involvement outlined the problems that had been faced: 'More might perhaps have been accomplished, but the task was from the outset of the most formidable kind. There was no more than a small force of bombers available, and it had to operate at extreme range in thick weather, without fighter support and with information always inadequate and sometimes altogether lacking.' These operations saw the final transfer, discounting exceptional circumstances, of the medium bomber force from a day bombing organization into a night bombing one; the transition was to take nearly two years to produce a truly effective night bombing force.

FUTURE STRATEGY

The first significant change in the air bombing policy had been initiated with a Directive issued to Portal on 13 April 1940; as with so much that was to affect Bomber Command over the next few years, it was very much a reaction to events rather than the creation of a long-term strategy. Even in this the Directive was not clear-cut since it put forward two policies dependent upon which series of events transpired: no German invasion of the Low Countries but the start of general

air action, or a German invasion of Holland and Belgium. In the event of general air action being called for, Bomber Command was to implement the basic provisions of plan WA 8 (the night attack on Germany), the priorities being given as:

1. Identifiable oil plants (WA 6).

2. Identifiable electricity plants, coking plants and gas ovens (WA 5).

3. Self-illuminating objectives vulnerable to air attack (WA 8).

4. Main German ports in the Baltic—if specifically authorized.

To carry out this ambitious plan the Commander was to use Nos 3 and 4 Groups, plus that part of No 5 Group not engaged on mining tasks. If the situation permitted he could also call upon the squadrons of the AASF to join in the campaign. However, if the second condition prevailed and the Germans had invaded the Low Countries, then the entire plan changed, the emphasis being 'to attack vital objectives in Germany, starting in the Ruhr, to cause the maximum dislocation to lines of communication of the German advance through the Low Countries'. In essence this was a modified plan WA 4(c), the stated objectives being:

1. Troop concentrations.

2. Communications in the Ruhr, especially marshalling yards.

3. Oil plants in the Ruhr.

The additional notes to the Directive confused the issue somewhat by turning the second plan into a mini-version of the first, stating that the main weight of the attacks should be on the oil plants, with attacks on marshalling yards more of a 'harassing nature'. If crews could not find either of these targets, then they were to attack self-illuminating targets instead (meaning such installations as coke ovens, the targets being given away by the light of the industrial process). Two other comments were of significance: first, that operations by heavy bombers should be confined mainly to night to conserve the forces; and second, that the Command should be prepared to undertake a sustained effort.

It is significant to note that the targets included the comment 'identifiable'; there was no suggestion of a general bombing campaign. This was in line with War Cabinet guidelines, confirmed again at a meeting on 10 May, that 'it is preferable not to begin bombing ops in the Ruhr until we have definite news that the Germans have attacked targets . . . which would cause casualties to civilians'. This showed shades of the Hague Convention and a desire not to be the first to 'declare war' on the general civilian population; it could however be argued that the Germans had already done just that with their bombing campaign in Poland. Allied to this argument was the more widely held belief, strongly supported by the French, that the Luftwaffe was far better equipped to carry out a strategic campaign than its opponents. To launch such an offensive would be to invite a devastating response. Would it not therefore be best to leave well alone unless no other option remained?

THE GERMAN OFFENSIVE IN THE WEST

On the day that this meeting took place the German armed forces launched their offensive in the West with a lightning strike into Belgium and Holland. One of the primary objectives of the early German operations was the capture of airfields; troop-carrying aircraft landed at Ypenburg and Waalhaven in Holland, as well as at landing sites along the Dutch coast. All these locations were immediately targeted by the Blenheims of No 2 Group; crews reported causing much damage, but in the process lost three of their number. That night the attacks on the airfields were continued by a force of Wellingtons attacking Waalhaven, while nine Whitleys tried to bomb bridges over the Rhine and columns of troops on the surrounding roads. The Battle squadrons attached to the AASF were freed from their previous reconnaissance tasks and began what was to become a heroic, but suicidal, offensive against the advancing German columns. A problem that was to plague all

attempts at countering the enemy advance was an almost total lack of accurate, up-to-date intelligence. Bomber Command, and that part of it attached to the AASF (No 1 Group), began a period of sustained and intensive operations which bled much of its medium bomber strength away, and saw the loss of many aircrew—relatively experienced aircrew who could not easily be replaced. It was crisis management; equipment and tactics were ill suited for the tasks being performed.

The AASF squadrons had found operating from France difficult, partly because of the intransigence of the French authorities, and before the German offensive they had been confined to reconnaissance sorties along the border (and up to 10 miles into Germany). It had been reasonable experience. There had even been the odd sharp lesson of the vulnerability of the Battle to attacks from German fighters; four out of five aircraft had been shot down over Saarbrucken on 30 September 1939. Despite such incidents the 'Phoney War' continued into the spring of 1940, the Battle squadrons flying their recce sorties, sometimes with an escort of French fighters. In mid-April, as the overall situation deteriorated and a German offensive seemed likely, plans were laid to attack line of communication targets in the Rhine area. However, on 15 April the French 'Comité de Guerre' ruled these targets unacceptable because of the possibility of civilian casualties and German reprisal. This left the only target system available as troops on open roads. It was pointed out to General Gamelin that this was a most unsatisfactory situation. The launch of the German offensive in May, although expected, still caught the Allied forces by surprise and made rapid gains.

The bomber task was stated as: 'To delay and weaken in every way possible the advance of the German mechanized forces and try to relieve the pressure on the Allied armies sufficiently to enable them first to hold the enemy and then to mount an effective counter-attack.'

The weak point in the offensive was obviously the bridges over the rivers, natural choke-points for reinforcements, the destruction of which would have a great impact on the battle. Battles of the AASF were thrown into the fray in an effort to stem the flood of German armour and troops; unco-ordinated and often unescorted attacks were made against such targets as the bridges over the Meuse. Losses were enormous and yet time after time the gallant crews returned to try to destroy their targets. Despite some successes, it was a one-sided battle. As exponents of the art of air-to-ground operations, the Germans had developed that other essential element—effective anti-aircraft defences. Having crossed the Meuse, the German forces spread out and the chance to stem the tide was lost. It had not been through lack of effort on the part of the AASF and No 2 Group. The Blenheims had joined in the attacks on German columns and positions—and had suffered equally heavy casualties. By 21 May the Germans had reached the sea at Le Touquet and the Allied armies could do nothing to save the situation. British and French forces withdrew to Dunkirk and in Operation 'Dynamo', one of the most amazing operations of the war, some 340,000 men were lifted off the beaches and taken to Britain. To the troops on the beach the RAF's part in the evacuation was treated with scorn as the only aircraft they saw were German—'Where was the bloody RAF?' Fighter Command had, however, tried to stem the waves of German aircraft, before they reached the beaches, and paid a heavy price; while Bomber Command flew hundreds of sorties for 'Dynamo' between 27 May and 4 June to 'put a curtain of bombs around the port'.

Throughout the period of the German offensive, the heavy bombers undertook missions against lines of communication, the Meuse crossings, and points of congestion behind the enemy lines, to disrupt supply and reinforcement. Between 11 May and 15 June these squadrons carried out 27 major raids. The first of these operations was mounted on the night of 10/11 May when 36 Wellingtons attacked Waalhaven airfield and nine Whitleys went after bridges and concentrations of enemy MT. The following night a force of Hampdens and Whitleys attacked road and rail communications at Mönchengladbach, the first raid of the war on a German

The attacks by Battles against bridges and German troop movements decimated the squadrons.

town, although it was argued that the town itself had not been the target.

In the period from 10 May to 25 June—when the Franco-German Armistice became effective—the Blenheim squadrons operated on all but four days, an incredible level of effort. The total of sorties ran to 1,616 against a wide range of targets, the nature of which depended on the phase of the campaign. The overall losses of 104 aircraft (although very few of the aircrew survived) seem to suggest a reasonable loss rate; this, however, is a false picture. During the first week of the German offensive the Blenheims flew against airfields, bridges and troop columns and in 168 sorties lost 36 aircraft—a 20 per cent loss rate. The worst day was 17 May when eleven out of twelve Blenheims from No 82 Squadron were shot down while attacking troops near Gembloux; the twelfth aircraft was badly shot-up but managed to crash-land in England. The intensive pace and heavy losses continued up to 25 May. From then until 3 June the squadrons were tasked with supporting Allied forces around Dunkirk. On 31 May 93 Blenheims flew against German positions around Dunkirk, with no losses. However, despite the reduced level of losses in the Dunkirk missions it was obvious that the pace of operations could not continue. An urgent directive was sent to Air Marshal Barratt, AOC-in-C British Air Forces in France (BAFF), on 30 May: 'It is imperative that some reduction in their effort should be made in order that the force be maintained as its present operational strength and efficiency.'

With the evacuation of Dunkirk complete, the Blenheims continued to operate against German columns and occupied airfields, such as Schipol and Merville, although the scale of effort had been reduced in accordance with the recent instruction.

As operations moved further into France the equally depleted and battered squadrons of Battles were withdrawn to Britain to rest and re-form. It was the end of an episode for Bomber Command. Valuable lessons had been learnt but little could be done about re-equipping with more appropriate aircraft as resources were limited, and in the face of 'imminent' invasion of the home base every aircraft would be needed. Thus, although the Battle had been shown to be of limited operational value, squadrons were brought back up to strength and others formed. There was simply no alternative.

THE START OF THE STRATEGIC OFFENSIVE

On 14 May the Luftwaffe launched a heavy attack on Rotterdam, the first overt bombing of a town by either side in the western theatre of operations. A number of other towns in Holland and Belgium had been hit during the previous days, although in most instances this was connected with the general flow of the advance. Nevertheless, many in the War Cabinet were of the opinion that 'the gloves were off' and that the Ruhr towns were now a legitimate target.

On 15 May Churchill authorized bombing east of the Rhine. With the attack the same night by 99 bombers on oil and rail targets in the Ruhr the strategic bombing offensive, which was to reach its climax in late 1944 and early 1945, was under way.

Having just explained the basis for the reduction in the Blenheim support operations, Barratt had the unenviable task of informing the French High Command that the RAF's heavy bombers were switching away from direct support of the land campaign; but with the guarantee that if a 'critical situation' developed the full weight of Bomber Command would be immediately available. The Air Staff had decided that 'in the absence of moonlight, experience proves that the heavy bombers cannot operate with sufficient accuracy against road objectives and defiles in the forward area to make an effective contribuition to the land situation by this means'. They decided, therefore, to concentrate on industrial targets in Germany, 'to cause the continuous interruption and dislocation of industry, particularly where the German aircraft industry is concentrated'.

Within a week of this statement, on 4 June, a new directive had been sent to Bomber Command, the opening comments of which were revealing: 'The initiative lies with the enemy; our strategical policy is liable to be deflected by the turn of events from the course we should like it to follow'. Although an accurate statement, it was not very reassuring to those whose task it was to plan and implement strategy. The inevitable result of living in such a hand-to-mouth fashion was to have the wrong equipment and training, which was then thrown into unsuitable and often unviable situations on the grounds that there was no alternative. There was indeed little choice in the matter in view of the crisis being faced by Britain in 1940. It was not that the senior commanders did not appreciate the difficulties, or that they failed to grasp the required solution. Early in 1940 the Senior Air Staff Officer (SASO) of Bomber Command had said: 'In view of the changing tactical conditions which are likely to lead us more and more to night operations, I think we need to stress the importance of maximum training in night bombing.' He was right, but it would take time to put into effect, and even longer before that effect could be made obvious at the front line of Bomber Command operations.

It was stressed to Portal that in the event of a further German advance into France, he would be called upon to give maximum support to the ground forces, but in the meantime he could look to a more strategic employment of his forces. The Air Staff would continue to try to persuade the French that their best interests would be served by Bomber Command hitting Germany—'a really suitable and profitable objective'. The target systems list was headed once more by oil, with the added proviso to hit oil stocks, as reports indicated that the German situation could become critical following a concerted anti-oil campaign. Bomber and fighter assembly plants were proposed as alternative targets, with self-illuminating targets as a last option. It was further stressed that 'in no circumstances should night bombing be allowed to degenerate into mere indiscriminate action', this being contrary to the policy of His Majesty's Government. It was suggested that the Command should conserve its effort during the dark moon period so as to be ready for a maximum effort when conditions were more favourable. As for the Blenheim squadrons, they should be employed on any suitable target, 'except naval dockyards and vessels under construction'.

It appeared that Bomber Command was to be allowed to implement its long-cherished plan for striking a mighty blow at the heart of German industry—the Ruhr.

To return to that first operation of 15 May. The 39 Wellingtons, 36 Hampdens and 24 Whitleys were sent against sixteen different industrial targets throughout the Ruhr; most claimed to have bombed their targets without too much difficulty. The only loss was a Wellington of No 115 Squadron which crashed in France. A few bombs were recorded as falling on Cologne and Munster, but overall the raid appears to

Left top: Battles of No 88 Squadron with (very rare) a French fighter escort of Curtiss Hawk 75As.

Left: Signals briefing in June 1940.

The Whitley squadrons faced a daunting task both in finding their targets (lack of navaids) and struggling against the weather and the German defences. Some aircraft returned with extensive damage, like this No 58 Squadron machine. [58 Sqn records]

have been ineffective, no damage being recorded at any of the target industries. With the addition of operations against German positions in Belgium, the total effort for the night was 111 sorties—the first time that Bomber Command had exceeded 100. The Ruhr was visited again the following night, but this time by only twelve aircraft looking for oil targets. Most nights throughout the remainder of May saw 60 or so bombers in action against industrial targets or in conjunction with battle-field requirements, attacking communications or troop concentrations.

WHY THE RUHR?

Virtually all British plans for an air offensive specified the Ruhr as the most critical area to be attacked; this was true from the earliest WA plan of the pre-war period right up to the major offensive planned and executed by Bomber Command in 1943–44. It is worth examining the reasons why this emphasis was made.

The Ruhr area was often referred to as 'the weapon-smithy of the Reich', an area of critical importance to German heavy industry and munitions. At the start of

the war about two-thirds of the total German production of hard coal and coking coke came from the Ruhr area. With this as a basis, and the fact that the area was situated at the meeting point of various trans-continental communications routes (road, rail and water), it was an obvious location for heavy industry. It was also a compact region, the main industrial belt being no more than 30 miles from east to west. This included the eleven main industrial towns, the most significant ones being Essen, Duisburg, Dortmund, Bochum and Gelsenkirchen. Of these, Essen, with the huge Krupps arms and engineering factories, was the most important. The town contained many other vital war industries in addition to the Krupps complex, such as the Goldschmitt chemical and metal works. The outskirts of Essen joined with the towns of Mulheim,

Oberhausen and Gelsenkirchen, an area containing numerous foundries and engineering works, coal mines and coking plants. Near Gelsenkirchen were two of the most important targets, the hydrogenation plants of Gelsenberg-Benzin and Hydrierwerke-Scholvern, which together produced some 575,000 tonnes of aviation petrol per year. The largest Ruhr town, Dortmund, contained a variety of engineering works as well as three large iron and steel works. Bochum, situated between Dortmund and Essen, was a centre of the coal and coke industry and as such had the usual accompanying industries of petroleum and chemicals, including explosives manufacture. It also included many of the principal high-grade steel works, producing such items as gun barrels, armour plate and aircraft components. Duisburg occupied the key position at the junctions of the Rhine and Ruhr rivers, and in Duisburg-Ruhrort had the largest inland port in Europe. As a centre of the coal, iron and steel industry it produced millions of tons of iron and steel each year, much of it going to supply munitions factories throughout the Ruhr. The list of industries was almost endless and there could be little doubt of the critical importance of this relatively small and compact area. Furthermore, it was also the nearest part of Germany to the bombers based in Britain and was thus a most suitable target. A glance at the map on pages 72–3 will show just how compact and interlinked this area was.

The question that remained to be answered was:

The Wellington provided the backbone of the night bomber force for more than three years. This aircraft belonged to No 12 OTU, a training unit.

could Bomber Command carry out an effective campaign against the Ruhr?

Crews were learning as they went along. The difficulties of navigating at night in a wartime environment had been brought home in a forceful manner, many a navigator 'suddenly' finding that he was 100 miles away from where his plot said he should be. It came as a shock to the peacetime-trained crew; nevertheless, there was a reluctance among some to admit the problem and place greater reliance on the Direction Finding (D/F) information provided by the Wireless Operator (WOP). Fixes using D/F could even be obtained from German beacons, a favourite being that on Texel. By August 1940 new long-range D/F stations, such as Butser Hill and Acklington, meant that D/F bearings could be obtained over western Germany, although the possible errors at such long ranges from the beacon had to be considered. Given the right weather conditions, a drift could be obtained by dropping a 4½lb incendiary down the flare chute and then getting the tail gunner to track it using his Drift Scale.

After the week of intensive day and night operations around Dunkirk, the night bombers returned to the offensive against the Ruhr, with occasional forays farther afield to such places as Hamburg. A great deal of effort was expended against communications, especially rail, in a continued attempt to assist the battle being fought in France.

ITALY JOINS THE WAR

With the probability that Italy would join the war alongside her Axis partner, plans were made for a bomber offensive against industrial and military targets

in the north of that country. In view of the distance to the targets it was decided to operate from airfields in southern France; 'Haddock' Force was formed and Wellingtons were deployed to Salon, near Marseilles. The attack planned against Milan had to be cancelled when the French authorities prevented the aircraft from getting airborne, the reason being that they had not received authorization to allow such a raid. Although the problem was soon sorted out it was too late; the aircraft returned to England and the idea of using these southern airfields was abandoned. Instead No 4 Group deployed Whitleys to the Channel Islands on 10 June. The next day 36 aircraft took off from the very small airfields, almost too small for a heavily-laden bomber, en route to attack the Fiat works at Turin. 'As we flew over France,' reported one crew, 'the weather deteriorated and when we reached the Alps we ran into electrical storms. Lightning flashed constantly around us and ice built up on the leading edges of the wings and tailplane. We were thrown around like a pea in a bucket by the turbulence and as conditions got progressively worse we were unable to climb to an altitude that allowed us to cross the mountains.' This Whitley, like 26 others, was defeated by the weather and had to turn back. Nine aircraft reached and bombed Turin, causing some damage; a further two machines bombed Genoa. Whitley N1390 of No 77 Squadron (Sgt Songest) crashed in France.

The next operation against Italy did not take place until 15/16 June when eight Wellingtons took off from Salon to attack Genoa. Only one aircraft claimed to have bombed the target. Genoa and Milan were again the targets the following night for 22 Wellingtons, fourteen of which bombed their targets. Raids were then suspended as other tasks took priority.

The increasing weight of RAF bombing attacks upon Germany brought a corresponding increase, and re-organization, in the German defences. By the summer of 1940 the area Germany/Western Front mustered 2,628 heavy and 6,720 medium/light anti-aircraft guns, together with 2,256 searchlights. The totals look impressive but it was a huge area to defend; the major concentrations were around the most obvious and critical areas such as the Ruhr and Berlin. The fighter threat remained minimal, a total of 164 aircraft being available in the second half of 1940, all of them still single-engined types. RAF crews reported occasional sightings of fighters but 'they appeared to be not very aggressive'. This aspect of the defensive system was about to change; within a year it was to become formidable.

For a variety of reasons the offensive task was becoming increasingly difficult, and the almost 'care-free' period of early 1940 was coming to an end. The war had become more clinical and impersonal; bomber crews were becoming part of a huge machine over which they had little influence, but the comradeship of the squadron kept them together. Gradually friends began to disappear. In this respect this was perhaps the worst period of the war as pre-war-trained comrades who had been together for quite some time would not return from a mission.

From the commencement of the strategic offensive against Germany and Italy the scale of Bomber Command operations increased markedly. It was also a very diverse range of missions, day and night. There is not the space in this account to detail every operation undertaken by Bomber Command, so the authors have chosen to highlight typical and/or specifically 'important' missions for discussion; the rest are covered in period summaries. (For a day by day statistical account of Bomber Command's war, see *Bomber Command War Diaries* by Martin Middlebrook and Chris Everitt.)

TAKING THE WAR TO GERMANY

The loss of France and the now direct threat to the British Isles led to much re-thinking of policy. Throughout 1940 the situation was to remain critical and the reactive nature of British strategy, especially air strategy, led to directives flowing thick and fast from the Air Staff to Bomber Command. No fewer than nine major directives, plus numerous signals, memos and letters, brought new policy statements for Bomber Command to implement. It was an impossible situation, even though some rather more consistent threads were maintained, and would have caused enormous difficulties if followed to the letter. Fortunately, many of the directives were couched in terms that allowed, intentionally or otherwise, a degree of flexiblity—or, as Harris would later state with the directives he was issued, a degree of 'interpretation'.

First of this flood came on 20 June with the statement that: 'The primary offensive must be directed towards objectives which will have the most immediate effect on reducing the scale of air attack on this country.' To achieve this the German aircraft industry and associated equipment depots were given top priority and a list of suitable targets was detailed. Second priority was to be given to communications targets, in view of the difficulties of forward supply being faced by the German forces. The best targets in this category were the marshalling yards in the Ruhr/Cologne area, the yard at Hamm, the largest and most important in Germany, being seen as the most important single target in this group. Oil was kept on the list, and fourth place was given to crops. This latter came from a suggestion that the harvest was likely to be poor and that Bomber Command should use the new 'pellet' incendiary to attack crops and forests (some of which were suspected of being major military storage areas).

Tasks for the medium bombers (meaning the Blenheims) were along the same lines, with attacks on

ARMSTRONG WHITWORTH WHITLEY

'The Whitley was a sturdy aeroplane with few vices. It could take a lot of punishment, and was a pleasure to fly—if a trifle on the slow side, but well liked by those crews who had to fly them on operations.'

Unlike the Hampden and Wellington, the Whitley was the only one of the original trio of heavy bombers to be designed for night operations. It played a key part in Bomber Command operations until the advent of the more potent four-engined aircraft of 1942. When Specification B.3/34 for this aircraft was laid down it promised to be an advanced and capable aircraft; unfortunately, developments rapidly overtook the type and by its entry to service in March 1937, with No 10 Squadron at Dishforth, its 192mph maximum speed was somewhat restrictive. When the prototype (K4586) made its first flight on 17 March 1936, the situation had been somewhat different; the case of the Whitley aptly demonstrates the rapid progress of military aviation in the mid-1930s and the inherent problems of getting aircraft from specification to operational service before they became redundant.

The Whitley received a number of improvements over the next two years as new variants entered service, including the Mk IV with its revolutionary Nash and Thompson four-gun power-operated rear turret. The introduction of such powerful defensive armament to a British bomber was proof of the realization of the increasing vulnerability of heavy bombers to the new generation of fighters. At the same time, more powerful engines were installed, improving performance, although the Merlin-engined Mk V Whitley could still only reach 222mph maximum and cruise at just 185mph.

Nevertheless, the Whitley was a great improvement over the lumbering Heyford which it replaced; at least it looked like a 'modern' aircraft. At the outbreak of war No 4 Group had six operational Whitley squadrons and they were in action over Germany from the first night—a 'Nickel' sortie by Nos 51 and 58 Squadrons, dropping leaflets over the Ruhr. It was in this nightime leaflet-dropping role that the Whitleys first tackled the problems of night operations and night navigation, including the first 'Berlin run' in October 1939. However, the squadrons were soon tasked with bombing missions as an integral part of the Bomber Command campaign to Germany and Italy. The third arm of the offensive, minelaying, also occupied many hundreds of Whitley sorties, as did numerous anti-submarine patrols—with a number of U-boat kills.

Having played its part, the Whitley bowed out from the Bomber Command's front-line with a raid against Dunkirk on the night of 27 April 1942. It was not the end of the aircraft's war as it continued to serve with OTUs and Coastal Command, and as a glider-tug.

WHITLEY V DATA
Crew: Five
Engines: Two 1,010hp Rolls-Royce Merlin X
Span: 84ft
Length: 72ft 6in
Height: 15ft
Weight empty: 19,330lb
Weight loaded: 28,200lb
Max. speed: 222mph at 17,000ft
Ceiling: 17,600ft
Range: 1,650 miles with 3,000lb bombs
Armament: Single 0.303in in nose turret, quadruple 0.303in rear turret; 7,000lb maximum bomb load

Squadrons (Bomber Command): Nos 7, 10, 51, 58, 77, 78, 97, 102, 166

The Armstrong Whitworth pioneered night operations. The pilot of this aircraft was F/Sgt Moore and the front gunner P/O Elliott.

VICKERS WELLINGTON

'The arrangements in the cockpit of the Wellington were almost totally unlike those of any other aeroplane. Nearly everything but the instruments appeared to have been designed and built by Vickers to their own ideas. . . . There was a warning on the main spar that the aircraft must not be dived at more than 280mph. We had just pulled out at 360mph and were still flying.'

Without doubt the Wellington, with its excellent payload/range performance, was the single most important bomber of the early war years, shouldering the Bomber Command offensive battle until the introduction of the four-engined 'heavies'. Designed to 1932 requirement (Specification B.9/32 for a twin-engined bomber), the Wellington prototype (K4049) flew in June 1936 and two months later the Air Ministry placed an order for 180 production Mk I aircraft. It had double the performance capability of the existing Heyford bombers, together with what was considered to be a heavy self-defence armament. However, it was not until October 1938 that the type entered service, with No 99 Squadron at Mildenhall. At the outbreak of war Bomber Command still only had six operational squadrons of Wellingtons. Fourteen of these aircraft took part in the first bombing mission over Germany on 4 September 1939.

These early raids soon revealed that the Wellington was incapable of surviving in daylight over the skies of Germany in the face of determined fighter opposition. By the end of the year most daylight operations had been terminated and Bomber Command turned its attention to night operations.

However, with its unique fabric-covered geodetic metal construction the aircraft was able to take a tremendous amount of damage and still keep on flying; many a crew testified to the rugged nature of the 'Wimpy' as they nursed a badly crippled bomber back to England. The Mk IC became the main variant for the squadrons in the first years of the war as the pace of re-equipment quickened, a total of 2,685 of this mark being built—most, although not all,

serving with Bomber Command. By mid-1941 the Mk II and Mk III had entered service, and gradually the latter variant came to hold the most prominent position among the medium bombers. Nevertheless, it was obvious from mid-1942 that the Wellington was reaching the limit of its useful employment as part of the Bomber Command Main Force and the scale of operations gradually decreased. The final Wellington operation with Bomber Command took place on 8/9 October 1943.

During its three years of operational flying the Wellington had achieved notable successes, despite what at times were severe limitations. The type played an important role in the introduction of new techniques (Pathfinders) and new weapons (4,000lb bomb) and in general terms was well liked by the crews. In addition to its service with Bomber Command, the Wellington played a vital role with Coastal Command and was used extensively by the OTUs and as a crew trainer; as the T.10 it remained in service in this role until 1953. In all, 11,461 Wellingtons were built—the largest total ever of any British multi-engined aircraft.

WELLINGTON IC DATA

Crew: Six
Engines: Two 1,000hp Bristol Pegasus XVIII
Span: 86ft 2in
Length: 64ft 7in
Height: 17ft 5in
Weight empty: 18,556lb
Weight loaded: 29,500lb
Max. speed: 235mph at 15,500ft
Ceiling: 18,000ft
Range: 1,200 miles (4,500b bomb load) or 1,550 miles (1,000lb load)
Armament: Nose and tail turrets with twin 0.303in guns. Beam positions for single 0.303in guns; max. bomb load 4,500lb

Squadrons (Bomber Command): 9, 12, 15, 37, 38, 40, 57, 75, 99, 101, 103, 104, 109, 115, 142, 148, 149, 150, 156, 158, 166, 192, 196, 199, 214, 215, 218, 300, 301, 304, 305, 311, 405, 419, 420, 424, 425, 426, 427, 428, 429, 431, 432, 458, 460, 466

Wellington ICs of No 311 (Czech) Squadron, which operated with Bomber Command until transferred to Coastal Command in April 1942.

airfields high on the list. The airfields in France and the Low Countries would be suitable targets for the Blenheims and were to be kept under harassing attack. The entire Command was also warned to stand by for anti-invasion duties. Two days later (22 June) France signed the Armistice and the British Commonwealth stood alone. It is important to realize what a significant part the Commonwealth played in the British war effort with the provision of material, training establishments and manpower. The contribution to the aircrew strength, of Bomber Command in particular, has all too often been ignored. It is a thread we shall pick up again in this account.

The weeks since Dunkirk had seen a continuation of the night attacks on Germany, often by 100-plus bombers. At this stage of the war there was no thought of concentration of effort on a single target or of complex co-ordinated raid planning. Having been given the target it was up to each crew, led by their captain, to work out a route and, within certain constraints, a time over the target—it was very much an individual (crew) war. Oil and rail targets remained top of the list; in the absence of solid intelligence it was impossible to know just what damage was being inflicted. From late June onwards the Blenheim squadrons were given an additional task: to carry out daylight raids on the targets attacked the previous night, the idea being to make use of cloud cover to sneak into and out of Germany. There was a double aim to this policy: to acquire post-raid photography for use in damage assessment; and to drop a few 'harassing' bombs and so keep the air-raid sirens going and the ARP organization under strain. The vast majority of these raids ended up abortive through lack of cloud cover. The philosphy survived to be reborn when the de Havilland Mosquito entered service with Bomber Command some years later.

THREAT OF INVASION

As the military situation continued to deteriorate invasion seemed imminent. Bomber Command had been attacking enemy shipping in the occupied ports of Europe for some time but a review of bombing policy in early July led to a new directive (4 July). This called for an increased effort against enemy ports and shipping, ranging from the capital ships, such as *Scharnhorst* at Kiel and *Bismarck* at Hamburg, to barges and merchant shipping in the occupied ports. The mining effort, which had been carried out by one squadron of Hampdens, was to be trebled, with the Hampdens now to concentrate on the Kiel Canal, Kiel Bay and the Belts. Any spare capacity was to be directed against the German aircraft industry and oil industry. The Air Staff also directed that the crop attacks should go ahead. For the medium bombers there was no change, except that Norway was added to the list.

In the words of one Bomber Command summary:

Invasion barges gathered at Antwerp.

'The invasion ports face us in a crescent, centred on Calais, some of the world's greatest cargo and passenger installations; in fact, if the enemy had built the ports himself for the express purpose of invading this country, he could hardly have improved on their actual layout— Amsterdam, Rotterdam, Flushing, Bruges, Zeebrugge, Ostend, Antwerp, Dunkirk, Calais, Boulogne, Dieppe, Le Havre and Cherbourg, plus all those on the "flanks" of this crescent.' The planning for Operation 'Sealion', the German invasion, rapidly took a material definition as large numbers of barges and other vessels were collected in the above ports. British estimates showed that in Holland alone there were (pre-war) 18,000 registered barges, the majority of 2-300 tons but some as large as 3,000 tons, and added to this now German-controlled total were many thousands more in Belgium, France and Germany. By the latter part of May at least 3,000 barges had been collected together, enough to transport 1 million tons, together with shipping for another 4 million tons. The urgency of attacking this target led to an immediate and heavy commitment of the bomber force, the Blenheims being tasked particularly heavily. Even crews still in training were included in the battle, partly as the nearness of the targets tempted planners to look upon them as 'Nursery Slopes' which would provide a good operational introduction for 'fresher' crews. Nevertheless, the defences were heavy.

While the Blenheims visited airfields such as Merville, Amiens and Abbeville, and from 3 July the ports where the barges were being gathered, the night bombers were active over the Ruhr and Hamburg. Among the references for the night of 30 June/1 July, when 82 bombers attacked Darmstadt, Hamm, Hamburg and Hanau, is one to 'fire-raising'; this probably refers to the use of two special lighting munitions, 'Razzles' and 'Deckers', designed to destroy crops and forests. These weapons consisted of small phosphorus pellets in celluloid strips (3in by 1in for 'Razzle' and 4in by 4in for 'Decker'). The

idea was that they would ignite as they dried out, and thus set fire to their surroundings (including in a few reported cases the pockets of those who had collected them for souvenirs!). These 'incendiary leaves' were stored in tins of alcohol and water, about 500 to a tin, the idea being to pour them down the flare chute when the time came. It appears that they caused very little damage to the Germans, but they did cause concern in some of the dropping aircraft as leaves stuck on the machine, dried out and caught fire.

Among the bombers operating on 1/2 July was a No 83 Squadron Hampden flown by Flying Officer Guy Gibson. In his attack on *Scharnhorst* at Kiel he dropped the first 2,000lb bombs used by Bomber Command. It had been realized early on that the standard 250lb and 500lb bombs were inadequate, but it would be some months before the Command had even the basis of a suitable range of weapons.

A revised directive issued on 13 July re-emphasized the primary aim as being to 'reduce the scale of the air attack on this country' but also provided for a small additional effort against communications. However, the most important element of this Air Staff statement was its implication that Bomber Command could be making better use of its resources by concentrating effort on fewer targets and maintaining pressure on those targets until the requisite amount of damage had been achieved. To facilitate this the directive listed fifteen primary targets, ten in the aircraft industry and five oil plants. Furthermore, it was estimated that the destruction of each aircraft plant would require 140 of the

Another Blenheim bomb load for a daylight op.

standard 500lb bombs. This was one of the first instances in which the directives had included precise statements regarding effort required to destroy particular targets. Such strategic 'guesswork' became a regular feature of Air Ministry directives; most looked reasonable on paper, but almost all proved totally fanciful in reality.

As secondary targets a number of communications elements were listed, particular emphasis being placed on the aqueducts north of Munster and the shaft lock and aqueduct at Minden. Meanwhile, for the medium bombers it was to be a case of keep hitting the invasion ports and airfields, and attempt to hit three oil targets in France. Portal considered that this directive was too restrictive and that it did not appreciate the tactical difficulties under which his Command laboured. Having questioned this with the Air Staff, he was given a supplementary instruction confirming the general provisions but giving more flexibility by allowing a wider range of targets within the overall general categories. Furthermore, it said, the Air Staff was drawing up a list of targets 'selected primarily for their intrinsic industrial and pyschological values', and this would be forwarded in due course. A week later, on 30 July, the list duly arrived and it also added a new target system—power, the latest assessment from the expert advisers being that damage to any one powerplant would cause a serious reduction in industrial output.

The Blenheims of No 2 Group had already devoted

much effort to the anti-airfield campaign, and increasing attention to the invasion ports. From the date of this directive to the end of July they were engaged on all but one day (and even on that day, 21 July, Blenheims joined in a night attack), on average with fifteen aircraft. During this period they flew 304 daylight sorties, their losses (eight aircraft) being remarkably light considering some of the targets attacked. The Blenheims also contributed to most of the night attacks as nightly ops by all Bomber Command types, including Battles, continued. The philosophy was still to attack a wide range of pinpoint targets each night. A significant development on 18/19 July was the inclusion of 3 Operational Training Unit (OTU) aircraft in the plan— leaflet-dropping over France. The employment of OTU crews in the operational tasking was to become standard policy for Bomber Command, the theory being to send them to 'easy' targets as a means of increasing their experience. It was a philosophy that was to cause much argument and dissent.

By the end of July the strain of intensive operations was beginning to tell; many of the crews were rapidly becoming worn out as night after night they either flew, or were on standby for, operations. Despite earlier attempts at trying to fix a limit on the amount of time each crew member had to serve before being rested, there had been little progress and in most cases it was left to the discretion of the Squadron Commander. This, added to the shortage of trained bomber aircrew, meant that many just carried on until they either dropped from exhaustion or were shot down. It was a situation that was to get worse before it got better. Discussions on this matter continued throughout the summer, each Group Commander having his own views on the subject but all being in general agreement that some sound policy had to be reached. At one stage 'tired crews' were rotated to the Reserve Squadrons rather than to OTUs; this was all very well but by this stage of the war most of the Reserve Squadrons were virtually operational units, carrying out a wide range of tasks including minelaying. It seemed that the only real solution was to impose a limit on the amount of operational flying a crew performed before it was rested. An initial figure of 200 operational hours, equating to 30 to 35 missions, was put forward as the maximum figure before an aircrew member was given a 'long rest'. A letter outlining this policy was sent out to

Whitley crew; note the variety of flying kit.

all Group Commanders on 29 November. The whole question of tour lengths and what constituted a 'rest tour' was to plague the Command for its entire wartime career, a point we shall return to later.

The overall pattern of raids continued into August. On 12/13 August eleven Hampdens were tasked to carry out a low-level attack on the Dortmund–Ems canal near Munster, one of the specific targets listed in the July directive. This was a daring low-level attack by aircraft of Nos 49 and 83 Squadrons on a target of some importance. The flak defences were intense and two aircraft were shot down; the others, some damaged, put in their attacks, causing damage to the target which restricted barge traffic for many weeks. No 49 Squadron's record book for this raid states: 'M25 successfully attacked and bombed, aircraft P4403 severely damaged'; behind these few words lay a VC for Flight Lieutenant Learoyd.

The following night Bomber Command returned to Italy, 35 Whitleys attacking Milan and Turin. Periodic raids on Italy remained an element of Bomber Command strategy, although Germany always held priority unless some direct strategic requirement was being met, as was the case in later months.

It is worth examining the procedure by which strategy was turned into operational missions. The overall

Wellington T2739 of No 99 Squadron damaged by a night fighter.

strategic aim of the British armed forces was decided at War Cabinet level, in close consultation with the Chiefs of Staff. This policy was turned into a directive (plus additional letters, memos and signals as required) for transmission to the various Commands. It was the task of the Commander-in-Chief of a Command to determine the most effective and appropriate way of employing his forces to achieve the aims of the directive (it was on this point that many Commanders, not least Arthur Harris, were to have much disagreement with higher authority). Some directives were couched in unequivocal terms and included details, or 'advice', as to the best way to proceed. In some cases this 'advice' amounted to a detailed tactical plan for a specific target.

The heart of Bomber Command was the Operations Room; it was from here that the Commander ran his war. On the main wall of the Ops Room were three blackboards showing the Order of Battle (ORBAT) for the Command by Groups and squadrons. On the right-hand wall were the meteorological situation maps and a phase-of-the-moon chart. To the left was a 4in-scale map of Europe showing the main targets, with pins and coloured labels giving the target code numbers (all the targets had a code number and this was used in the tasking message). The back wall was covered by a similar map of Italy. In the centre were three large tables: one with maps of the current night's operations, plus a photo mosaic of the Ruhr; one with a map of Europe showing routes, nightfighter defences and general target maps; and one with a series of graphs of recent attacks, plus a map of Berlin and photographs of the main targets. The Commander would select the targets for attack and, after the 9 a.m. conference, nominate a primary and a secondary, or a selection of primary targets. Having determined the targets and the overall level of effort required of each Group, this information was transmitted to the Groups by telephone and teleprinter. The Air Officer Commanding the Group would follow a similar process and then task his stations to provide the requisite level of effort.

The station took little part in the process, relaying the tasking to the squadron commanders who would decide the route and times, and perhaps an adjustment to the stated fuel and bomb loads. It was then up to the groundcrew to prepare the right number of aircraft ready for the mission. Entering the briefing room, one of the first things the aircrew would see would be a sign along these lines: 'It is better to keep your mouth shut and let people think you're a fool than to open it and remove all doubt.' It was a variation on the 'careless talk' theme; as soon as the target had been revealed the crew were expected to keep it to themselves. The station would be shut off from the outside world—no telephone calls in or out, a sure sign that the base was operating that night! Although briefing formats changed somewhat, the overall procedure was fairly routine with details of the target, and its importance, defences and suggested routeing (later in the war the routes were firmly laid down), signals and intelligence information—until every last detail had been covered and the crews 'retired to a corner' to finish their planning.

Although the approach route to the target had been suggested it was up to the crew to decide the actual routeing. The navigator was given a simplified target map, printed in colour to show woods, water, etc, with the target itself marked in red or orange. Although a target photo was shown to the crew it usually proved of little value—it was a daylight photo and the target would look very different at night. With the planning complete and all the crew in the picture, there was usually time for a rest before the pre-flight meal. After the meal it was a case of collecting the flying kit and picking up the rations—biscuits, apple/orange, chocolate, barley sugar, chewing gum, raisins, and a thermos of hot drink. The poor old 'nav' had the most to carry as he packed into his green canvas bag the Very pistol, astro tables, nav instruments and charts, questionnaires on 'met' and photography, and the 'flimsies'. These rice-paper documents contained details of emergency procedures for wireless assistance, frequencies, etc—the rice paper being so that they could be eaten rather than captured—although 'the taste of the ink left much to be desired'. Also at the briefing the crew would obtain their escape packs, consisting of a small pouch of appropriate currency. Other escape aids were already provided—silk maps sewn into tunics, magnetized fly-buttons with a tiny white dot to show north. Later, more effective escape and evasion kits were used, handed out at briefing and returned at debrief. These consisted of a small perspex box containing silk maps, money, benzedine tablets, malted milk tablets, water bottle and purifying tablets.

Meanwhile the groundcrew had been completing work on *their* aircraft, making sure that everything was as ready as could be; as stated in a Bomber Command booklet, 'The success of the attack and the lives of the flying crew depend in the last resort on their labours. The aircraft is checked from nose to tail.' The vital work of the groundcrew, including the substantial number of WAAFs serving at Bomber Command stations, played a key role in the success of the offensive; on the nights that 'maximum efforts' were called for the groundcrew worked like demons to get as many 'kites' up as possible.

The aircraft would already have had its night flying test and be ready to go. Each member of the crew ran through his pre-flight checks, the WOP checking in with the Watch Office: 'Hello Parsnip, Hello Parsnip, E for Edward calling, E for Edward calling, are you receiving me, are you receiving me? Over to you, over.'

At the take-off point a green light would be the signal that the aircraft was clear to go. Turn on to the runway,

A pensive-looking Wellington crew member.

through the checks, power on and away into the night sky. In those early years of Bomber Command from that point on the crew were on their own, rarely seeing another bomber. Once over the sea the bombs would be made live. The nav would be working his DR plot and obtaining D/F from the WOP, and perhaps trying an astro shot or two, while the gunners would be scanning the sky—and passing visual information to the nav if appropriate. The W/T (Wireless Telegraphy) sets were not always very reliable and often the pilot would look around to see the nav and WOP huddled over the table with bits of the set, or valves, spread all around—prior to putting it back together in the hope that maybe it would work.

Inside the aircraft crew discipline was tight (every crew varied of course), the intercomm (i/c) being left as free as possible for operational use—such as a sudden call for evasion.

Approaching the target run, the nav would put down his nav instruments and take his place in the nose as the bomb-aimer. The i/c in most aircraft was of poor quality and to avoid confusion directions were given in a standard format . . . 'Left, Left' . . . 'Right' . . . 'Steady'. If the 'Skipper' had not heard left or right, he would know from the fact that the word was repeated that it must have been left. Different crews adopted their own variations of the basic techniques.

The crew having made it back to England, and found the airfield, the flare-path was switched on to recover the aircraft, with a bright 'T' at the start and the Chance Light illuminating the ground at the entrance to the flare-path. Back on the ground, hand the aircraft back to the groundcrew—who have waited to see their kite and their crew safely back—and into the debrief, filling in a questionnaire presented by the Intelligence Officer. A welcome-home breakfast—after hours in the cold and dark with only a few, but welcome, rations—and off to bed. A few hours' sleep and ready to start the routine again if the crew's name was on the Battle Order.

One significant event during August was the instant promotion of all air-gunners to the rank of at least sergeant, a move that many considered was long overdue—and some argued should have been made

retrospective to give the rank to all those who had already lost their lives.

When German bombs fell on London on 24 August Churchill demanded an immediate retaliatory raid on Berlin. The following night a force of 81 (some records say nearly 100) bombers, attacked industrial targets on the outskirts of Berlin. Arriving in the target area, the bombers were faced with thick cloud, making identification of the target difficult and resulting in poor bombing results. Nevertheless, the point had been made. British bombs had fallen on the German capital—despite all the claims of the Nazi leaders. Three Hampdens were lost and a further three were forced to ditch in the sea on the way back, Berlin being at the extremes of their range.

Berlin was attacked twice more before the end of August, although not on quite the same scale as the initial raid. At a speech in the Sportspalast on 4 September Hitler, in fury at these 'unprovoked' attacks, declared, 'When the British air force drops two or three or four thousand kilograms of bombs, then we will in

Wellington crews collect their kit.

PIGEONS

Every Bomber Command aircraft carried at least one pigeon. It was part of the pre-flight routine to go and pick up the container with the pigeon. The idea (as in the First World War) was that if the aircraft came down in the sea, then the crew could send the pigeon back to base with a message of where they were; the Air-Sea Rescue service would then come out to rescue the crew. The birds were given a thorough training at the regional training centres, such as Finningley, including being released from an aircraft. The message container was made of bakelite and included a partially completed message—station, aircraft number, date of issue). The crew would then, in the event of an emergency, completed the rest of the form with location, time and message. If there was no time to take the container apart and carry out this procedure, then they could simply write on the white strip on the outside of the container.

Each station with a Pigeon Service also had a trained staff to look after the birds—one corporal and two airmen, all of whom were usually pigeon-fanciers.

The authors can find no reference to Bomber Command pigeons being released in anger! However, some crews did comment, sadly, that when they had the misfortune to crash back at base they were in such a hurry to vacate the burning aircraft that they forgot about the poor old pigeon.

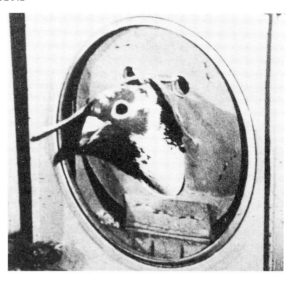

An unsung pigeon of Bomber Command.

one night drop 150-, 230- or 400,000 kilograms. When they declare that they will increase the attacks on our cities, then we will raze their cities to the ground. We will stop the handiwork of these air pirates. . .' The gloves were definitely off.

Up to this point Bomber Command had kept its effort concentrated against the target systems specified in the various directives, as shown by the fact that 41 per cent of total bomb tonnage had been directed against targets associated with the Luftwaffe, and a further 21 per cent directed against oil.

The anti-invasion task remained high on the Command's target list, both for small-scale daylight attacks and larger night-time efforts. By the beginning of September German statistics showed the strength of the invasion fleet standing at 168 transports, 1,600 motorboats, 419 tugs, and 1,910 large barges. This large and vital target had to be attacked at every opportunity. The critical period had obviously arrived. The British Government issued the Invasion Warning on 7 September, and aircraft were prepared to undertake anti-invasion tasks; but at the same time the bomber force was thrown into the attacks on the ports.

By the end of the month confirmed German losses included 12 transports, 4 tugs and 51 barges, plus 9 transports and 163 barges seriously damaged. Added to this was varying degrees of damage around the port areas; for example, an ammunition train was blown up during an attack on Rotterdam. While the German resources remained impressive they *had* been dented, and it had been made plain that they could not simply sit in port and wait. The invasion ports were visited day and night, although many of the daylight raids were aborted through lack of cloud cover. In addition, anti-shipping searches and minelaying had the same effect of damaging the German naval build-up. Although the night bombers continued to attack industrial targets, they also went after the invasion ports. With a raid on the U-boat base at Lorient on 2/3 September by 39 Hampdens, Bomber Command opened its attacks on the U-boats.

During an attack on the barges at Antwerp on 15/16 September, a Hampden of No 83 Squadron was badly damaged by flak. Sergeant John Hannah, the WOP, managed to put out the flames, thus enabling the aircraft to limp back to base. For this courageous act, during which he was badly burned, he was awarded the Victoria Cross.

Despite the 15 September turning point in the Battle of Britain, the invasion threat still seemed very real. This was reflected in the directive of 21 September which instructed Bomber Command to maintain the highest level of pressure against the invasion forces, 'so as to dislocate the enemy's means of mounting and despatching the expeditions'. It was considered essential to keep a proportion of the offensive forces engaged over Germany—No 4 Group (Whitleys) was suggested for this task—and to bear in mind that the destruction of the enemy's oil resources was still the basis of the Command's long-term strategy. The attack on key component factories could proceed alongside the continued pressure on communications. However, the three squadrons engaged on mining should be switched to meet a growing threat from the German U-boats in the North-West Approaches. These squadrons must now be tasked against U-boat building yards, according to the list provided, and other suitable targets as provided by the Naval Staff; in this latter group came the principal submarine crew training establishment. Berlin was given a special mention: 'Although there are no objectives in the Berlin area of importance to our major plans, it is the intention that attacks on the city and its environs should be continued from time to time when favourable weather conditions permit. The primary aim of these attacks will be to cause the greatest possible disturbance and dislocation both to the industrial activities and to the civilian population generally.'

In the midst of the anti-invasion campaign came a significant milestone. On the night of 23/24 September Bomber Command concentrated its main effort against a single target—Berlin. Some nineteen individual targets—rail yards, power stations, aircraft factories, gasworks—were listed as aiming points for the 129 bombers taking part. In a three-hour period the bombers searched for their targets, a difficult task because of thick haze and searchlight glare. Some of the target areas were damaged but three aircraft were lost. Over the next few years the 'Big City' was to claim many more Bomber Command lives.

A week later the overall situation appeared different, with a lowering of the immediate threat of invasion, due partly to the deterioration in the weather and partly to the failure of the Luftwaffe to gain air superiority. This led to a reappraisal of the role of the RAF's offensive aircraft. The outcome was to point to a transfer of additional effort to the offensive over Germany; however, the heavy bombers were also to keep an anti-invasion role by maintaining attacks on ports such as Le Havre, Antwerp and Rotterdam.

NIGHT OFFENSIVE

By mid-October the decision had been taken to return the major effort to the night offensive over Germany, while the Blenheims would continue the anti-shipping sweeps and cloud-cover raids. Numerically the Blenheim squadrons comprised the major element of Bomber Command, but their employment caused difficulties to the planners, many of whom would have happily replaced them with 'real' bombers.

So on 13/14 October the bombers attacked Kiel, Wilhelmshaven and the Ruhr; in addition, a few aircraft raided the Channel Ports. The results of the evening were poor as many machines turned back in the face of bad weather. The nine Battles included in the forces employed on 15/16 October, their targets being Calais and Boulogne, brought to an end this type's operational life with Bomber Command. It had not been a happy association; the crews had fought hard and fought well,

No 58 Squadron Whitleys in the gathering dusk. [58 Sqn records]

Whitley cockpit.

in full knowledge of their vulnerability, but they had demonstrated the courage and determination for which Bomber Command became renowned.

Bad weather was a major problem during October, not only the weather over the target area but also the weather at base, fog being the greatest hazard. For example, of 73 aircraft operating on the night of 16/17 October, three were lost in action and fourteen others (ten Hampdens and four Wellingtons) crashed in England because of fog covering their base areas.

Arrival back over England was also no guarantee of safety from the enemy; four days after the above incident, a Whitley from No 58 Squadron was shot down near Thornaby-on-Tees by a German intruder aircraft. The threat from these roving predators grew over the ensuing years and it was quite common for returning bombers to be given the signal to hold off away from base because of prowling fighters.

With Portal moving to become Chief of the Air Staff, Air Marshal Sir Richard Peirse was appointed as the new head of Bomber Command on 25 October. A few days later, following the now standard practice, there was a policy review of the air campaign for the coming winter period and, on 30 October, a new and lengthy directive to Peirse. It was intended to be an extensive review to determine 'the extent to which we can achieve a more decisive effect, both in the material and moral spheres by a greater concentration of our offensive air attacks'. There were two primary target systems: oil, of first importance, and aircraft component and aluminium factories. In addition, Bomber Command was left with the 'additional targets' list from previous directives. The stated aim was that: 'Regular concentrated attacks should be made on objectives in large towns and centres of industry, with the primary aim of

Bombing up a Whitley, June 1940.

Hampden crews of No 83 Squadron, 1940.

causing very heavy material destruction which will demonstrate to the enemy the power and severity of air bombardment and the hardship and dislocation which will result from it.'

This admirable military precept of concentration of effort was lessened by another phrase in the same document which called for widespread attacks so as to 'impose ARP measures with the resulting interruption of work and rest and dislocation of industry'. Along the same lines was the tactical suggestion that the maximum damage and disruption could be caused by using an initial assault with incendiaries, followed by subsequent waves dropping mainly HE and DA (delayed-action) bombs, plus a few mines.

As if this did not spread the small resources of Bomber Command thinly enough, the Command was also enjoined to continue its attacks against Italy, marshalling yards in Germany, anti-submarine targets, enemy-occupied ports and airfields and night bomber airfields in France, and to continue sea-mining. It was hoped to reduce the mining and anti-submarine work but this would need the agreement of the Admiralty. This agreement was forthcoming and the mining effort was again reduced to a single squadron, although the C-in-C was given authority to use more aircraft for this task if he considered it of use for the training of new crews. At the same time that this was confirmed (10 November) it was also stressed that the main directive

was intended to imply that oil was the *only* primary target system; all other objectives were secondary and only to be attacked if oil attacks were not possible.

While there was increasing doubt as to the success of the night raids, there was no doubt of the rising casualties. The operations of 14/15 November, mainly to Berlin and Hamburg, cost Bomber Command ten of the 82 aircraft involved—the greatest number of losses on a single night so far recorded.

In the meantime, the Luftwaffe carried out a number of highly successful and destructive attacks on British cities. The raid on Coventry (14/15 November) caused great anger amongst the British public and led to calls for retaliation on a massive scale. As we have seen, the massive scale simply did not exist.

However, on the following night (16/17 November) Bomber Command carried out its largest raid to date when 130 aircraft attacked targets in Hamburg. Only half the crews reported attacking their targets, with another 25 bombing alternative targets. It was not a particularly effective response.

Once again the post-raid intelligence evidence did not quite support the accounts of the crews. This was not to say that the crews were trying to distort the picture; quite the reverse, as crews went to extraordinary lengths to try to identify the target area and bomb the aiming

NIGHT PHOTOGRAPHY

'After each raid an account was pinned up on the ops board in the briefing room. Also displayed were the target photographs taken by the automatic camera in each aircraft. This camera started operating when the air bomber pressed the bomb tit and continued to make exposures until the calculated moment of bomb impact; the pilot had to continue flying straight and level on the bomb run for over half a minute in order to obtain accurate photographs.'

During the first six months of the war Bomber Command acquired only 150 usable night photographs from bombing missions, the definition of usable being a photograph showing ground detail that could be plotted to discover where the aircraft was at the time of exposure. The reasons behind taking such photos were expressed in the *Bomber Command Quarterly Review*: 'Indeed, night photography has contributed no small part of the knowledge available about the progress of our bomber offensive, permitting comparisons of the success of different tactics and methods of attack. Thus a night photograph taken with bombing gives the crew positive evidence of where their bombs were dropped. If this proves not to be the intended target, then all the relevant factors can be checked and the necessary corrections in procedure made the next time. Night photography is thus playing an important part in getting more bombs on to the target. No doubt the development of a competitive spirit between squadrons, as reflected in the interest shown in the "squadron raid assessment table", has also played a part in the general improvement in night operations.'

One of the limitations early in the war was the lack of cameras; even in early 1941 the establishment was only four night cameras per squadron. If the number of equipment failures is added, then the percentage of possible photographs becomes quite small. A cloud-covered (or thick haze) target will reveal no ground detail; and if the bomber takes violent evasion then the detail may be unplottable. Some photographs show ground detail but it is simply impossible to work out where it is. The prospect of having to stay straight and level for another 30 seconds did not meet with great favour among crews, who considered that having dropped the bombs the job was done.

The F.24 was an open-plate camera which took a series of pictures during the time that it was being exposed, light being provided by the photoflash but also by other light sources such as target indicators, searchlights, flak, and the burning target. The track of objects showed the attitude of the aircraft—a curved light meaning that the aircraft was taking evasion. In September 1941 a memo was sent to

Enough ground detail here to be plotted. Note aircraft at top of photo.

all Group Commanders: 'The purpose of night photography in this Command can be defined as follows: 1. To confirm the location of the bomber at time of attack. 2. To pinpoint the bomb bursts. 3. To provide general information.—it is not intended as a means of damage assessment.' This was not strictly true as the photos were used as a comparison with the post-raid PR, whose primary function was damage assessment.

The films were examined at the stations to see if ground detail had been recorded and then at Group HQ as part of the Group raid analysis. The Command Photographic Interpretation Section carried out more detailed analysis, as did the Central Interpretation Unit. The maximum amount of information was extracted from each photograph. Harris kept a book of the best photographs to show visitors as he explained the effect that Bomber Command was having on the enemy; the material in this 'Blue Book' convinced many a sceptical visitor. For the crew, especially the bomb-aimer, obtaining an aiming-point photo was a great thrill; an 'unusable' photo brought a sense of frustration.

Various changes were made during the course of the war, including the use of automatic cameras and, in October 1943, colour film. Although the latter did show the TIs quite well, it was too slow and there was a loss of ground detail for plotting.

The Intelligence Officer had the vital job of interpreting the photos.

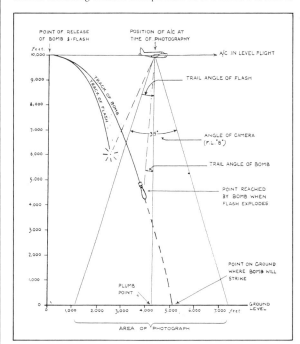

points. The advent of increasing numbers of bombing cameras had a two-fold advantage: first, it provided data for the analysts to examine, a task which was very carefully undertaken; and secondly, it provided an element of 'competition' in that the photographs were displayed for crews to see—each crew, and especially the bomb-aimer, was keen that their photo should show the aiming point!

The value of bombing-camera evidence was stressed at frequent intervals: 'Some of you occasionally forget, in the stress of the moment, to use your night cameras. I must impress upon you again how important it is that we should have photography regarding the fall of your bombs. Don't be afraid of letting it be known that your bombs have not hit the target—we all make mistakes and the fact that you know where your bombs have gone will help you to do better next time.' At squadron level it was a harsher reality—any 'wayward' bombing would have to be explained!

The only positive way to assess the amount of damage would have been to have walked the streets of a target town or toured the 'pinpoint factory' the following day.

Air Council 341 in session, March 1941: (left to right) Air Marshal Sir P. Babington (AMP); Capt. H. H. Balfour (US S-Air); The Rt. Hon. Sir A. Sinclair; Air Chief Marshal Sir C. Portal (CAS); Sir Arthur Street (PUSS-Air); Air Chief Marshal Sir Wilfred Freeman (VCAS); and Air Marshal A. G. Garrod. Out of shot are Sir Harold Howitt and Air Marshal Sir C. Courteney (AMSO)

This, of course, was not possible, although the intelligence organizations did have access to sources in enemy territory and these did provide information. The next best bet was photo reconnaissance. As has always been the case, it was a question of too few resources and too many tasks, plus the added problems caused by the weather. The Blenheims of Bomber Command flew many PR sorties, but these aircraft from No 2 Group faced enormous difficulties, not only the weather and poor (almost non-existent) navigation equipment, but also an inferior aircraft in which to take on the German defences. The results they brought back were useful, the casualties they suffered were high. From November 1941 onwards, Spitfires from the Photographic Reconnaissance Unit were tasked with post-attack recce and this certainly helped; these aircraft could penetrate areas where the Blenheims dare not go unless conditions were just right. Although the science of photographic interpretation had progressed in giant strides since the outbreak of the war, it was by no means infallible. It was in the interest of the Nazi authorities to play down the amount of damage being caused; one way of doing this was to conceal, against photo recce, the extent of any damage. This was hardly practicable for extensive areas of housing but it was certainly viable, and exploited, for key targets such as factories and installations.

While the majority of the night effort was still against Germany, oil installations such as those of Leuna and

Gelsenkirchen being frequent targets, the bomber force at times went farther afield—for example, on 19/20 November to the Skoda works at Pilsen, Czechoslovakia. The general level of operations in late November and early December was light, aircraft being tasked on most days and nights but only in small numbers. The 16/17 December attack on Mannheim was somewhat different. As Operation 'Abigail Rachel' this was intended to be a devastating raid on the centre of a city by a force of over 200 bombers—an attempt at an effective reply to the German 'Baedeker Raids'. In the event only 134 aircraft (still the largest force yet sent against a single target) took part, led by an incendiary force of Wellingtons in an attempt to emulate the successful German tactic. Despite good weather the raid was not a great success, damage being scattered and light. The major significance of this raid was that it was the first planned 'area' attack rather than precision raid. In another move that was to become accepted tactics later, Mannheim was revisited on the next two nights, but only by small numbers of bombers.

An overview of 1940 did not make promising reading for the leaders of Bomber Command; it had been a year of great effort and endeavour but one of little material success. What cannot be denied, however, is the enormous psychological impact on both British and German public opinion and perception (plus to an extent 'neutral' opinion) of the offensive operations undertaken. At the very least it showed that Britain was not a defeated nation; the spirit to fight—and win—was there. Among the Group Commanders of Bomber Command there were mixed feelings; some saw the fruits of all their labours just around the corner—*if* they were given the resources of aircraft, equipment and trained personnel; others thought that a major shake-up of the Command was the only way forward. All agreed that 1941 was going to be another difficult year.

CHAPTER THREE

The Uphill Struggle Continues

THE NEW YEAR opened well with an accurate attack on industrial targets in Bremen on 1/2 January, a number of important factories, including the Focke-Wulf works, being damaged.

The economic warfare experts consulted their charts and predictions once more and concluded that the oil offensive was having an effect, but not as great as was needed; furthermore, the first six months of 1941 were likely to be a critical period for the Axis. It was imperative, therefore, that the oil offensive be stepped up before Germany could rectify the approaching crisis. An estimate issued in December had claimed that a 15 per cent reduction in supplies would be effective—and should only take up 6.7 per cent of the total Bomber Command effort. After some discussion this was translated into a new instruction for Bomber Command. The directive of 15 January stated: 'The destruction of German synthetic oil plants will reduce the enemy to such a shortage of oil within the next six months that there will be widespread effects on German industry and communications, while it is even probable that within this time an appreciable effect may be felt in the scale of effort of her armed forces.' It did indeed, therefore, promise much. To clarify the situation, the directive added a list of seventeen synthetic oil plants, the destruction of the primary nine of which would reduce internal output by 80 per cent. Sceptics pointed out that this would have little effect following the capture of stocks of petrol and oil products and production capacity in conquered territory.

A large raid, 135 aircraft, had been mounted against the oil plants at Gelsenkirchen just a few days before (9/10 January) the directive came into effect. Less than half the crews claimed to have attacked the target, no damage appears to have been caused but only one Whitley was lost.

The Blenheims had seen little action since November the previous year but in mid-January a new role was found for them. On 10 January six aircraft of No 114 Squadron took part in the first 'Circus' operation, the idea being that the bombers would attack a target in Occupied Europe to encourage the German fighters to take action; the Blenheims' escort, in this case 72 fighters, would deal severely with the enemy aircraft, thus wearing down the overall German fighter capability. The bombers were only included in the plan to make sure that the German defences reacted; a pure fighter sweep would almost certainly be ignored. The target for this first operation was an ammunition depot in the Forêt de Guines, near Calais. Although the tactic was not repeated until early February, it was to become a standard task later in the year.

Of the German towns attacked during the first weeks of 1941, Wilhelmshaven was one of the most frequently visited, partly because of the presence of the battleship *Tirpitz*. A particularly successful raid took place on 15/16 January when 96 aircraft caused extensive destruction, for the loss of only one Whitley.

As part of the 222 bombers sent to Hannover on 10/11 February, No 3 Group contributed 119 Wellingtons—a record for any group. Crews reported an accurate attack and light defences but four aircraft were lost, with a further three being shot down in England by intruders.

Although the directive implied that oil should take precedence over all other target systems, it was not until the middle of February that another raid was planned against the designated oil plants. On the night of 14/15 February 44 Wellingtons attacked the Nordstern plant at Gelsenkirchen; only nine claimed to have hit the target. The following night two oil plants were scheduled for attack. Seventy-three aircraft attacked the Holten plant at Sterkrade, for the loss of one Whitley and one Wellington, while 37 Blenheims and 33 Hampdens attacked the oil installations at Homberg. Neither raid was very successful as crews complained of difficulty in finding the target; in the case of Homberg this was attributed partly to glare from the searchlights. Connected with the bombing of oil plants was the attack on oil storage depots. The largest raid was that mounted on 10/11 February when 43 aircraft bombed the storage tanks at Rotterdam. Although the raid was not very successful it was highly significant in that it saw the operational debut of the Short Stirling. This was summarized in No 7 Squadron's records: 'The squadron carried out its maiden operational trip, three aircraft successfully bombed the target area at Rotterdam, all returned safely—well pleased with the Stirling aircraft.' Each of the three aircraft (N3641, N3642 and N3644) carried a sixteen-500lb bomb load.

A few days later, on 24 February, the second of the new heavy bomber types went into action, six Avro Manchesters (L7300, L7288, L7279, L7284, L7286 and L7294) of No 207 Squadron making individual attacks

SHORT STIRLING

'... the mid-upper gunner observed a single Me.109, 700 to 800 yards astern and about 700 feet above. The enemy aircraft fired a long burst and the mid-upper gunner replied with a long burst, but the former broke off the engagement and disappeared. During evasive diving the Stirling went out of control and the tail hit the sea when pulling out of the dive'—a hair-rising sortie for a No 214 Squadron aircraft, but a suitable testament to the rugged nature of the Stirling.

One of the series of heavy bombers designed to Specification B.12/36, the Stirling was the first to enter service, with No 7 Squadron at Leeming in August 1940. However, it was to exhibit severe limitations which restricted its operational life to less than four years and led to its replacement by the Halifax and Lancaster.

When the engineers at Short's, led by Arthur Gouge, started work they faced a major restriction in the limit of 100 feet for the aircraft's wingspan, imposed by the size of current hangar doors. This led to the adoption of a low-aspect ratio wing, which included a number of Sunderland features, resulting in an aircraft with poor high-altitude performance and, with operational loads, a restricted ceiling. One novelty was the use of a half-scale flying model to provide the basic data on aerodynamics and handling. The first true Stirling prototype (L7600) flew on 14 May 1939 but crashed on landing and it was not until December that the second aircraft (L7605) could take up the flight test programme. The aircraft's basic limitations were soon obvious but at this stage of the war did not seem too serious; there was also the pressing need to introduce new bomber types to replace inadequate existing types. When No 7 Squadron re-equipped it gave up its Hampdens, and a 4,000lb bomb load, for the Stirling with its 14,000lb bomb load—a critical consideration when bomb tonnage delivered was a major factor.

In fact the Stirling's bomb bay arrangement, a neat system of cells in the fuselage and wings, was to prove another drawback as the largest single bomb that could be taken was of 4,000lb; as the war progressed the bombs got bigger and the Stirling was left behind. The operational debut of the type came when three aircraft of No 7 Squadron took part in an attack on the oil storage tanks at Rotterdam on 10/11 February 1941.

As the number of Stirling squadrons increased in No 3 Group they began to take on a wider range of targets, including a substantial number of day raids over Occupied France. During the early months of 1941 the aircraft achieved a reasonable reputation for survivability, both in its ability to take punishment and for its self-defence capability against marauding German fighters. 1941 continued to be a good year and the Stirlings ranged far and wide over Germany, Italy, and even further afield to targets such as the Skoda works in Czechoslovakia. In December the new, and excellent, navaid 'Oboe' received its operational debut with the Stirlings. The following year brought an increase in tasks with No 7 Squadron moving to join the newly formed Pathfinder Force, while the other squadrons continued to provide a major element of Main Force. Towards the end of the year the Mk III, with four 1,650hp Hercules XVI engines and a new type of dorsal turret, was introduced and gradually replaced the Mk Is.

Stirling 'MG-D' of No 7 Squadron.

However, improving German defences, especially flak, meant that the aircraft's poor ceiling gave increasing cause for concern; the Stirling squadrons began to bear the brunt of the punishment rather than the higher-flying Halifaxes and Lancasters. This, and the bomb restriction, led to most of the squadrons re-equipping with Lancasters as these became available; by early 1944 the main Stirling bombing role was over, although the last raid was not flown until September (No 149 Squadron).

In the meantime, the Stirling went on to play a part in the RCM war fought by No 100 (Bomber Support) Group, with No 199 Squadron, and later No 171 Squadron, playing a key role. However, from mid-1944 onwards the aircraft was to see its greatest use with airborne forces duties, including glider-tug, the Mk IV being purpose-designed for this, and with the Mk V as a transport. In this last role the type soldiered on until mid-1946. Of the bomber variants, 712 Stirling Mk Is and 1,047 Mk IIIs were built.

STIRLING III DATA

Crew: Seven or eight
Engines: Four 1,650hp Bristol Hercules XVI
Span: 99ft 1in
Length: 87ft 3in
Height: 22ft 9in
Weight empty: 46,900lb
Weight loaded: 70,000lb
Max. speed: 270mph at 14,500ft
Ceiling: 17,000ft
Range: 590 miles with 14,000lb bombs; 2,000 miles with 3,500lb load
Armament: Nose and dorsal turrets with twin 0.303in guns, tail turret with four 0.303in guns: max. bomb load 14,000lb

Squadrons (Bomber Command): Nos 7, 15, 75, 90, 149, 171, 196, 199, 214, 218, 513, 620, 622, 623

Stirling 'LS-J' of No 15 Squadron. Note the pronounced cockpit area and blunt nose. [15 Sqn records via Peter Green]

Above: The ill-fated Avro Manchester, an excellent basic design but grossly underpowered by its unreliable Rolls-Royce Vulture engines. Heavy losses led to the Manchester's removal from operations.

Below: Manchester crew stations.

on the *Hipper*-class cruiser in Brest harbour. Led by Wing Commander N. C. Hyde, the aircraft dropped a total of seventy 500lb SAP bombs, but the results were not observed because of 'insufficient field of vision for the bomb-aimer to see the bomb bursts'. Bombing from between 8,000 and 15,000 feet, the Manchesters met no opposition; however, L7284 (Flying Officer P. R. Burton-Gyles) had hydraulic failure and crash-landed at Waddington, fortunately with no injuries to the crew. Subsequent investigations showed that the emergency air system had been wrongly assembled, thus preventing one of the main undercarriage legs from lowering.

On 10 March a message from the AOC was received by No 35 Squadron at Linton-on-Ouse: 'Good wishes to 35 Squadron and the heavyweights on the opening of their Halifax operations tonight. I hope the full weight of the squadron's blows will soon be felt further afield.' At 1900 hours Halifax I L9486/B, piloted by Wing Commander Collings, took off and set course for the primary target—the docks and shipping canal at Le Havre; five more aircraft followed, the seventh aborted with hydraulic failure. Collings' report stated: 'Took off from Linton at time stated for target (Le Havre). The weather was excellent to the French coast where 8/10 cloud was encountered. Le Havre was located first by searchlights and flak, and then seen through a good break in the cloud, the dock area being clearly visible. A level attack was delivered from 13,000 feet in one stick of twelve 500lb SAP; the bombs were seen to burst along the edge of the main docks. Only slight heavy flak and scattered searchlights were encountered. Landed base 2309.'

Three other aircraft attacked the primary, a fourth could not find the primary or secondary (shipping at Boulogne) and so bombed Dieppe, while the remaining Halifax circled the area, failed to find any target and so returned to base, jettisoning its bombs (safe) in the Channel. Over the target L9493/G (Flying Officer Warren) was hit by flak: 'Shrapnel from a very near heavy shell-burst holed the aircraft in many places and injured the navigator; with commendable fortitude this NCO carried on his duties, including aiming and releasing the second stick of bombs. The radiator of the starboard inner was punctured causing overheating of the engine, which had to be switched off; also hydraulic failure caused the starboard undercarriage to fall. The aircraft returned to base at the time stated [0035] on three engines and with one leg down.'

For L9489/F the sortie had a tragic ending. Having successfully bombed the target despite heavy flak, 'On return flight aircraft was mistaken for enemy by British fighter and shot down in flames at Normandy, Surrey, at 2240 hours. The Captain, Squadron Leader L. P. Gilchrist, DFC, and the flight engineer, Sergeant Aedy, escaped by parachute, but the remainder were killed in the crash.' (Sergeant Lucas, Pilot Officer Arnold, Sergeant Broadhurst and Pilot Officer Cooper.)

HANDLEY PAGE HALIFAX

'We were very favourably impressed by the flying qualities of the Halifax B.III with its powerful Bristol Hercules engines, which gave it a lively climbing ability and good all-round performance.'

Designed to the same twin-engined bomber specification (P.13/36) as the Manchester, the HP.56 was redesigned as the HP.57 to take four Merlins instead of two Vulture engines when it appeared that the latter were likely to be in short supply. Quantity production of the Halifax was ordered in October 1938 as part of the Air Staff's heavy bomber programme, although the prototype Halifax (L7244) did not make its first flight until 25 October 1939.

A year later the first production aircraft took to the air and within weeks No 35 Squadron at Leeming was giving up its Blenheim IVs in favour of the new type. The first operational sortie was on the night of 11/12 March 1941 to Le Havre, the Halifax being the second of the four-engined bombers to undertake bombing operations. The squadrons of No 4 Group gradually re-equipped over the next twelve months as the Halifax began to play an increasingly important part in the bombing offensive. However, there were problems and as early as October 1942 Bomber Command's Operational Research Section was trying to find out why the Halifax squadrons were suffering a higher loss rate than other types. The conclusion recommended that 'the pilots posted to Halifax squadrons should be detailed to complete at least three, preferably five, sorties as second pilot, or against lightly defended targets before being employed on main operations' in order to gain experience. However, this was not always possible and higher than average loss rates continued. A further report in July 1943 put the onus on training as the Halifax had acquired a bad reputation for instability during hard manoeuvres.

Nevertheless, the Halifax was a sturdy and reliable aircraft and was generally well liked by its crews, very few of whom expressed any desire to swap their aircraft for the 'superior' Lancaster. The Halifax played a full and integral part in the offensive, with a short lull in late 1943 after the investigations and pending the introduction of improved marks such as the Mk III.

A number of variants and sub-variants served with Bomber Command, the main ones being the Mks I, II, III, V, VI and VIII. The major visual differences, other than engines, revolved around the shape of the nose and the presence or absence of an upper turret. The type had a successful career in other roles, including Special Duties, although by far its most central role was as part of Main Force. Of the 6,176 Halifaxes built, just over one-third (2,238) were Mk IIIs.

The only 'surviving' Halifax, 'W' of No 35 Squadron, re-emerges from a Norwegian lake. It is now on display in the RAF Museum.

HALIFAX I DATA

Crew: Seven
Engines: Four Rolls-Royce Merlin X
Span: 98ft 8in
Length: 70ft 1in
Height: 20ft 9in
Weight empty: 33,720lb
Weight loaded: 58,000lb
Max. speed: 265mph at 17,500ft
Ceiling: 18,000ft
Range: 1,552 miles
Armament: Nose turret with twin 0.303in guns, rear turret with four 0.303in, beam guns on some aircraft; bomb load 13,000lb

Squadrons (Bomber Command): Nos 10, 35, 51, 76, 77, 78, 102, 103, 158, 171, 192, 199, 346, 347, 405, 408, 415, 419, 420, 424, 425, 426, 427, 428, 429, 431, 432, 433, 434, 460, 466, 578, 614, 640

Halifax VI of No 346 (French) Squadron, one of two French heavy bomber squadrons formed within the RAF.

It was a tragic incident but it was not unique. Throughout the war 'own goals' were scored on Bomber Command aircraft—by fighters, ground defences (the Navy were famed for shooting at *any* aircraft that went near them), and even other bombers. The theory was that by firing the 'colours of the day', the aircraft would ward off any friendly fighter or AA threat, but it did not always work like that. At times the bombers had actually to shoot down the offending friendly fighter, but resist temptation to bomb the ship!

No matter what destruction the recent series of attacks had created, or how the predictions of the experts were shaping up, Bomber Command was called away from its strategic campaign to help in another crisis. In many ways it was a useful diversion as it enabled Portal to get away from the oil offensive, although in reality very little of the Command's effort had been devoted to this task; certainly, Portal was losing confidence in the predictions he had been given. The oil plants at Gelsenkirchen, Homberg and Sterkrade, together with a number of storage depots, had been attacked but Bomber Command was denied the chance of undertaking a sustained anti-oil campaign by the dictates of the new crisis.

THE BATTLE OF THE ATLANTIC

To sustain its war effort Britain relied on the flow of men and supplies—and also food, to prevent the nation from being starved into submission—brought into its ports from around the world. This lifeline was still under threat. February and March provided hard statistics: 350,000 tons of merchant shipping sunk in February and 500,000 tons sunk in March. The situation had grown so serious that Churchill decreed that the defeat of this menace was all that mattered; it was a life or death struggle and all possible resources should be employed to ensure victory. For Bomber Command this meant a new directive, issued on 9 March. It started by repeating Churchill's position: 'We must take the offensive against the U-boat and the Focke-Wulf wherever and whenever we can. The U-boat at sea must be hunted, the U-boat in the building yard or dock must be bombed. The Focke-Wulf, and other bombers employed against our shipping, must be attacked in the air and in their nests.' It was good solid Churchillian stuff.

The directive was kept as broad as possible in the circumstances by giving a list of targets and suggesting that priority be given to those 'in congested areas where the greatest morale effect is likely to result'. It also allowed that all other targets from the previous directives were permissible as secondary targets. However, the primary list consisted of: Kiel (Germania Werft, Deutsche Werke, Howaldtswerke dockyard), Bremen (Deschimag and the Fock-Wulf assembly factory), Vegesack (Vulcan Werke), Hamburg (Blohm & Voss, Howaldts), Augsburg (diesel engine factory), Mannheim

(diesel engine factory), Dessau (Ju 88 factory), the U-boat bases at Lorient, St Nazaire and Bordeaux, and the Focke-Wulf Fw 200 Condor bases at Stavanger and Bordeaux-Mérignac. Ten days later the target list was amended to remove three targets and add five more in Cologne, Hagen and Stuttgart. A further amendment was issued when the warships *Gneisenau* and *Scharnhorst* were discovered to be at Brest, making the destruction of these two powerful vessels a priority. During their previous foray into the Atlantic they had sunk a total of 22 ships.

The first major raid in accord with this directive took place on 12/13 March when 88 aircraft attacked Hamburg, the Blohm & Voss yards being a specific target, and 86 aircraft attacked Bremen, with the Focke-Wulf factory being the main target. A further 72 aircraft went to Berlin. The following night Hamburg was the target for 139 bombers and further damage was caused to the Blohm & Voss yards. The campaign was off to a good start. The 14/15th saw the main effort directed against Gelsenkirchen, causing extensive damage to the Hydriewerk Scholven oil plant. With a raid on the U-boat base at Lorient the next night, Bomber Command had clearly expressed its intention. In the period up to mid-July the offensive against naval targets intensified, specific targets being attacked by night and anti-shipping searches being flown by Blenheims during daylight. On one of these sweeps, on 29 March, six aircraft were sent to find and attack *Scharnhorst* and *Gneisenau* as they moved towards Brest after their Atlantic foray. The Blenheims were frustrated by the weather but two days later the ships, now in Brest harbour, were attacked by 109 bombers—the first of many attempts to destroy these two warships.

Included in the bombing forces on the night of 31 March were six Wellingtons sent to Emden; among the weapons dropped were a number of 4,000lb HC blast bombs, usually refered to as 'Cookies'. It had been realized for some time that the range of bombs was inadequate for the type of targets being attacked. As soon as Bomber Command started large-scale area attacks it was decided that a blast bomb was needed; this would not require the thick casing of a penetrating bomb and could contain more explosive for a greater blast effect. This was the basic theory behind the entire range of blast bombs used by Bomber Command, bombs that looked more like oil drums or containers than bombs but which had a devastating blast effect.

March also brought another change in the tour-length saga, with 200 hours being laid down as the 'standard' tour length, to be followed by a six-month rest and then a second tour of 200 hours. There was still a great degree of flexibility within this system, each commander interpreting the overall rules to suit different circumstances. By early 1942 the system had changed to one that required a total of 30 ops to be flown in the first tour

```
SECRET. STATION OPERATIONAL ORDER. Serial No.2920. 23/4/41.

M.S.I      51 Squadron            M.D.S 885-555-668

E.T.D 2000 HRS ONWARDS

TARGET.    PRIMARY    C.C. 49

AREA 1. THE SCHARNHORST and GNEISENAU at BREST harbour.

        ALTERNATIVE Any invasion port.


ROUTE   OUT Base- COTTESMORE (Light-house) - ABINGDON - BRIDPORT -

AREA 1      Target

        RETURN. Same route.


BOMB
LOAD 4 X 500 lbs S.A.P ) T.D. 012
     6 x 250 lbs S.A.P )

SPECIAL INSTRUCTIONS
1. OBJECT. To inflict maximum damage on the battleships.
2. HEIGHT FOR BOMBING. Not below 12,000 feet.
3. Left hand circuits to be maintained in the target area.
4. YEOVIL Balloon Barrage to be close hauled 1000 feet from
   2100 to 0300 hours.
5. Other A/C on same target: Topcliffe 9
                             Middleton 9
                             Leeming   7
```

before the crew could be 'screened'. It was still not a satisfactory situation; the crews were not sure of what they had to do to qualify—what, for example, constituted an 'op'. This basic system remained in force for the remainder of the war, but with numerous variations such as the use of a points system, the number of points being determined by the location of the target. At certain times the second tour was specified at 20 ops; but for the Pathfinders the basic was to be 50 ops without a break. There were many variations, although the general rule of 30 ops was the most common yardstick applied.

The attacks on *Scharnhorst* and *Gneisenau*, nicknamed 'Salmon and Gluckstein' by the RAF, intensified in early April. Following the raid of 4/5 April *Gneisenau* was moved away from her drydock because of an unexploded bomb; while in the open water of the harbour she was torpedoed by a Coastal Command Beaufort and sustained serious damage. Returned to drydock she was hit again on the night of 10/11 April by at least four bombs. Such was the determination to destroy these ships that Brest was the target of day and night operations and became the recipient of a huge tonnage of bombs.

By 9 April Kiel had been subjected to four major attacks, causing damage and hold-ups in the production of U-boats. The final two raids were so successful that civilians began to flee the city in panic. However, with the pressure relaxed they soon returned and the Nazi Party organization took steps to ensure that such flights were not repeated. Meanwhile the Blenheim squadrons, now joined by Hampdens on the daylight sweeps, met with more success in April when attacks were made against a number of coastal convoys. On 28 April six Blenheims of No 101 Squadron, with fighter escort, flew the first 'Channel Stop', an attempt to close the narrows to German shipping operating by day. It was to become a fierce conflict as the Germans increased the strength of the defences; flak ships began to take a severe toll of the attackers. When three Blenheims attacked a convoy off Holland they found a single tanker with an escort of eight flak ships, plus prowling Bf 110s; fortunately, only one Blenheim was shot down.

A new record was set on 8/9 May when a total of 364 sorties were flown (for the loss of ten aircraft) on two major raids against Hamburg and Bremen and a variety of minor operations, including an attempt to block the Kiel Canal. The 27th May saw 52 Wellingtons and

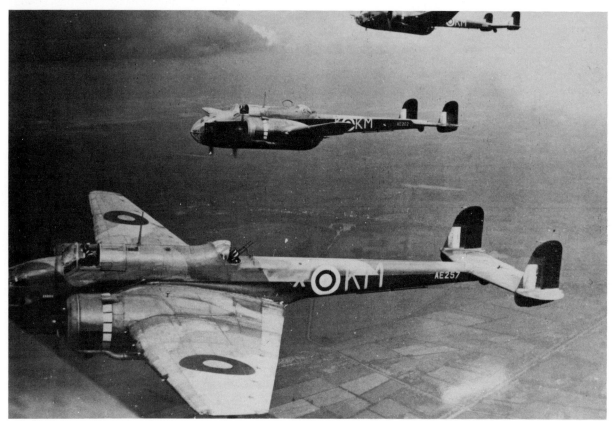

twelve Stirlings out hunting for the cruiser *Prinz Eugen*, thought to be heading for Brest following the loss of *Bismarck*. It was a fruitless search, but a week later the cruiser turned up at Brest, and so joined the target list at that port.

As a total change from the recent run of attacks, the night of 12/13 June was devoted to attacks on rail yards at Soest, Schwerte, Hamm and Osnabruck. None of the attacks was particularly successful and six of the 311 bombers were lost. Included in the 84 aircraft attacking Schwerte were four Wellingtons of No 405 (Vancouver) Squadron, the first of the many Canadian squadrons to operate with Bomber Command. No 405 had formed at Driffield on 23 April. Schwerte was attacked again on 13/14 June.

The heavy bombers were still being called upon to make daylight raids. On 28 June three Stirlings were tasked to attack Emden or any other suitable target. The weather prevented them from finding any target but as they turned for home two of the bombers were attacked by Bf 109s. The encounter was recorded thus in the squadron record book:

'Three aircraft were detailed for a daylight raid on EMDEN or any other suitable target. S/Ldr. R. D. Speare, F/Lt. J. K. Collins, and F/O. G. B. Blacklock (DFM). S/Ldr. Speare found no target and returned to base but F/Lt. Collins and F/O. Blacklock were attacked by a number of hostile aircraft.

'*1543*: At 3000 feet 3 M.E.109s. attacked and broke away after 3 minutes. F/Lt. Collins formated on F/O. Blacklock and the Stirlings finished the encounter at sea level.

'*1548*: Six to nine yellow nosed M.E.109s. attacked mostly from port side but some from behind and starboard. One E/A from ahead and one from astern. The rear gunner saw the engine of this hit and the propellor (*sic*) stopped. It is claimed as destroyed. One from the port beam came in to 25 yards with mid-upper and rear turret bearing on it. The enemy aircraft passed straight over the top of the Stirling and turned back with smoke pouring from beneath it. It is claimed as damaged. One more came in from ahead and turned off to port as the front gunner gave it a burst. He did not return to the attack.

'*1553–1622*: During these encounters F/Lt. Collins formated on the other Stirling but after the second encounter his starboard outer engine was seen to be U/S. A hole was visible behind the port outer and the guns in turrets were not seen to move throughout the action. The aircraft maintained height but flew too slow (*sic*) for formation. F/Lt. Blacklock flew back and forth to ward off further attacks though none came. All attempts to communicate by Aldis Lamp were fruitless

and the aircraft finally sank down on to the surface. Although the approach was made with the tail well down the nose actually struck first and the fuselage broke in half by the door. The rear part stood vertically in the water but eventually sank leaving no trace of crew or dinghy.

'*1740*: Off SOUTHWOLD two Hurricanes came in from starboard. The Verey (*sic*) pistol could not be fired from the socket and during the delay in detaching it one of the Hurricanes opened fire at 6–700 yards. Rear gunner replied with burst; recognition signal was at length fired and the Hurricane sheered off. No damage was done.'

Among the daylight naval raids was that of 4 July by twelve Blenheims against Bremen, led by Wing Commander Hughie Edwards of No 105 Squadron. Despite the lack of cloud cover the raid went ahead at ultra-low level and in the face of very heavy light flak. Although four of the Blenheims were shot down it had been a successful attack, damage being caused to the harbour areas. For his leadership and example, Edwards was awarded the VC.

The major night offensive against naval targets ended on 6/7 July so that Bomber Command could return to its offensive against German industry. During the four-month period the effort expended had been enormous, Brest alone receiving 24 major raids—most of which appear to have done little damage, although *Prinz Eugen* was badly damaged and lost 60 crew killed on the night of 1/2 July. Even though the ships had not been destroyed they had also not been repaired, and were thought unlikely to be able to put to sea to endanger Allied shipping. The campaign was not in fact yet over. Of the other stated targets most had been attacked on numerous occasions—Kiel (14), Bremen (14), Hamburg (8), Mannheim (6), Lorient (4)—and the others had all received at least two visits from the bombers. There had been nights when the naval targets had been unsuitable and so Bomber Command had kept up its pressure against German towns with attacks on Cologne, Munster, Berlin, Dortmund, Wilhelmshaven, Hannover, Duisburg and Düsseldorf.

The previous few months' operations had brought the realization that Bomber Command was not the precision weapon which many had believed it to be (at least in public). The 9 July instruction was the first directive to put this belief into words and as such was a significant turning point in the operational status of Bomber Command: 'It is accepted as a principle of this plan that the successful attack of a specific target at night can only be undertaken in clear moonlight. It follows, therefore, that for approximately three-quarters of each month it is only possible to obtain satisfactory results by heavy concentrated and continuous attacks on large working-class and industrial areas in carefully selected towns.' The reasoning behind this was that 'the

Left: Two photos showing Hampdens of No 44 Squadron; the nearest aircraft, AE257, went missing on 21/22 October 1941.

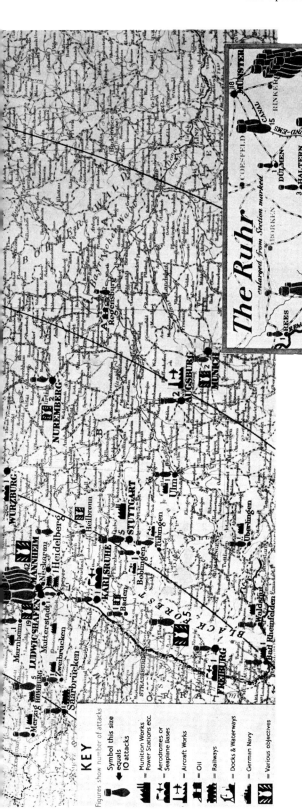

ATTACK AT THE HEART :
THE RAIDS ON GERMANY.

A fully-documented map of the places in Germany which have been attacked by Bomber Command.

The bombs are grouped and sized according to the number of raids, which is stated in each case.

Symbols show the type of target bombed.

The map is completed to 26th July, 1941.

Bomber Command map of attacks up to July 1941. [44 Sqn records]

A Short Stirling surrounded by flak bursts.

weakest points in his armour lie in the morale of the civilian population and in his inland transportation system . . . direct main effort towards dislocating the German transportation system and to destroying the morale of the civilian population as a whole and of the industrial workers in particular'. The directive was therefore aimed at covering precise targets, but only when conditions were suitable, and 'area' targets which contained elements of the primary target systems.

With the assistance of the Railway Research Service a list of nine major rail centres was drawn up—Hamm, Osnabruck, Soest, Schwerte, Cologne (2), Duisburg (2), and Duisburg-Ruhrort. These nine targets were to be considered the primary objectives. The towns of Cologne, Düsseldorf and Duisburg were scheduled for attack on moonless nights—each having important industrial areas as well as being major rail centres. The communications element was also to include inland waterways with attacks on the Dortmund–Ems Canal, the Ems–Weser Canal and the River Rhine. It was considered that roads were unprofitable targets and that the best way to reduce road transport was to destroy the two main synthetic rubber plants (Schopau and Huls). Finally, a list of secondary targets was provided— Hamburg, Bremen, Hannover, Frankfurt, Mannheim and Stuttgart.

Even before this directive was issued a report examining recent operations was in the process of preparation, a report which would come as a shock to many of the most ardent supporters of the bomber offensive. The Cherwell Commission had been examining night raids undertaken in June and July with a view to determining the accuracy of the attacks. The period in question, 2 June to 25 July, involved 100 raids against 28 different targets on 48 nights. The data under examination were the aiming point photographs taken by the aircraft, some 650 photographs being available for study. The idea was to look for the aiming point on the photograph; if that could not be found, then to try to identify what the photograph did show and thus work out the position of the aircraft at bomb release. The Butt Report, issued on 8 August, did not make enjoyable reading for Bomber Command. Of all the aircraft claiming to have

attacked, and for which usable photographs were available (i.e., one showing ground detail), only one in three was within 5 miles of the aiming point: taking only targets in the Ruhr, only one in ten was within 5 miles of the target. Other conditions which affected the results included thick haze (one in fifteen), phase of the moon (one in fifteen during new moon) and the amount of flak. It did not look good, but—and this is often ignored in modern summaries of this report—the conclusions emphasized the difficulties of working with the amount of data provided, and the possible areas of error in the methods used. It also stressed that these figures should be checked over a wider sample; and, as Bomber Command later pointed out, 'Do photographs indicate such important factors as the loss of skilled workers killed and injured, or the loss of time during periods of air-raid alarms and post-raid disorganization, the disruption of transport facilities serving factory and building yards, aggravated by the adverse impressions made on the employees' morale?' However, there could be no denying the basic conclusions of the Butt Report: Bomber Command was not achieving the accuracy, and therefore level of destruction, that had been thought. The question now was what could be done about it, especially in the face of ever-increasing German defences.

REASONS FOR LOSSES

Those who thought that they had only the German defences to worry about were sadly mistaken; many aircraft were lost, and crews killed or wounded, to a variety of other causes. At certain periods this 'non-operational reason for casualties on operations' reached over 2 per cent of sorties; the picture was somewhat complicated and the damage caused by enemy defences must often have been a contributory factor. Of these losses the greatest number (26 per cent) were to fuel shortage; it was always a case of balancing the bomb load against the fuel load, with the desire to get the maximum of the former while allowing for adequate reserves of the latter. Bomb and fuel loads were specified by Group as part of the tasking instruction to the Station, although the Station, and to a lesser extent the squadron, could query the figures and adjust them if they thought it prudent so to do; the crew, however, had no choice—they had to make the best of what they were given. It was usually knowledge of the fuel load that gave the first hint as to where the target might be—a visit to the aircraft once the Battle Order had appeared, a chat to the groundcrew to find out the fuel load, and guessing would begin.

The later addition of the flight engineer to the crew of the heavy bombers helped share the workload of aircraft management; looking after the fuel was one of his major concerns. It was treated as a matter of some pride to get the best out of the engines, including the economical use of fuel. Some squadrons ran competitions to see which crew could achieve the most economical fuel consumption, although many crews were happy to come last as long as it meant that they could use the full capability of their aircraft to get away from the defensive zone as quickly as possible! There were many unknowns once the aircraft was airborne; any change in cruising altitude, 'met' conditions, evasion of enemy defences, would all have an effect on the fuel consumption—and hence the fuel reserve. Many crews began the return journey knowing that they were short of fuel and that it was going to be a close-run thing between ending up in the sea or back at an airfield. Having reached England safely . . . another glance at the gauges . . . land at the nearest airfield or risk pressing on back to base? At least, having made it back to England, the crew could always bale out on dry land; but a night parachute descent was always a hazardous prospect and even the cold uncomfortable bomber seemed better than a step into the dark—unless it was about to crash. There were strong reasons to press on home; it was part of the mission to get the aircraft back so that it could be made ready to go again; it was a familiar environment—

Handley Page Halifax JG244 'MH-K' of No 51 Squadron shot down over Holland. [51 Sqn records]

the rest of the squadron, the Mess, the local pub. Many crews pressed on, some made it back, others took to their parachutes, some crashed. The prudent answer was to land at the nearest airfield, and many did just that.

The next highest figure (24 per cent) was put down to bad landings. Every flying incident of this sort was the subject of an enquiry in an attempt to discover what had happened and, if appropriate, to apportion blame. Here again there were many cases of battle damage being a major factor, with aircraft staggering back to Britain to make a dramatic landing. Even in cases such as this the pilot might find himself on the wrong side of the CO's desk. There were too many cases of plain bad landings of undamaged aircraft. But that is too simple a statement; the arrival back in Britain after a long, usually hazardous, operational mission in uncomfortable conditions brought an inevitable relaxation, despite all the many warnings about this problem, and this occasionally produced errors, in both inexperienced and experienced crews.

Of the other reasons for such losses one of the most tragic was that of aircraft hitting the ground. In these days of modern navigational and flying aids, including very accurate instruments and ground radar, we still read of aircraft flying into high ground—with the

obvious catastrophic result. The bomber crew returning to England had little to help them, although the situation improved slightly with the advent of new navigational devices: navigating by DR, assisted by astro and D/F, they would have to find their home airfield in the wartime darkness. On a clear night this would prove reasonably easy by locating a few visual features to help point the way to the general area; then the welcoming sight of the airfield beacon, join the landing pattern and—home again!

However, with thick, heavy cloud covering the country it was a different story. It was essential to get down below cloud at some stage. A descent based upon the DR plot, with all its possible errors, was fraught with inherent danger: it was a descent towards the ground— and ground kills. What height to go down to (on a not very accurate altimeter)? Where would the cloudbase be? Are we over the valley west of base—or could we be 10 miles further north-east and so over the high ground?

'A widespread and unpredicted deterioration in the weather at our home bases occurred. No diversion areas were available and many deplorable accidents resulted while our aircraft were endeavouring to break cloud and land.'

'We could see nothing of the ground of course, and no beacons either because of the cloud, but I throttled back and gingerly lost height, collecting a little white ice on the way down and flying on a northerly heading hoping to be over the valley. It was a horrid feeling as we got to 1,500 feet with still a couple of hundred feet to go before we broke cloud. If we happened to be only 10 miles out on either side we might have just a few feet to spare with luck—or fly smack into a hill otherwise. We were all holding our breath as the cloud thinned and we broke free into reasonable visibility with no snow shower in the vicinity.'

RENEWED OFFENSIVE

The 'return to Germany' had started even before the new directive had come into force, Cologne, Osnabruck, Munster and Mönchengladbach being attacked on 7/8 July. There were also minor ops that night to Frankfurt and Boulogne. It was to remain a feature of Bomber Command operations for some time that small raids, by up to 30 aircraft, were made against a variety of targets as an adjunct to the main effort of the night. Wellington L7818 of No 75 (New Zealand) Squadron was attacked by a night fighter near Munster and seriously damaged; fire broke out in the starboard wing, threatening to destroy the aircraft. Sergeant James Ward, RNZAF, the second pilot, clambered out onto the wing, kicking foot and hand holds into the fabric, and was able to beat out the flames. In due course he was awarded the Victoria Cross.

In the midst of this renewed offensive it was discovered that *Scharnhorst* had moved from Brest to La Pallice for sea trials. Bomber Command was tasked to destroy the ship. The opening shots were fired by 30 Whitleys on 23/24 July, followed by a major day attack on the 24th. This raid, divided between Brest and La

W/C MacDougall lands back at Polebrook after the first B-17 Fortress op by No 90 Squadron [90 Sqn records]

Pallice, and with a fighter-escorted Blenheim attack on Cherbourg, was planned to give the heavy bombers a chance of putting in an accurate daylight attack—with fighter escort. To Brest went 100 bombers, including three of the new Boeing B-17C Fortress Is being flown by No 90 Squadron. The hope was that this aircraft would fly well above the range of the defences and with this immunity carry out accurate daylight bombing. In the event this was not to be the case and the experiment was short-lived, although later versions of the Fortress subsequently returned to the Bomber Command inventory as an RCM (radio counter-measures) element in No 100 Group.

The plan fell down badly with La Pallice and fifteen Halifaxes of Nos 35 and 76 Squadrons went in unescorted. The bombers were bounced by fighters and lost five of their number. The flak was intense and accurate but could not prevent the bombers scoring five hits on the warship; three bombs went straight through the bottom of the vessel. In view of the damage *Scharnhorst* returned to drydock at Brest—a success for Bomber Command. All three of these major warships were to remain bottled up in Brest for some time to come.

In the first seven weeks of the tasked anti-rail campaign, very few of the stated targets had been attacked: Hamm (3), Cologne (2) and Duisburg (2). Most of the effort had been directed against German towns, many of which were also important rail centres. The list included Osnabruck, Monchengladbach, Munster, Aachen, Wilhelmshaven, Bremen, Hannover, Hamburg, Frankfurt, Mannheim, Kiel, Karlsruhe, Essen, Krefeld, Berlin and Magdeburg.

Having expended a great deal of effort on some of the targets listed in July, Bomber Command could feel reasonably pleased with its summer campaign to date—assuming that it was hitting the targets as hard as it appeared to be (and the Butt Report had called this into question). On 30 August the general directive was extended to include small towns on the rail network, with the intention of spreading the disruption, and associated ARP requirement, over a wider area, and also by hitting more than one point on the rail network at the same time, thus increasing the overall disruption. It was considered that there might be an additional benefit of reduced losses through attacking less well defended areas. The German defence system in the West had been greatly strengthened, and reorganized, by the summer of 1941. In August the XIII Air Corps was formed, incorporating two searchlight divisions, three signal regiments, the day fighter units, and the Nachtjagd-division. The increasing level of fighter activity was made evident in a report relating to the number of interceptions of night sorties during August. Of 3,449 sorties, 6.9 per cent reported interceptions and of these 36 per cent turned into attacks. As an overall level of

Two photographs showing Blenheim IVs of No 21 Squadron carrying out an attack on Rotterdam docks, 16 July 1941.

only 2 per cent of all sorties were intercepted, this was still not a drastic figure, but it did point to the increasing effectiveness of the German night-fighter defences.

The raid of 29/30 August on Frankfurt included the first Royal Australian Air Force (RAAF) participation, a Hampden of No 455 Squadron, which had formed at Swinderby on 6 June. The same night saw Bomber Command operating in support of Resistance groups in occupied countries, sorties being flown by No 138 Squadron. This squadron had been formed out of No 1419 Special Duties Flight at Newmarket on 25 August and used Whitleys and Lysanders. These Special Duties (SD) missions—dropping arms, supplies and agents—were of great importance and highly classified. Although the squadron was part of Bomber Command, being attached to No 3 Group, tasking came direct from the Air Staff through the office of the Assistant Chief of the Air Staff (Intelligence).

In the ten days following the extension of the directive to include smaller rail centres, none of the original targets was attacked, most of the effort being expended on the standard targets of Cologne, Essen, Frankfurt and Berlin, plus other industrial centres. The attack of 8/9 September on Kassel did inflict severe damage on a factory making rolling stock, although this factory had not been scheduled as a primary target. The scale of German rail movements can be appreciated from the statistic of 10,000 movements a day through the rail centre at Hamm. Disruption of rail communications remained a key bombing aim. Italy had not been

NOSE ART

The temptation to paint symbols and motifs on military aircraft has proved irresistible since the birth of military aviation. The official attitude to the decoration of aircraft has never been easy to divine, different organizations and different commanders taking different stances. Throughout the Second World War aircraft of Bomber Command 'sprouted' nose art, both the standard use of symbols to denote missions completed (usually bombs in the case of bombers), and an aircraft name/symbol at the whim of the crew. There were, of course, other motif types: squadron designations, favoured by some of the Allied squadrons such as the Poles, and special devices such as the family crest on the Stirling 'McRobert's Reply'. Most nose art, however, was of the decorative sort devised by the crew and painted on the aircraft by the nearest thing to an artist that the crew could lay hands on—and some of the artwork was of a very high standard. There was no hard and fast rule to the creation of designs—'Decided to name and paint artwork, needed official permission but this was informal and caused no delay . . . to be of feminine sex, and therefore pilot's name and aircraft letter (C), therefore had to be "Charlie's Aunt". Chose Varga pin-up from *Esquire* magazine—curvaceous redhead in a seductive green dress'.

The range of nose art was very impressive and much of it followed the basic precept of that applied to 'Charlie's Aunt'. An entire volume could be devoted to the subect but regrettably colour photography arrived too late to record more than a few samples of RAF Bomber Command nose art.

Above: Whitley 'Schwartz Nemesis', September 1941.

Below: Wellington of No 300 (Polish) Squadron.

Below: Wellington 'The Sundowner'.

Above: Halifax 'Intuition', with a good array of mission symbols and an Adolf Hitler cartoon.

Above: Halifax 'Winsome WAAF' of No 51 Squadron.

Below: Lancaster 'Mickey the Moocher' with 112 mission symbols.

forgotten and on 10/11 August Turin was attacked by 76 aircraft.

As CAS, Portal was still pressing the War Cabinet for an ever greater slice of resources so that the bomber force could be expanded and enhanced. Although the events of the summer, including the Butt Report, had given Churchill pause for thought he nevertheless continued to support the expansion programme; but, as was to be stressed again before the year ended, this was largely due to the lack of any alternative. Bomber Command was still the only offensive weapon the British had. Earlier in the summer the Air Staff view had still been that it was better to attack specific critical targets ('the most vulnerable cogs of the enemy's war machine'), but there was increasing pressure for a review of this in view of 'the apparent failure of the current communications offensive and of the previous oil offensive; towns were more pushed to the fore as the most profitable targets of all'. This target system, although given such a high priority, was not included in the Bomber Command autumn campaign; neither were many of the primary rail targets. Instead, Bomber Command spread its effort throughout the Ruhr and to a number of other German towns. The period also saw the last daylight raid in Europe by the RAF's Fortress Is; their hoped-for accuracy and invulnerability had not materialized and there had been too many problems. Added to this was American reluctance to supply any more of these heavy bombers as this would disrupt their own expansion plans.

While the general target systems list remained in force, an important additional target was specified on 11 September—Schweinfurt. This important rail junction was also the centre of Germany's ball-bearing industry; the experts suggested that 70 per cent of the supply to the aircraft industry, armoured fighting vehicles (AFVs) and military transports came from these plants at Schweinfurt.

The concentrated, almost non-stop anti-shipping searches by the Blenheims of No 2 Group in the period from March to October 1941 involved 2,320 sorties, from which 126 aircraft failed to return. All these attacks were carried out at low level by day, sometimes with fighter escort, and almost always against ships in known locations—rather than as sweeps for opportunity targets. There was a 30 per cent success rate in finding the targets and an associated loss rate of 18 per cent, with a further 7 per cent seriously damaged; of the losses it was estimated that 51 per cent fell to anti-aircraft fire from the ships, 18 per cent to enemy aircraft, 5 per cent through running into the target ship (most of these aircraft had probably already been hit by flak), and 25 per cent to unknown causes (including flying into the sea—the Blenheims operated at ultra-low level, climbing to deliver their attacks). Of the 456 ships attacked, 72 were estimated to have been sunk and a further 65

seriously damaged; thus, although losses were heavy, the result appeared to be worth it. One of the major problems was the quality of the bombs being used; the 250lb GP and 250lb SAP bombs were not really suitable for the anti-shipping task, the GP version being particularly poor, and far too many of the bombs were duds.

An important development in September had been the establishment of a new Bomber Command Operational Research Section (ORS), under Dr B. G. Dickins. The organization was given four main areas of study:

1. Study of bomber losses.
2. Study of the success of bomber operations.
3. Study of the vulnerability of bombers.
4. Study of radar and radio problems.

(A fifth, the study of daylight operations, was added later.)

It was a move that was long overdue. Bomber Command was in need of a central organization able to take an overview of various aspects of the offensive, an organization removed from the daily 'battle' but with close links at operational and command levels. This is what the ORS set out to become, a combination of scientists and airmen working together to solve the myriad problems related to the bomber offensive. It certainly did not become a Bomber Command 'yes' machine; many of its reports had hard-hitting criticism of the way things were being done. Throughout this book the reader will find references to ORS reports; this is a reflection of the amount and importance of work undertaken by the ORS. Very few Bomber Command personnel below Group level knew much of the existence of this organization, or of the influence it had on the development of equipment and tactics, which is understandable bearing in mind the highly classified nature of its work.

From spring 1942 onwards ORS was also given the task of producing the *Bomber Command Quarterly Review* (prompted by the C-in-C's seeing a copy of a similar magazine produced by the Coastal Command ORS). Harris was later to comment that 'the purpose of this review is to enable all concerned to learn more about the far ranging operations of Bomber Command, and to have a better understanding of what it has achieved and is achieving'. The tone of the magazine was always upbeat, with its list of the achievements for the period in question, and had the general feeling of a public relations product, which to an extent it was, the circulation ensuring that all those in the right places should receive it and be suitably impressed. Although the distribution of this secret document was fairly

Right top: Daylight raid by No 35 Squadron Halifaxes seen en route to Brest on 31 December 1941.

Right: Halifaxes over Brest; warships in dry dock to right of picture.

No 35 Squadron raid on Brest, 17 December 1942:
Top: Bombs away!
Centre: W/C Robinson, CO of No 35 Squadron, with both port engines out.
Bottom: W/C Robinson ditches.

widespread, it does not appear to have filtered down to many of the operational stations, although a few aircrew do recall seeing a copy in the Intelligence Section.

Having appraised the achievements and losses of 1941, it was not altogether a happy picture; however, the future looked much brighter with new and more capable aircraft in the pipeline, together with the expected improved navigation/bombing systems. This could only be seen with hope if Bomber Command had a solid basis from which to exploit its new power, but it was essential that a policy of conservation be introduced to prevent the Command being bled to death. This was reflected in a new directive, dated 13 November, which outlined the War Cabinet's view that it was vital to 'conserve our resources in order to build a strong force to be available by the spring of next year. Air Marshal Peirse was requested to bear this principle in mind when planning future operations. It was further suggested that the Command should not press attacks if the weather was unsuitable—a distinct comment on one of the major reasons for the losses of 7/8 November. This caused much upset at Bomber Command HQ, with Peirse considering that his tactical judgment had been called into question, which in some ways it had. He was quick to point out that most decisions were taken in close consultation with a wide range of experts and in consideration of the overall tactical requirements—and that plans sometimes went wrong. This was the kind of disagreement that should not occur between Command levels, but it was symptomatic of the problems facing Bomber Command.

The Command had a 'rest' from 10 to 15 November, bad weather precluding operations, the same being the case later in the month. As soon as the weather improved the bombers were active again. The raid on Brest on 7/8 December saw the first operational use of 'Oboe', Stirlings of Nos 7 and 15 Squadrons conducting a trial on the new blind-bombing aid. These trials continued throughout December but results were inconclusive; the risks of a set falling into German hands led to its withdrawal until sufficient equipment was available and suitable tactics devised.

On 10 December a signal from the Air Ministry instructed Bomber Command to give 'highest priority to the destruction of enemy capital ships' and proposed that a series of daylight attacks should be made against Brest. Six Hampdens went to Brest the next day, but aborted the sortie through lack of adequate cloud cover. However, Brest was attacked most days or nights until the end of the year, the scale of attack varying from six aircraft to a major raid by 121 bombers on 17/18 December. Cologne, Düsseldorf and Wilhelmshaven were also attacked during this period. For the hardworking Blenheims a new task was forthcoming on 27/28 December, six aircraft being assigned to carry out a night attack on the German airfield at Soesterberg in

'OBOE'

Undoubtedly the most accurate of the electronic aids to enter service during the war, 'Oboe' was developed by the Telecommunications Research Establishment (TRE) as a result of research into German beacon systems. Early trials of blind-bombing on a ground signal used a CHL (Chain Home Low) ground station plus an IFF set in the aircraft. One of the trials team thought that the CHL signal sounded like an oboe, and the name stuck.

The system, as devised by early 1941, consisted of two ground stations, the 'Cat' (a tracking station sending a dot-dash signal) and the 'Mouse' (ground station sending the release signal). In essence use of the system was simple. The aircraft would aim to fly to the target along an arc of a circle from a start point 10 minutes' flying time from the target. With the 'Oboe' switched on the crew would then receive the series of dots-dashes from the 'Cat' which indicated which side of the planned approach track the aircraft was, on track being indicated by a steady tone. If the aircraft was well off track, then a morse letter would be transmitted, the letter depending on the distance off track. The 'Mouse' sent signals indicating time to go to bomb release signal itself. At that point the aircraft transmitter would cut out, thus indicating to the ground stations the point, and time, of release.

The fact that the procedure took 10 minutes was its only major drawback; only one aircraft could use the system during this time frame. This limit of six aircraft per hour caused objections in the Air Staff and a delay in the development of the system. The answer to the problem was to develop a wider range of frequencies or build more ground stations. Additional limitations were those of any electronic aid: it was limited in range and it could be jammed. The range problem meant that the aircraft had to operate at 26,000 feet over the Ruhr; only the pressure-cabin Wellington VI and the Mosquito could achieve this. Trials decided in favour of the latter, the limited bomb load of the Mosquito leading to suggestions for its use as in a marker technique. The initial pairs of ground stations at Dover and Trimingham gave adequate coverage of the Ruhr. By autumn 1943 there was confirmation of German jamming of 'Oboe' Mk I; however, the 10cm Mk II variant, 'Album Leaf', was just entering service. This went on to become the standard variant, having a theoretical accuracy of 0.01 of a mile!

The need to improve the accuracy of the bomber force meant that 'Oboe' went into service before it was really ready. On the night of 20/21 December 1942 six Mosquitoes of No 109 Squadron attacked the power station at Lutterade in Holland. On this first 'Oboe' attack three aircraft dropped using the system, the equipment in the other three aircraft being unserviceable. Unfortunately, the area around the target was so heavily cratered from previous raids that it was impossible to determine the accuracy of this atttack. The 'Oboe' Mosquitoes continued these small-scale trial attacks during December; more signifcantly, on the night of 31 December two aircraft acted as markers, dropping TIs for a small force of Lancasters attacking Düsseldorf. The trial raids continued into early 1942, culminating in the first real test of the system with a major raid on Essen.

'Oboe' remained an effective and generally reliable blind-bombing (or marking) aid throughout the war. Numerous improvements and modifications were made; some, however, were curtailed in the trials stage by an unfounded over-confidence in the accuracy of H2S.

Holland. These intruder raids became a standard routine for the squadrons of No 2 Group (and Fighter Command), with fighter and bomber airfields being attacked. The policy was intended not only to disrupt the German defensive network, and so assist the night bombers, but also to disrupt German bombing efforts against England.

On 31 December 1941 the Command mustered 56 squadrons, 27 per cent of which were 'heavies'—a significant improvement on the situation earlier in the year. During the year the Command had operated on 240 nights, dropping 31,700 tons of bombs (12 per cent of which were incendiaries), and in 1,250 mining sorties had laid 1,055 mines. These were reasonable statistics if all the munitions were finding their targets; however, despite the Butt Report and a desire to improve accuracy, little had been achieved in this respect by the end of the year. Nevertheless, some important changes had been made and developments were under way that would change the situation in 1942.

Overall it had been a frustrating year and the faith of many supporters of the bomber offensive had been shaken by the high losses and the apparent inability of the Command to hit its targets. Nevertheless, a number of positive aspects had been evident, not least the operational debut of the new generation of four-engined heavy bombers. Portal and the Air Staff had put forward positive proposals for the 1942 campaign and they had fought hard to counter all the detractors. The first few months of 1942 were seen as being critical, almost make or break for Bomber Command—succeed, or lose resources to other Commands.

CHAPTER FOUR

A Decisive Year

FOR BOMBER COMMAND, the year 1942 was destined to mark the turning point. After frequent changes of Commander, including Air Vice-Marshal Baldwin as acting AOC from 8 January for six weeks, in February 1942 Bomber Command acquired at its head the man who was to inspire and lead it for the rest of the war, Air Marshal Arthur T. Harris. Harris was convinced of the value, and necessity, of the bombing offensive and he gave a valuable boost to the morale of the Command at a time when its fortunes and spirits were at a low ebb. It was also under attack from the influential Ministry of Economic Warfare; a report of 4 February was scathing about the Command's, or perhaps more accurately the Commander's, determination to achieve the tasks it had been set: 'The MEW depends directly on the Director of Bombing Operations to resist, in the higher levels, any unsound tendencies to dilute, by-pass or emasculate policies which have been agreed between ourselves (meaning the MEW, Bombing

Boston 'RH-J' of No 88 Squadron, May 1942. [88 Sqn records]

Target Information Committee) and the Air Staff as being sound in the respects which are within our respective provinces. ...Bomber Command is still paying more attention to techniques and operational problems than to economic strategy, though there are signs that this phase is now passing.' If it was, then it was to be the lull before the storm; the arguments would rage fierce and long when Harris was in command. Although willing to use statistics to ram home his points, he had little love of statisticians and even less for 'panacea merchants' and their ideas on strategy.

In one respect at least the Bomber Command effort was having an impact on Germany: a large proportion of her military resources was being put into defensive rather than offensive systems. By January 1942 the total number of flak guns had almost doubled, to 4,416 heavy and 7,452 medium/light guns, supported by 3,276 searchlights. The night fighter defences were also ready for another year; the Kammhuber Line had been deepened and elements of the system, including early warning and ground control, had been improved. A number of the great night fighter aces had opened their

AIR MARSHAL ARTHUR T. HARRIS

Without the guiding hand of its commander, Arthur Harris, it is most unlikely that Bomber Command would have become such a decisive offensive force; a lesser leader would have given way to some of the pressures that tried to push the Command in different directions. There has been much argument since the war as to the way that Bomber Command was used, and Harris has received a great deal of vituperation—being accused of running a 'vindictive campaign' against the German cities!

Born in 1892, Arthur Travers Harris went through an unremarkable schooling, leaving when 16 to go to Rhodesia. When war broke out in 1914 he became a bugler with the 1st Rhodesia Regiment and took part in the campaigns in German South-West Africa. Having decided that there was more to be gained elsewhere, he went to England to join the Royal Flying Corps. Tours on Home Defence and artillery-spotting over the Western Front saw him end the war as a Major. One of the few to be given a post-war position, Harris, as a Squadron Leader, went out to the North-West Frontier Province of India. It was here as a squadron commander that Harris, like many others, developed his theories of air power. By 1922 he was CO of No 45 Squadron in Iraq, where he converted his Vernon and Victoria transport aircraft into 'long-range heavy bombers' by cutting sighting holes in the nose and bolting on home-made bomb racks. Among his flight commanders were two other future bomber leaders, Saunders and Cochrane.

Harris's connection with bombers continued in 1925 when he was CO of No 58 Squadron, in England, equipped with the Vickers Virginia, the RAF's first post-war heavy bomber. A period at the Army Staff College (Camberley) and a tour as SASO in Egypt were followed by another squadron commander tour, this time with No 210 Squadron at Pembroke Dock with flying-boats. He was promoted to Wing Commander in 1927 and Group Captain in 1933. A series of staff appointments, such as Deputy Director of Operations and Intelligence, and then DD of Plans, gave Harris his chance to influence air policy. As a member of the Joint Planning Committee in 1936 he helped formulate the strategic bombing policy for the event of war with Germany. With the reorganization of RAF Command and Groups, he took over the newly formed No 4 Group in 1937 (being promoted to Air Commodore), based at Linton-on-

Ouse. The Group was equipped with Whitleys and Harris took a direct interest in everything that was being done, making frequent visits to his stations. It was a short-lived appointment as he was sent to the USA with the Purchasing Mission to acquire American aircraft, followed by another staff tour in the Middle East as Air-Officer-Commanding Palestine and Transjordan. Invalided back with ulcer problems, he was promoted Air Vice-Marshal in July 1939 and in September was appointed AOC No 5 Group, and so was back in the 'bomber business'.

As the war progressed so he became more concerned about the way that the offensive was being conducted. He appreciated the great strain under which his crews were operating and tried to adopt a policy of two nights' rest between each mission. All these aspects were to stand him in good stead when he took over control of Bomber Command. First, however, came another spell in the Air Ministry, as Deputy Chief of the Air Staff; he was promoted to acting Air Marshal in June 1941.

In February 1942 Harris was given the task of guiding Bomber Command for the remainder of the war; he was determined that the Command should be run his way and that the decisive nature of its offensive power should not be misused or bled away to other areas. It was a policy that brought many heated arguments, but it was undoubtedly a policy that, in general terms, was correct. There were of course errors and mistakes, areas in which a little more flexiblity might have produced a better result; but much of this can only be said with the benefit of hindsight. The cost of the campaign was high, earning him the name 'Butch' or 'Butcher' Harris from the crews, although in most cases this was not meant in quite such a blunt way as it sounds. To the Press he was also 'Bomber' Harris. What cannot be denied is his total devotion to the Command and those who worked in it; he fought long and hard to get recognition for their efforts.

As the war came to a close so the detractors of Bomber Command's bombing theory began to speak ever more loudly, calling into question the nature of some of the operations carried out. Harris stood by all that had been achieved. The acrimony grew in the post-war years, and has continued ever since.

'accounts' the previous year, men such as Helmut Lent of II/NJG 1 who shot down two Wellingtons on the night of 11/12 May 1941; by January 1943 he would be the first pilot to achieve a score of 50 night kills. 1942 was to be a year of difficulties, improvisation, and success for the German night fighter defences. This success was to cause Bomber Command great concern.

January and early February saw a continuation of Bomber Command's anti-naval campaign, Brest being the most frequent target, although Bremen, Hamburg and Wilhelmshaven were also hit. There were almost no daylight operations until, on 12 February, came the 'Channel Dash' when the three German warships *Gneisenau*, *Scharnhorst* and *Prinz Eugen* made a break-out from Brest to head for safer ports in Germany. It was a superbly planned and executed operation, catching the British off-guard. It was not until early afternoon that Bomber Command mounted operations against the warships; during the remainder of the day the Command flew 242 sorties, none of which scored hits on the vessels. Among the aircraft taking part were ten Douglas Bostons of No 88 Squadron, the new American bomber replacing the long-serving Blenheim IVs. During the next few months three of No 2 Group's

squadrons would receive the new type. However, both *Scharnhorst* and *Gneisenau* hit mines—which had been laid by Hampdens of No 5 Group—and were damaged; nevertheless, all these ships reached port safely. The enormous effort expended over Brest had failed to destroy the ships but it had kept them out of the sea lanes for almost a year. With the transfer of this threat, Brest was no longer a drain on Bomber Command's resources and the Command could concentrate on the offensive over Germany.

The week before Harris arrived to take command, a new and important directive had been sent by the Air Staff to Baldwin; this directive of 14 February was a confirmation and clarification of an Air Ministry letter of 4 February which had outlined a revised bombing policy. One of its central themes was the advent of TR.1335 ('Gee') and the suggestion that this would 'confer upon your forces the ability to concentrate their effort to an extent which has not hitherto been possible under the operational conditions with which your are faced . . . [and] will enable results to be obtained of a much more effective nature'.

The primary objective was stated as being 'the morale of the enemy civilian population and in particular of the

Above: Boston cloud cover raid—an opportunity attack on a dockside crane.

Above right: Low-level attack on Matford factory, Poissy, France, 8 March 1942; note aircraft at top right. Twelve Douglas Bostons of Nos 88 and 226 Squadrons attacked the factory to great effect, for the loss of one aircraft. [88 Sqn records]

industrial workers.' To achieve this the Air Staff provided a list of suitable towns, with Essen being given as the priority target. Once more the statistical experts had been at work and for each of the major towns listed gave an estimate of the bomb tonnage needed to create the required level of destruction; in the case of Essen this was estimated at 1,000 tons—based on the theoretical delivery of 7 tons per square mile. Berlin was included, but with the proviso that attacks should be of a harassing nature in order to keep aircraft losses to the minimum. One of the most important statements in the directive concerned the level of effort per target; in this the Air Staff proposed that Bomber Command should continue to hit a particular target until it was destroyed, this being one of the reasons for providing the list of estimated bomb tonnages. It was appreciated that 'Gee'

would not be available in all the Command's aircraft and that to take advantage of the new aid new tactics would have to be developed. The Air Staff suggested the use of an initial wave of 'Gee'-equipped aircraft to drop incendiaries as a guide for the rest of the bombing force. It was six months since the first operational trials of 'Gee', but at last an adequate number of sets had been delivered and Bomber Command was now ready to test it in battle.

It might appear from what has been said of the overall policy that all thought of precise attacks had been shelved, but this was not the case, and it was in this department that much was hoped for from 'Gee'. A list was included of eight precise targets within 'Gee' range, although with no stated priority. Somewhat more surprising was the list of four precise targets outside 'Gee' range. The final target systems listed covered locations in France, with special mention of the Renault factory, plus the standard element of 'other targets as called for'—meaning as called for by the Air Staff.

Baldwin was aware that his time as acting C-in-C was coming to an end and so he made notes on the directive, informing the Air Staff that he would pass these details to Harris on his assumption of command. In the

'GEE'

The search for an electronic aid to assist navigation and permit 'blind bombing' (i.e., accurate bombing even when the target was not visible) was of critical importance to Bomber Command. The earliest successful device, and then only partly so, was TR.1335, otherwise known as 'Gee'. The concept was fairly simple and relied on the reception of signals from a series of ground stations. The ground organization comprised three stations, a Master (A) and two Slaves (B and C) set along a 200-mile base line; each Slave station was locked to the Master. The time difference for signals A/B and B/C to reach the aircraft was measured and displayed on a display unit (cathode ray tube) in the aircraft. In essence, this gave the operator two position lines, the 'Gee' co-ordinates, and using a special 'Gee' chart he could plot the intersection of the lines and so obtain a fix of ground position. The theoretical accuracy was ½ to 5 miles, far better than any other navaid then in service. 'Gee's' main advantages were ease of operation and the rapidity of obtaining a fix—less than one minute. However, the system also had severe limitations, including range (line-of-sight or maximum of around 400 miles) and reliability.

A series of experimental flights was planned to determine the accuracy and potential range of the system. These 'Crackers I and II' trials by No 1418 Experimental Flight looked promising and so the system went into development. In July 1941 the Wellingtons of No 115 Squadron were fitted with 'Gee' sets in order to conduct operational trials. On the night of 11/12 August a force of 29 Wellingtons, including two 'Gee' aircraft, attacked Monchengladbach. This trial and others on the next two nights appeared to be successful, the navigators having no trouble obtaining 'Gee' fixes for most of the route. It was then decided to halt the experiment until sufficient sets were available to equip the majority of the bomber force, a figure of 300 bombers being set as the minimum. As was stated at the Chiefs of Staff Conference on 18 August, 'it made the

theoretically desirable policy of concentration in time and space practicable'. It was some months before the required number of aircraft had been equipped and 'Gee' was once more used operationally. It was an immediate success with the crews, not so much as a blind-bombing aid—it never achieved the accuracy for such a role—but as a general navaid to help the bomber get within the target area so that the crew could visually acquire the target. By August 1942 the Germans were jamming the system, thus reducing the effective range. A number of anti-jamming features were added, but the system remained of limited use as soon as the bombers approached the enemy coast.

However, another essential part played by 'Gee' was in helping the bomber find its way back to base. Statistics showed that after the introduction of this equipment, the number of aircraft landing away from base dropped. It also saved many a crew from the fate of flying on past England and ending up in the Atlantic as the petrol ran out.

Ron Tettenborn, an observer with No 9 Squadron, was among the first to use 'Gee' on ops: 'First impressions were of staggering accuracy, on practice use in UK—you could say to the pilot "we should hit the SW corner of the airfield in . . . minutes", and did, to the astonishment of the crew! The rest of the crew knew nothing about this highly secret gadget, full of detonators so we were told. "Gee" charts also had to be destroyed in emergency, but I doubt if this would have been possible with the rather clumsy equipment provided—rather like an explosive umbrella, just to the right of the nav table. On the Continent it was obviously not as accurate as over the UK, but was said to be within about a mile at Ruhr range; on a good night, with height, you could use it about as far east as Heligoland, with accuracy of 4–5 miles. After that the pulse became so small as to be more or less unreadable. It was most comforting on the way home, but tended to leave the lazy navigator in trouble if it failed!'

meantime his staffs continued to look at the requirements imposed by the new directive. The question of how best to employ 'Gee' was one which taxed many of the most experienced personnel in the Command. The initial tactical solution was to adopt what became known as the 'Shaker' technique. The basis of this technique was to try to make the best use of 'Gee' while at the same time overcoming some of the known shortcomings of night bombing, the main one being the problem of seeing the target at night. The tactical plan called for three waves of aircraft, the first two of which would comprise 'Gee'-equipped aircraft:

Wave 1—Illuminators. Drop triple flares from zero hour to illuminate the target.

Wave 2—Target Markers. Drop a maximum incendiary load from zero +2.

Wave 3—Followers. The bulk of the force, with a mainly HE load from zero +15.

Harris, who had finally taken up his post on 23 February, was determined to prove the detractors wrong and show that Bomber Command was the true war-winning weapon. This firm conviction was to set him on a collision course with some members of the Air Staff, but there can be no doubt that his driving force was to prove a key factor during 1942. When he took command it was still a time of dark days for the Allies, two years of defeat after defeat (with the odd success of course, such as the Battle of Britain), and every theatre of war calling for more and more of the military capability and

production capacity. Each new problem brought a fresh call for more supplies, more aircraft and more men. It would have been easy for the War Cabinet to vacillate and order continual changes of priority. It was only the determination of such leaders as Harris, ably supported most of the time by Portal, with the ability to convince Churchill of their case, that a longer-term and sound policy prevailed.

His time as a Group Commander had left Harris in no doubt of the many problems faced by Bomber Command. He was fully aware of its limitations, but also of its potential: 'The bomber force of which I assumed command on 23rd February 1942, although at that time very small, was a potentially decisive weapon. It was, indeed, the only means at the disposal of the Allies for striking at Germany itself and, as such, stood out as the central part in Allied offensive strategy.' He now set about trying to rectify some of the problems. In this he was fortunate that much of the groundwork, at least regarding equipment, had already been carried out— 1942 was to be the year in which many of the projected systems became operational. On the date that he took command the operational strength of Bomber Command (aircraft with crews) totalled 378, of which only 69 were 'heavies'. He summarized the overall position as 'lack of suitable aircraft in sufficient numbers, absence of efficient nav. aids, and deficiency of trained crews'—and then set about putting each right.

Expansion of Bomber Command was one of his first

priorities, the principle of taking ever more aircraft, each with an ever greater bomb load, to the target area. Although heavy bomber production had been given priority in late 1941, it would take some time for this to have a material effect on the number of aircraft entering service. Beaverbrook had made great progress with the expansion of aircraft production, despite the increasing complexity of the machines being produced; nevertheless, heavy bomber production was slow, only 67 aircraft being produced each quarter during 1942. This was hardly sufficient to allow for the re-equipment of squadrons to full operational requirements, and gave no flexibility for losses. The entry into the war of the United States brought the ending of Lend-Lease, at least for the time being, as the US armed forces needed every item of military equipment for their own use; although certain types of equipment, including some aircraft, were not affected.

The period immediately following the policy change did not see a massive return of effort against Germany. In fact, there was a marked lowering of overall effort with very few large-scale raids, the 98 aircraft to

Manchester cockpit.

Mannheim on 14/15 February being the largest. This slack period was to end with a spectacular and effective raid.

A modified version of 'Shaker' was employed on 3/4 March when 235 aircraft attacked the Renault factory at Billancourt, near Paris. This attack, although not employing 'Gee', did use the flare technique outlined in 'Shaker'. Attacking in three waves the bombers, including 75 'heavies', achieved both concentration and accuracy. The first wave, of experienced crews, had the task of identifying the target in the light of flares and then dropping 1,000lb bombs. The second wave also dropped 1,000lb bombs, while the aircraft of the first wave kept the target illuminated with flares; the third wave carried 4,000lb bombs. The target was only lightly defended and so the bombers were able to attack from a lower altitude, 6,000 feet on average, thus increasing the accuracy and, hopefully, keeping to the minimum the number of French casualties. It was a record-breaking attack; not only the largest number of aircraft attacking a single target but also the most concentrated attack timewise (roughly 120 aircraft per hour). Crews returned reporting excellent results. This was confirmed by PR the next day; the factory buildings had indeed received heavy damage. Later reports showed that 300 bombs fell on the factory, causing the destruction of 40 per cent of the buildings and halting production for many weeks. Despite the accuracy of the attack, French casualties were heavy.

This night was also significant in that the first Avro Lancaster operational sorties took place, four aircraft of No 44 Squadron laying mines off the coast of Germany—'It is noteworthy that this is the first occasion that Lancaster aircraft have operated and this squadron was the only one operational with this type'. Each aircraft dropped four mines from 600 feet—L7546 (Squadron Leader Nettleton) and L7568 (Flight Lieutenant Sandford) at 'Yams' (code-name for Heligoland Approaches) and L7549 (Warrant Officer Crum) and L7547 (Warrant Officer Lamb) at 'Rosemary' (Heligoland). It had been an uneventful introduction to operations. A week later, on the 10th, the squadron sent three Lancasters on the type's first bombing mission, as part of a force of 126 aircraft tasked against Essen. The first of the 'Lancs' over the target was L7536 (Flying Officer Ball) at 2148—'height 18,000 feet, bombs 14 SBCs each 90 × 4lbs dropped in area believed to be SE of "blitz" area. 16 bundles of Nickels G.1 dropped over target area. At this height not worried much by searchlights and flak activities, but on leaving target area, flak very accurate both for height and direction'. The other aircraft on the raid—Wellingtons, Hampdens, Manchesters and Stirlings—had to struggle at lower altitudes. It was another disappointing raid, little damage being done, and four aircraft were lost.

The first true 'Shaker' operation took place a few days

later with an attack on Essen. A force of 211 bombers, over half of which were Wellingtons, led by 'Gee'-equipped aircraft, tried on the night of 8/9 March finally to deal with one of Bomber Command's long-standing trouble spots. Although the new aid meant that most crews had little difficulty finding the approximate area, the usual industrial haze once more provided a protective blanket so that the bomb-aimers could not see the target itself. At this stage of the war the instruction was simply to get to the area using 'Gee' and then, in the light of the flares, make a visual acquisition of the aiming point. Analysis of the results showed that the main target area, Krupps, had escaped undamaged and that very few bombs had fallen on Essen. The attackers lost eight aircraft (3.8 per cent), although with two out of 22 Avro Manchesters failing to return their particular loss rate was nearly 10 per cent.

Following the principle of concentrating on a particular target, Essen was attacked again on the two subsequent nights. On the 9/10th a force of 187 bombers again had trouble with haze and only light damage resulted to Essen; it was a similar story on the 10/11th when 126 bombers were defeated by the haze. A further seven aircraft were lost on these two raids.

AVRO LANCASTER

'Starting a Lancaster was a four-handed job until one is used to it, and pilot and engineer work together. The engineer has control of the main fuel cocks, booster pump, booster coil switch, and starter buttons; while the pilot operates engine master cocks, magneto switches and throttles. Invariably one of the engines will refuse to start, so one works on the principle that one starts the remaining engines, thereby providing the stubborn unit with what one hopes is a good example!'

The most famous of RAF bombers and one which had a first-class war record, the Lancaster was the last of the series of four-engined bombers to enter service. The Lancaster grew out of the failed twin-engined Manchester, the prototype being a converted Manchester airframe with four Rolls-Royce Merlins. The prototype Lancaster (BT308) first flew in January 1941, with the first squadron (No 44) re-equipping in December the same year. This squadron was also the first to undertake bombing operations with the type, an attack on Essen on the night of 10/11 March 1942 being the start of what was to become an almost endless stream of Lancasters over Germany.

One of the aircraft's most notable features was the expansion of its bomb capacity from the original 4,000lb weapon to the giant 22,000lb 'Grand Slam' bomb, the Lancaster being the only aircraft capable of taking this particular weapon. In almost all other aspects of operations the Lancaster played a key, often crucial, role—special operations (such as the Dams Raid), Pathfinder techniques, Special Duties (radar counter-measures, jamming and spoofing), and many more. It also had a lower percentage loss rate than the other four-engined bombers, thanks partly to its higher ceiling, and was the only type not to have been the subject of a loss-rate review by the Bomber Command Operational Research Section (other than as a comparison).

The classic lines of the Avro Lancaster: LL854, a Lancaster I, probably of No 15 Squadron.

The major production versions used by Bomber Command were the Mks I and III, the main difference being the mark of Merlin engine used. By early 1945 there were 56 squadrons of Lancasters, making it the most significant aircraft in Bomber Command, not only in terms of numbers but also of bomb load.

In all, 7,377 Lancasters were built (including 430 in Canada), the last being delivered in February 1946. The last RAF Lancaster bomber squadron re-equipped with Lincolns, in many ways a follow-on Lancaster, in 1950. However, the 'Lanc' served in a number of other roles, the most notable being Maritime Reconnaissance (MR), in which capacity the last aircraft (RF325) was not retired until October 1956.

LANCASTER I DATA
Crew: Seven
Engines: Four 1,280hp Merlin XX or XXII
Span: 102ft
Length: 69ft 6in
Height: 20ft
Weight empty: 36,900lb
Weight loaded: 68,000lb
Max. speed: 287mph at 11,500ft
Ceiling: 24,500ft
Range: 1,660 miles (14,000lb bomb load)
Armament: Nose and upper turrets with twin 0.303in guns, tail turret with four 0.303in guns; single 22,000lb bomb (no upper turret) or 14,000lb max. bomb load

Squadrons (Bomber Command): Nos 7, 9, 12, 15, 35, 44, 49, 50, 57, 61, 75, 83, 90, 97, 100, 101, 103, 106, 115, 138, 149, 150, 153, 156, 166, 170, 186, 189, 195, 207, 218, 227, 300, 405, 419, 420, 424, 425, 426, 427, 428, 429, 431, 432, 433, 434, 460, 463, 467, 514, 550, 576, 582, 617, 619, 622, 625, 626, 630, 635

THE BOMBER CREW

'In the prolonged night bomber offensive every Captain of aircraft has an individual responsibility higher than his equivalent in any other sphere of military operations. Once he has become airborne from his base he is the sole arbiter of the destiny of his share of the attack.'

The crew was the heart of the bomber, a close-knit team of experts who relied upon each other not only for the success of the mission but also for each other's lives. This was a unique situation; the battles over Germany each night were battles between one crew and the whole of Germany. When Bomber Command entered the war it was badly equipped in aircraft and training for the roles it was called on to perform. The hard lessons of war taught that much had to be changed—including the composition of the bomber crews and the responsibilities of each man. An early rule had been: 'It is a guiding principle in laying down the composition of crews of large bombers that there must be at least two men capable of carrying out each major task. Thus, if any one member of the crew should become a casualty there is another man available to take on his work and play his part in carrying out the task allotted and bringing the aircraft safely back to its base.' With a standard heavy bomber crew of two pilots, navigator/bomb-aimer, wireless operator, and air gunners, this principle was just about workable. The Captain, always referred to as 'skipper', led the team and managed the sortie based on information from the other members of the crew. It was his decisions that were final; there could be no other way in the skies over Germany.

As aircraft and equipment became more complex, and in the light of experience, changes were made. The second pilot was removed when a shortage of pilots became apparent and the luxury of two per aircraft could no longer be afforded; instead, one of the other crew members was given training as a pilot's assistant. With the increased specialization of both navigation and bomb-aiming, the two jobs were split and an 'Air Bombardier' added to the crew. Likewise, the increased complexity of the four-engined bombers called for a specialist and so the Flight Engineer was created. So, the standard crew of a Lancaster would comprise: pilot, flight engineer, navigator, bomb-aimer, wireless operator, mid-upper gunner, rear gunner. Each was an expert in his field, each a vital cog in the overall crew machine. Rank played no part in the airborne life of the crew; a sergeant pilot would have command of his officer navigator and gunners. It was important that the individuals worked as a team; there was no room for personal friction.

No 149 Squadron crew of Stirling 'P-Peter', Methwold, July 1944. Left to right: F/Sgt Martin (Australian)—WOP; P/O Lukey (NZ)—bomb-aimer; Sgt Chamberlain—mid-upper gunner; F/O Tenduis (Dutch)—pilot; F/Sgt Crisp—navigator; Sgt Grames—rear gunner; Sgt Rowland—flight engineer. [Peter Rowland]

Lancaster crew of No 61 Squadron, Skellingthorpe. [H. Parsons]

'Then they go to the OTU where they are formed into a crew and begin to learn team work. The duties of all members of the crew are carefully defined as far as the principal tasks are concerned, but the captain of each aircraft is responsible for arranging the duties of his crew and for seeing that they carry them out punctually and efficiently.' A new pilot would start the trawl to find the rest of a crew, the decision being left to the individuals as far as possible rather than the 'system' just putting names together. It worked remarkably well and gradually the crew would come together.

Once formed and trained, the crew would fly together on the squadron whenever possible, although individuals were borrowed from time to time to make up numbers for a particular sortie. This was not a popular move as it meant that the crew would become out of step with the number of ops each individual had to perform—the hope of all being that they would complete the tour together and be 'screened' together. It was equally bad luck to go sick and miss a few ops with one's crew; it meant catching up by flying with another crew for a while. In the highly superstitious world of bomber aircrew this was seen as a great hazard; a crew member who had completed his 30 ops would often agree to do one or two more to see the rest of the crew through to their total.

At some stage during the tour, having survived a certain number of ops and 'risen' up the experience ladder within the squadron, the crew would become a 'gen crew'—they knew what it was all about, they were all 'gen men'. The navigators of No 51 Squadron were given this advice on how they could become 'gen men' (it could equally apply to the other aircrew trades): 'As a smart young cadet with a white flash in your cap, you may, at one stage of your career, before you became "disillusioned", have gazed in wonder and admiration at the tour-weary, so-called gen-men of Bomber Command. Later on during your training you may have wondered in romantic moments how people earn that title. Later still some instructor may have half-heartedly mentioned the word "crew-co-operation" but as it is such a mouthful and apparently meaningless, you probably forgot all about it and put the whole business down to plain luck. Actually there is such a thing as crew co-operation and it consists of knowing your crew members. It also means knowing something about their jobs and worries and of their knowing how they can help you—making your life easier and therefore their lives longer. Every member of a crew is a specialist in his own work and although it is a "good thing" to let your admiring aunts and uncles think that you, "Little Jimmy", are the gen man of the crew, nevertheless you must know that it takes seven men in an aircraft to bomb a target and not one gen man and six of an audience. As we were saying, you, too, can be a gen man.'

The comradeship forged by the battle to survive over Germany has seldom been equalled in any other field of experience; many of those crew friendships survive to this day.

Three nights later it was Cologne's turn to receive a 'Gee'-led raid, and this was to prove the most successful of the early series of such raids. Only one aircraft, a Manchester, was lost from the 135 bombers that attacked Cologne, again using the flare technique and with incendiaries dropped by the first wave. It was estimated that 50 per cent of the bombs fell within 5 miles of the aiming point. Damage was extensive and many factories were hit; one rubber factory was reduced to nil output for one month, and then taking a year fully to recover. Essen was attacked twice more at the end of March but without much success; it seemed that the ever-present haze was defeating the use of the new aid. The raid of 26/27 March brought a 10 per cent loss from the 115 aircraft involved. The previous night had seen the loss of nine aircraft (from 254), including no fewer than five of the 20 Manchesters. One of the penalties of attacking the same target too frequently was that the defences were ready and waiting.

Although incendiaries had been included in the series of Ruhr raids they were not really intended as 'fire-raising' raids, as proposed by the Air Staff directive. To test the incendiary concept Harris chose Lübeck as the target. There were two good reasons for this choice: it was easy to find, being a coastal town, and many of its buildings were made of wood and therefore a good target for incendiaries. The raid took place on the night of 28/29 March. Using the now established technique of experienced crews going in first to find and hit the target, thus revealing its position to the subsequent waves, 191 of the 234 crews claimed to have made good attacks. No less than 62 per cent of Lübeck's buildings were burnt out. It was the most successful raid to date, but once again a raid in which conditions favoured the bombers—good weather, a coastal target and light defences (although twelve aircraft were lost). Damage was estimated at 200 million Reichmarks and just over 300 people were killed. In the British press it was reported thus: 'Over 200 aircraft of Bomber Command tonight launched a shattering raid on the Baltic port of Lübeck, a shipbuilding and industrial centre. Hundreds of tons of incendiaries and high explosive were dropped, and about half of the built-up area has been destroyed by fire. The RAF has begun a round-the-clock offensive against German arms factories, German-controlled industries in France and German gun emplacements in the Calais area.' It was the kind of news to hearten those at home who had been used to reading of defeats; it was justified revenge against the bombing of British cities; it was the only way to deal with the

Manchester of No 83 Squadron, nicknamed 'Pepperpot', 29 March 1942. Repaired, it went on to serve with No 1656 Conversion Unit. [83 Sqn records]

Stirling at low level, 10 April 1942.

Nazis. Now that the glorious days of the Battle of Britain were over, many of those waiting to join the RAF wanted nothing more than to take part in this great offensive.

The Lübeck attack infuriated the Nazi leaders and the Luftwaffe was called upon to make a series of reprisal raids on English cultural towns, the so-called 'Baedeker Raids'.

Since Harris had taken over, Bomber Command had been working at almost maximum effort, other than a spell in mid-March when bad weather precluded large-scale operations, and the cost was beginning to tell. Some 90 aircraft, and crews, had been lost during the six-week period to the end of March and the strain on the Command was showing. During March Harris conducted a series of studies into aspects of aircraft crewing and crew training in an attempt to streamline the system. Air Council agreement was given to a change in the crewing arrangements to remove the two-pilot criterion in favour of pilot and pilot's assistant (PA), which in the case of the 'heavies' would be the Flight Engineer and in the case of the medium bombers another member of the crew. In order to get the most out of the trained personnel he had, Harris was determined not to let them be posted away to what he considered to be non-effective jobs; in general terms he expected two operational tours and two OTU tours from each of his aircrew. So that the Command could operate at maximum strength when weather conditions were suitable, he decreed that when the weather was not suitable then squadrons should be stood down to rest—and to give the groundcrew a chance to repair aircraft and achieve maximum availability. Although this policy did not always work in practice, it certainly overcame one of the biggest criticisms of earlier years, that of having to battle against the weather as well as the enemy. It was a philosophy to which Harris attempted to adhere; conserve effort when conditions were not quite right in order to have a bigger punch available for when they were.

At the time these crucial decisions were being taken, Harris's plans for expansion received a blow with an Admiralty bid, on behalf of Coastal Command, for eight and a half squadrons to be transferred from Bomber Command, two for the Indian Ocean and the others to help in the Battle of the Atlantic. Harris argued long and hard, especially against the loss of Lancaster squadrons, but eventually had to agree to lose six squadrons, which he stated should comprise three Whitley, two Wellington and one Hampden.

The Bomber Command Spring campaign was outlined as: 'Our bombers have two main tasks: 1. To destroy the enemy ports, ships and the mainspring of his great offensive against our ocean convoys. 2. To inflict the maximum damage on German and German-controlled war industries ... in the course of such operations it is now part of our policy to create havoc in those German towns and cities which house the workers on whose efforts the Nazi war machine is dependent.'

The never-ending round of experts were still plying their opinions, including Lord Cherwell who proposed to Churchill a 'de-housing' campaign to disrupt the German economy and break the spirit of the people. To support his arguments he listed German towns and the bomb tonnages required to effect their destruction. Portal supported the plan; it became the very theme he was to take up in November 1942 at the Chiefs of Staff Committee. Others, including Sir Henry Tizard, disagreed. The War Cabinet decided to seek arbitration and established an enquiry under Mr Justice Singleton with the remit: 'What results are we likely to achieve from continuing our air attacks on Germany at the greatest possible strength during the next six, 12 and 18 months respectively?' While the Committee was in session Bomber Command carried out a number of operations that proved of major significance to the outcome of the enquiry. Early April saw a concentrated effort against industrial installations in France, with attacks on the Ford works at Poissy and the Gnome et Rhône factory at Gennevilliers, both sites being near Paris. Main Force attacks were also sent against Cologne, Hamburg, Essen and Dortmund. While this campaign continued, an experimental daylight raid by Lancasters was carried out.

THE AUGSBURG RAID

The choice of the MAN diesel-engine factory at Augsburg was an interesting one. It could be suggested that Bomber Command wanted to find out exactly what the new Lancasters were capable of in terms of range and accuracy—and of looking after themselves in a hostile environment. Although the MAN factory was one of the anti-U-boat targets, as a manufacturer of engines, it was also 1,000 miles away, deep in the heart of Germany. The plan was for a low-level raid *in daylight*.

The choice of squadrons was relatively straightforward as only two, No 44 at Waddington and No 97 at Woodhall Spa, were fully operational on the type. Chosen to lead the raid was Squadron Leader John Nettleton, a 23-year-old South African, who had joined No 44 Squadron in June 1941. The factory as Augsburg was no bigger than a football pitch and so pinpoint accuracy would be needed. The route out was planned so that the squadrons flew 2 miles apart, in two sections

Despite increasing losses Stirlings remained an important element of Main Force. [7 Sqn records]

of three. The attack was to take place at last light, thus allowing the bombers to return back over Germany under the cover of night.

Just after 3 p.m. on 17 April the twelve Lancasters took off and set course. As they crossed the enemy coast, diversionary raids were made by fighter-escorted Bostons to try to keep the defences occupied. The ruse certainly brought the fighters up but it also led to near-disaster; one group of fighters returning to base spotted a section of Lancasters and gave chase. In a 30-minute fight all three of the aircraft in Nettleton's second section were shot down. The fighters then turned on the leader's section. His No 3 was quickly shot down and both the other aircraft were hit again and again; just as the end seemed likely the fighters broke away, short of fuel. The No 97 Squadron formation had not been seen and carried on, as did Nettleton with his two remaining aircraft. These two made their attack on the target, but on the approach the No 2 was hit by flak, crashing just after releasing his bombs. Nettleton, the sole survivor from the six Lancasters of No 44 Squadron, turned for home. The two sections from No 97 Squadron were over the target minutes later, each losing one aircraft to the intense light flak. The others bombed the target and made their escape.

Rostock, 25/26 April 1942, photographed by F/Sgt Fletcher of No 97 Squadron. [97 Sqn records]

Of the 85 men who had taken part in the raid, 49 were missing; it was later discovered that twelve had survived to become PoWs. Although most of the Lancasters claimed to have bombed the target, only twelve bombs appear to have hit the factory, causing damage which held up production for a number of weeks. For his outstanding leadership John Nettleton was awarded the Victoria Cross.

In the aftermath of this raid there was heated argument between Bomber Command and the MEW as to its value. The MEW believed that a far more useful attack could have been made on other targets—'gravest doubts whether this attack was planned, in the light of the intelligence available, to hit the enemy where it would hurt him most'. In reply Harris stated that 'MEW allows no weight to the other, and over-weening, factors which strategy, tactics and technicalities bring to bear on such an operation'. His paper continued by outlining the reasons for the choice of Augsburg, with such factors as forcing the enemy to spread his air defences over a wider area.

The same night, 173 aircraft attacked Hamburg, while a further 41 bombers were engaged against other targets. It is worth stressing, again, the diverse nature of Bomber Command's operations, and of the 'other tasks' mine-laying remained the greatest commitment with, on some nights, up to 100 aircraft engaged on 'Gardening'.

ROSTOCK

On the night of 23/24 April a force of 161 aircraft attacked the Baltic coastal town of Rostock, a target similar in many respects to Lübeck. Part of the force was briefed to attack the Heinkel works on the southern outskirts of the town, while for the remainder the aiming point was the centre of the old town. Results appeared to be disappointing, but only four aircraft were lost. Rostock was attacked again on the three subsequent nights, each time by a force of over 100 bombers. The results were better each night, extensive damage being caused to the town and its industries, including the Heinkel factory. Losses for the four nights came to eight aircraft from the total of 520 taking part, a remarkably low figure. Once again it came as a shock to the German leadership, although the propaganda empire of Goebbels made the most of it by talking about the English *Terrorangriff* (terror raid).

April saw the passing of the Whitley from the front line of Bomber Command, the last operation taking place on 27/28 April when two aircraft from No 58 Squadron took part in a small-scale raid to Dunkirk. There had been concern for some time at the higher than average loss rates of the Whitley, a problem that was attributed to the aircraft's inferior manoeuvrability. The OTUs, however, continued to send their Whitleys on leaflet raids, part of the process of preparing crews for operational squadrons, for some further months.

On 5 May Harris received a modified directive which, whilst stating that the primary aim was as before, harked back to the instructions of 1941 with the German aircraft industry receiving mention for special attention by Bomber Command on the grounds that 'the outcome of the critical operations on the Russian Front will depend largely on the enemy's ability to maintain in operation a certain strength of fighter aircraft. Similarly the success of our own attempts at Combined Operations on the Continent will be crucially affected by the number of fighter aircraft with which the enemy can oppose us.' To clarify the position, the directive included a list of five towns containing vital aircraft factories—Augsburg, Regensburg, Leipzig, Wiener-Neustadt and Warnemünde.

This directive was to have crucial importance. It highlighted a number of important considerations: first, the need to support the Russians in any way possible, and at this stage of the war the only real means was through the bomber offensive; and second, the problems likely to be faced when (not if) the Allied forces went over the offensive on the Continent. Among all the many other variations that were to be put forward, argued about, ignored or enforced, this consideration of the need to attack the German aircraft industry was to continue to raise its head, and to be the cause of much friction between Harris and the Air Staff.

Industrial targets in France were added to the list of Bomber Command tasks with the instruction, dated 25 May, to 'discourage the nationals of enemy-occupied countries from working in German controlled factories'. Three requirements were given for target selection: economic importance, ease of identification, and maximum moral effect but with the minimum of casualties. Furthermore, three essential criteria were imposed: the targets were only to be attacked in good weather, by experienced crews, and crews *must* make a positive identification of the target before dropping their bombs. As it was already accepted that targets in other occupied countries were fair game, this directive included them within its general provisions. In the first instance the Command should attack only one target in each country, with special priority being given to the Philips works at Eindhoven. The highly successful attack on the Renault factory had shown that Bomber Command was quite capable of hitting such targets; the hope now was for similar destruction but without the level of civilian casualties in the Allied nations.

In the five weeks following the attacks on Rostock Bomber Command had attacked only one of the targets specified in the directive, Warnemünde (on 8/9 May), with a further three raids aimed at the Bosch factory at Stuttgart. The Gnome et Rhône works near Paris had been attacked twice, and other large-scale raids had been made on Cologne, Kiel, Hamburg and Mannheim.

On 20 May Mr Justice Singleton had made his report.

His conclusions were that overall accuracy had been low, except for the recent attacks on the Renault works, Lübeck and Rostock, and that TR.1335 did not as yet appear to be having a significant effect. He considered that a trained 'target-finding force' would greatly increase the efficiency of the bombing and that until greater accuracy could be assured, Bomber Command should stick to easily found targets. However, he considered that: 'The bombing strength of the RAF is increasing rapidly, and I have no doubt that, if the best use is made of it, the effect on German war production and effort will be very heavy over a period of 12 to 18 months, and such as to have a real effect on the war position.' It was an upbeat message and one that gave new heart to the proponents of strategic bombing. Harris knew that he still had a fight on his hands and that the best way to prove his point was to carry out a demonstration of the devastating power of a large bomber force.

THE THOUSAND-BOMBER RAIDS

To prove his point Harris planned a 1,000-bomber raid as a demonstration of the full power of a co-ordinated bombing plan. The target was the city of Cologne and the date the night of 30/31 May 1942. By scraping together every possible aircraft, including crews still in training, a force of 1,047 bombers was sent against the target. The force comprised:

No 1 Group—156 Wellingtons
No 3 Group—134 Wellingtons, 88 Stirlings
No 4 Group—131 Halifaxes, 9 Wellingtons, 7 Whitleys
No 5 Group—73 Lancasters, 46 Manchesters, 34 Hampdens
No 91 Group—236 Wellingtons, 21 Whitleys (OTU)
No 92 Group—63 Wellingtons, 45 Hampdens (OTU)
Flying Training Command—4 Wellingtons

Flying Officer Leslie Manser, flying Manchester L7301 of No 50 Squadron, took off from Skellingthorpe just after 11 p.m.; Cologne was to be his 14th op. With a full bomb load and overheating engines he could not get the Manchester to climb above 7,000 feet. Instead of turning back he decided to press on. Having reached the target and released his bombs, his aircraft was hit by flak. Manser put the nose down and went into a dive to 1,000 feet to dodge the searchlights and confuse the gunners. Clear of the target area, he climbed up to 2,000 feet and set course for England. The port engine caught fire and although this was extinguished the Manchester was unable to maintain height on one engine. He ordered the crew to abandon the stricken bomber but when handed his own parachute waved it away, indicating that he must stay to hold the aircraft steady while the rest baled out. As the crew descended on their parachutes they saw the Manchester hit the ground and burst into flames; it crashed near the Belgian village of

Bree. All but one of the surviving crew evaded capture and returned to England via Gibraltar. The full story was then told and, on 20 October, Leslie Manser was posthumously awarded the VC. In a personal letter to Manser's family, Harris wrote 'no Victoria Cross has been more gallantly earned'.

Although just under 900 of the bombers claimed to have attacked the target, damage was lighter than had been hoped. Nevertheless, a number of important industrial and administrative areas had been hit and the ARP organization had been overwhelmed by the sheer scale of the task they faced. Civilian casualties were 411 killed. The raid certainly had an impact on the population; almost a quarter of them fled the city in the next few days. For Bomber Command losses had been high, at 41 aircraft missing, but this was a small percentage of the force employed, thus seeming to confirm the theory that concentration of effort would swamp the defences. Fortunately for Harris and Bomber Command the raid was deemed a success, and this success silenced most of the doubters and persuaded the Government to allocate Bomber Command a higher priority for aircraft and, more importantly, scientific development of navigation aids and radar—vital for the accurate delivery of bombs to their targets.

'THOUSAND BOMBERS DEVASTATE COLOGNE'

Thus ran the headline in the British Press, going on to state: 'RAF chiefs today claimed to have destroyed more than 200 factories in last night's raid on Cologne. They said they had done more damage in one night than in the previous 1,300 RAF raids on the city. The scale of last night's attack was over four times bigger than the worst raid on London. That was on April 16th, 1941, when the Germans dropped 440 tons of bombs.'

The casualties in Cologne were kept down by the excellent defensive provision in the city, 500 public air-raid shelters (for 75,000 people) and 75,000 private shelters. Also, and in common with most German towns, the ARP was well organized and efficient, although they found it hard to cope with the scale of this attack. Some German commentators have expressed the opinion that the RAF raids on German towns had less effect than they might have done because of the small-scale nature of the raids in the early part of the war, the net result of which was to cause little damage but give plenty of practice in ARP procedures—training for the onslaught to come. The success of this attack was, however, the first serious loss of prestige for Goering; it was a blow from which he, and the Luftwaffe, never fully recovered in the eyes of Hitler.

On the following day (31 May) five aircraft from No 105 Squadron undertook the first Bomber Command operation by Mosquitoes, operating as single aircraft. The first took off at 0400 and the last at 1710. The Mosquito IVs (W4072, W4064, W4065, W4071 and

Bombsight training.

W4069) were tasked to bomb, and photograph, Cologne. Three aircraft reported bombing the target but no photographs were taken, the weather being too bad; W4064 (Pilot Officers Kennard and Johnson) took off at 0630 but did not return, there being no clue as to the reason for the loss.

During May Bomber Command's training system had been reorganized, with Nos 6 and 7 Groups becoming Nos 91 and 92 (OTU) Groups. The route to becoming operational aircrew had changed at frequent intervals to reflect availability of resources and front-line requirements. There was never a shortage of volunteers—and it is important to remember that all Bomber Command aircrew were volunteers. The route started with three days at the local Aircrew Selection Centre, followed by ten days at the ACRC (Aircrew Reception Centre) where the main task was to get kitted out. Next came the hardest phase, twelve weeks at an Initial Training Wing, with a mass of ground training on technical and air related subjects but, in the opinion of many, far too much 'bull'. At last came the flying training elements, basic, advanced and OTU. The whole system at this stage of the war took about eighteen months for a pilot from early into the RAF to arrival on the first squadron as a 'freshman'.

Two nights later (1/2 June) the '1,000-bomber' force was in action again, this time against the Command's jinx target—Essen. Despite the extensive use of flares, the 956 bombers (over half of which were Wellingtons) had difficulty identifying the target aiming points through the thick ground haze. Bombing results were

DE HAVILLAND MOSQUITO

Another of the all-time British 'greats', the Mosquito started in October 1938 as a private-venture for a high-speed, unarmed wooden bomber. At the time, the Air Staff general attitude towards future bomber aircraft was for a move away from light bombers to medium and, ideally, heavy bombers. The first prototype Mosquito (W4050) flew on 25 November 1940 and its outstanding performance was immediately apparent; by mid-1941 the Mosquito was in full-scale production and variants began to appear to cover a wide range of roles. However, development towards operational employment was slow and the prototype of the first definitive bomber version, the Mk IV, did not fly until September 1941. Two months later the first aircraft were delivered to No 104 Squadron at Swanton Morley.

Although intended as a general light bomber, the Mosquito soon established a reputation for accurate low-level attacks and was involved on many special missions such as pinpoint attacks on specific rooms within a building. However, the Mosquito was no 'lightweight' bomber as it proved by taking part in many raids over Berlin, often being used as bait to draw German night fighters away from the real target being attacked by the Main Force bombers. Likewise, by early 1944 the Mosquito was operating with the 4,000lb 'block-buster' bomb—four times the bomb load of the original design concept, and equal to the standard load of USAAF Fortresses bombing Berlin.

The high survivability of the Mosquito—thanks to its high speed—also made it ideal for operational trials of 'sensitive' equipment and extensive use was made of Mosquito variants for this work. This, plus the undoubted success and accuracy of the low-level bombing operations, led to the aircraft's use as one element of the Pathfinder Force.

As with any successful design, additional variants appeared, the main marks used by Bomber Command being the IV, IX, XVI and the Canadian-built XX and XXV. The bomber element was only one small part of the overall Mosquito story as the type had a very successful career in both its reconnaissance and fighter versions. With Bomber Command the Mosquito remained in service until 1953.

MOSQUITO IV DATA
Crew: Two
Engines: Two 1,250hp Rolls-Royce Merlin XXI
Span: 54ft 2in
Length: 40ft 9½in
Height: 15ft 3in
Weight empty: 13,400lb
Weight loaded: 20,870lb
Max. speed: 380mph at 17,000ft
Ceiling: 28,800ft
Armament: No defensive guns. Bomb load 2,000 to 4,000lb

Squadrons (Bomber Command): Nos 105, 109, 128, 139, 142, 162, 163, 192, 571, 608, 613, 627, 693

The Mosquito was one of the greatest aircraft of the war; it had the lowest loss rate of all Bomber Command types. Illustrated is a No 571 Squadron Mk XVI with bulged bomb bay.

AIRSPEED OXFORD

'Early take-offs were often crescent-shaped until pilots got used to the swing, but once in the air the Oxford handled well. It was responsive to the controls and generally stable. Single-engine flying was hard work, but was largely a demo exercise as the Cheetah was a very reliable power plant.'

Almost every bomber pilot at one time or another received training on the 'Ox-box' as by the early years of the war this sturdy little aircraft had become one of the RAF's standard training types. A development of the Airspeed Envoy, the Oxford was constructed to Specification T.23/36 as the RAF's first twin-engined monoplane advanced trainer. Although the prototype (L4534) did not fly until

The Airspeed Oxford was an essential part of the training routine.

19 June 1937, 136 aircraft had been ordered off the drawing-board the previous autumn.

Production increased as war loomed and eventually a number of other companies were involved in building the type as the need for training aircraft became ever greater. The Mk I was intended as a general aircrew training aircraft and so included an Armstrong Whitworth turret for air gunnery training. The Mk II, however, had this removed and was used primarily as a pilot trainer. Some 8,500 examples of these two marks were produced and, as well as use by the training units in Britain, saw extensive service with the Empire Air Training Scheme in Australia, Canada, New Zealand, South Africa and Rhodesia.

The Oxford's handling qualities were intended to match those of its larger service brethren, although with certain docile aspects built in to suit its training role—such as easy-to-control stall characteristics. It was more demanding than the Anson and so better suited as a training aircraft for future heavy bomber pilots. Oxfords also proved well suited to the work of the Beam Approach Training Flights (BATF) which were established to teach the art of blind flying recoveries—and which saved the lives of many a bomber crew in the later years of the war. Like all training aircraft this was an unsung hero of the expansion period.

OXFORD II DATA
Crew: Three
Engines: Two 370hp Armstrong Siddeley Cheetah X
Span: 53ft 4in
Length: 34ft 6in
Height: 11ft 1in
Weight empty: 5,380lb
Weight loaded: 8,000lb
Max. speed: 188mph
Ceiling: 19,500ft

poor and 31 aircraft were lost. A smaller force, 195 aircraft, returned to Essen the following night, with no more success and losing fourteen aircraft. Over the next three weeks Essen was attacked three more times, with Emden being attacked four times and Bremen once. The '1,000-bomber' force was called to action just once more, the target being Bremen on the night of 25/26 June. This time 1,067 aircraft, including 102 from Coastal Command, were dispatched, the majority being ordered to attack the centre of the city. However, the bombers from No 5 Group were given the Focke-Wulf factory as an aiming point and the Coastal Command aircraft were tasked against the Deschimag shipyard. The attack was moderately successful, damage being caused to numerous industrial works including the Focke-Wulf factory. With 48 aircraft missing it was the most costly of the raids. It is interesting to note that the German authorities in Bremen estimated the attacking force at no more than 80 aircraft. As on previous occasions, the aircraft of No 2 Group flew supporting intruder missions against German night fighter airfields. Bremen was the target on three more nights in the following week, but with far smaller numbers of bombers involved.

Of the three 1,000-bomber raids, it could be argued

De Havilland Mosquito IV DZ464 'XD-C' of No 139 Squadron. [139 Sqn records]

that only that against Cologne was truly successful, but it was impossible to keep the force together for an indefinite period; the OTUs needed to return to their usual training routine and other contributors, such as Coastal Command, could not afford the diversion away from their own tasks. Harris had hoped to prove that, given a sufficient number of bombers, the power of the bombing offensive was enormous. The arguments continued almost without pause; there were even some who saw little more in these raids than the 'wholesale bombing of civilians' and so called the whole concept into question. Harris was undaunted by the opposition and put his case to as many people as possible. In a letter to Churchill on 17 June he summarized his thoughts, and his anger: 'An extraordinary lack of sense of proportion affects outside appreciation of the meaning, extent and results of Bomber Command's operations. What shouts of victory would arise if a Commando wrecked the entire Renault factory in a night, with a loss of seven men! What credible assumptions of an early end to the war would follow upon the destruction of one third of Cologne in an hour and a half by some swift-moving mechanized force which with but 200 casualties withdrew and was ready to repeat the operation 24 hours later! What acclaim would greet the virtual destruction of Rostock and the Heinkel main and subsidiary factories by a Naval bombardment! All

this and far more has been achieved by Bomber Command: yet there are many who still avert their gaze, pass on the other side, and question whether the 30 squadrons of night bombers make any worthwhile contribution to the war.'

It was typical Harris material, making references to the other Services and what would be the comment if they had achieved similar results. It was the style of argument likely to appeal to Churchill; for a while at least the wolves at Bomber Command's door were silenced. However, there was still a great deal to rectify and the ever-present problem of bombing accuracy held prime position. There were two possible ways of improving the overall accuracy—provision of blind bombing aids, and the use of experienced crews as a target-finding force. Both of these had been under discussion since 1941, the latter having received special mention in the Singleton Report of May 1942.

The 1,000-bomber raids involved the first serious attempts at streaming and concentration to overwhelm the defences, and so reduce losses, as well as the ground organization. The risk of mid-air collisions in such a tight mass of aircraft was looked at, but discounted as

Lancaster I L7540 of No 83 Squadron. Note the overwritten code of its previous unit, No 44 Squadron. 4,000lb bombs in the foreground.

being far lower than the risk from the defences if the bombers did not stay together.

In early July the Press carried the following comment: 'The German people have been told to expect devastating air raids "every night and every day, rain, blow or snow". The man who gave them this message, in a broadcast in German, is Air Marshal Sir Arthur Harris, who took over as Chief of Bomber Command last February. He promised to "scourge the Third Reich from end to end".'

The heavy bombers (except for the Lancaster) had been operating for some time and all had been found lacking in various important respects. Of the three, the Manchester was fairing particularly badly, its loss rate of 4.4 per cent being almost double that of the Stirling. It also appeared that the Manchester was far more vulnerable to flak than any of the other types. This was ascribed to the fact that 'The Manchester has two main petrol tanks and two small ones, whereas the Stirling has fourteen', the implication being that critical levels of damage were thus sustained more easily by the Manchester. Having made this comment about the Manchester, ORS had even harsher things to say about the Halifax, the loss rate of which had risen to an average of

5.3 per cent from its 1,467 sorties in the year to June 1942. This time the conclusion reached was that the losses were due mainly to night fighters, perhaps because unsatisfactory exhaust shrouds on its engines made the Halifax easier for the night fighters to pick up. The Halifax problem was the subject of many reports throughout 1942 and into early 1943, one conclusion reached in October being that it was 'essential that pilots posted to Halifax squadrons should be detailed to complete at least three, preferably five, sorties as 2nd pilot or against lightly defended targets before being employed on main operations'. The question of 'new' pilots flying as '2nd dickies' was one raised throughout the Command since the decision to go to single-pilot operation. The primary purpose of sending a new pilot on a number of sorties as second pilot was for him to gain a little operational experience before he took his own crew on their first mission; it was an attempt to pass on some of the essential lessons that could only be learnt through experience. For some it was their first and last mission.

A few more months of statistics and the Halifax was under review again, with particular reference to the experience levels of pilots in No 4 Group as a factor in loss rates: 'There is no reasonable doubt that pilots on their first two operations have a casualty rate well above the average and that those who had survived 20 sorties had a rate well below the average. This must be aircraft-

The unsung work behind the scenes: major overhaul of a Wellington. WAAFs played a major part in support roles at Bomber Command stations.

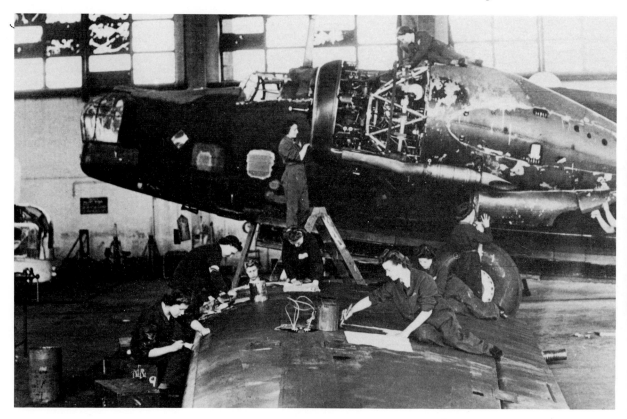

related as the Lancaster does not suffer the same problem. The record on lightly defended targets is good; the problem comes on highly defended targets. New pilots are a bit nervous of the aircraft, the aircraft having gained a bad name for instability in manoeuvres. It thus may happen that a new pilot is reluctant when he meets defences to manoeuvre his machine sufficiently in combat or that in a sudden emergency he puts his machine into an attitude in which he has had no previous experience of controlling it.' The solution proposed by the report was for more General Handling at the OTUs and fighter affiliation when on the squadron. Other reports had highlighted the benefits of fighter affiliation sorties, even suggesting that the loss rates of squadrons, flying the same type, were influenced by the number of such exercises undertaken. The crews quite enjoyed the chance to take their aircraft out over the sea to rendezvous with a Spitfire for a spot of mutual training, the gunners calling the evasions so that the pilot could throw his aircraft into a stomach-churning manoeuvre.

With the approach of summer Bomber Command had a limited arc of targets within its reach in the shorter hours of darkness. This had to be taken into consideration along with the many other factors, the most important being the overall strategic aim (in accordance with the latest directive—if Harris chose to apply it) and

Although it had a bad reputation at first, the Halifax went on, in later versions such as the Mk III, to become an excellent workhouse for Bomber Command.

the weather forecast for Germany. Although the advent of radio aids had made Bomber Command a little more independent of the weather, it was still the major consideration on a daily basis—not only the weather over the target area, but also the weather en route and, of special importance, the forecast for the period when the bombers would be returning to their home bases. By mid-1942 the 'met' briefing system was well established. The Central Forecast Station at Dunstable fed information into the daily conference, as did the Group Met Officers; the overall situation was then discussed and a general forecast produced from Britain and Germany.

The biggest single problem was the absence of observation stations over the sea and in enemy-occupied territory. The formation of a weather recce flight (No 1409 'Pampa' Flight) at Bircham Newton in January 1942 helped with the latter problem: these aircraft flew hazardous missions to bring back reports on the cloud structure and distribution, essential data for the 'met' forecasters to determine what was likely to happen over a period of time. It has always been the case, and still is, that aircrew never remember the instances when the 'met' man gets it right, but they have vivid recollections of the times he got it badly wrong! If you are expecting to have a clear run at 12,000 feet but then encounter thick cloud with heavy icing it creates an immediate problem. Icing and aircraft do not mix well; in the earlier years of the war the Whitleys and Wellingtons suffered badly from icing, including an unknown number of losses. It had been estimated that at least 2 per cent of Wellington losses were due to icing, the percentage of Whitley losses probably being much higher. The modifications introduced in late 1941, such as alcohol fuel for the Hampdens and Wellingtons, appeared to have little impact on the situation.

It was no better in 1942, or for that matter for the rest of the war; there was no truly effective anti-icing device provided for the heavy bombers, and certainly no de-icing system. The thick paste applied to some parts of the aircraft surface certainly helped retard ice formation but it was not a totally successful system. Engines stopped, guns and turrets froze up, control surfaces became solid; and if enough weight of ice accumulated or the engines were badly affected, the aircraft simply fell out of the sky. With luck the warmer layers of air lower down would start to thaw the ice enough for it to break loose; when it did, it would be flung at the sides of the aircraft with a heart-stopping series of thuds, and no small amount of damage. How many aircraft did not recover from the fall, to be recorded as 'missing' cause unknown, was never discovered. The best solution when the aircraft started to ice up was to get out of the ice layer. Unfortunately, few of the bombers had the option of climbing out of trouble; with a full load of bombs and petrol they simply did not have the perform-ance. To descend below the ice layer was also fraught with problems. To go too low—and who knew where the icing layer would stop?—would be to cause prob-lems with the fuel consumption, and most sorties already had little enough fuel margin, plus the increased risk from flak defences.

Issued in July, ORS Report R52 summarized Bomber Command's daylight operations for the six-month period to 30 June. This period included a number of special raids, such as Augsburg, but its main thrust was an examination of the 'Circus' operations undertaken by the three Boston squadrons of No 2 Group. Bearing in mind that the primary objective was 'to raise and engage that portion of Luftwaffe fighter strength based on the Western Front', it concluded that the results had not been too promising. Bomber losses had been low, less than 3 per cent for the 1,000 sorties, but the associated Fighter Command stastistics were not as had been hoped: in 9,486 sorties they claimed 118 enemy aircraft destroyed, but for the loss of 166 of their own aircraft. This should really have come as little surprise as the tactics employed were little different from those em-ployed, without success, by the Luftwaffe over Britain in 1940.

On 11 July, 44 Lancasters were tasked to make a dusk attack on the U-boat construction yards at Danzig; it would be a 1,500-mile round trip, the first half being in daylight! Routeing was carefully planned, the tactic being for the aircraft to split up over Denmark and then use cloud cover to make individual approaches to the target area. It worked reasonably well and only two bombers were shot down, both by flak over the target. A similar tactic was tried on 16 July by 21 Stirlings to Lübeck; only eight reached the target area, the others turning back, and of those eight, two were shot down. During this period small numbers of Mosquitoes were operating daily over Germany, attacking a wide range of targets and causing the defences great frustration. Major night raids were tasked against Duisburg, Hamburg, Vegesack, Saarbrucken, Düsseldorf and Wilhelms-haven. Increasing losses were, however, causing con-cern. Losses had been particularly high among the OTU participants; for example, at Duisburg on the night of 31 July, No 92 Group lost eleven of its 105 aircraft.

An ORS report of 10 August examined the losses against interception statistics for June (this was one of a routine series of studies into this subject) and concluded that: 'Losses have reached a very high level, since they have occurred mostly under conditions of heavy cloud and in the absence of searchlight co-operation it seems likely that effective GCI must be responsible. The proportion of attacks from below which result in serious damage emphasises the need for more protection from this direction.' The statistics behind this were an interception rate of 8.3 per cent of 4,788 sorties, some 25 per cent of the interceptions turning into full attacks.

In the week following this report, attacks were made against Mainz, Düsseldorf and Osnabruck, the last raid to Osnabruck (17/18 August) also being the last Blen-heim operation for Bomber Command, aircraft of No 18 Squadron flying intruder sorties over Holland.

THE CREATION OF A TARGET-FINDING FORCE

Since the spring debates as to the style of a target-finding force had been under way at Air Staff level; in March Group Captain Bufton, Deputy Director of Bomber Ops, had argued for a special six-squadron force. There was much support among the Air Staff for the concept of a separate target-finding, or marking, force with experienced crews who would then receive special training and equipment. Some aspects had already been tested in the 'Shaker' technique, led by experienced crews, often in the 'Gee'-equipped aircraft, finding and 'marking' the target. Harris favoured an extension of this concept rather than the creation of, as he saw it, an elite and separate force. His main argument against the latter, and in which he was supported by most of his Group Commanders, was that it would result in the Groups losing their best squadrons or crews, which would have an adverse effect on the

Group as a whole through the loss of experience. The Command was already suffering problems of experience levels, especially regarding Flight Commanders. Harris's compromise solution was that each Group should be led by the squadron which had achieved the best results the previous months, thus generating a healthy competition to be the best squadron. All parties were agreed as to the need for a target-marking force, but the manner of its inception and composition caused heated debate. At an Air Minstry conference in June Harris was forced to concede defeat: on the 20th of that month he instructed No 3 Group to set aside two Wellington and two Stirling squadrons to become the core of the new Pathfinder Force (PFF). He also commented that this was 'yet another occasion when a commander in the field was overruled at the dictation of junior staff officers in the Air Ministry'.

In the event, the initial composition of the force brought together squadrons from each of the bomber Groups: No 7 Squadron (Stirling) from No 3 Group; No 156 Squadron (Wellington), No 1 Group; No 35 Squadron (Halifax), No 4 Group; No 83 Squadron (Lancaster), No 5 Group; and No 109 Squadron (Lancaster/Mosquito). Group commanders were reluctant to release personnel and equipment and Bennett had an uphill struggle, although Harris, despite his earlier opposition, now gave him his full support. Fortunately, Bennett had a fierce determination, plus a fund of experience and knowledge—he needed them all. With its HQ elements at Wyton and Oakington, and satellites at Graveley and Warboys (squadrons being lodged on No 3 Group stations), the Pathfinder Force (PFF) was born. Bennett worked hard to make it a going concern as soon as possible; crews that did not meet his required standards were sent back, to be replaced by other, volunteer crews.

The PFF was officially formed on 11 August 1942 and seven days later it flew its first operation. This raid, on 18/19 August, to Flensburg saw 31 Pathfinder aircraft as part of a force of 118 bombers. It was not a good opening, 'met' forecast winds were in error and the force was blown to the north of its target. Sixteen PFF crews

---

AIR VICE-MARSHAL DONALD BENNETT

At a time when Bomber Command needed confident, determined leaders it found men of the calibre of Harris, Cochrane and Bennett. The establishment in 1942 of the Pathfinder Force (PFF) was of critical importance to the success of Bomber Command.

Donald Clifford Tyndal Bennett was born in Queensland, Australia, on 14 September 1910. He joined the Royal Australian Air Force in 1930 and was sent to England to complete his pilot training. Having qualified, Don Bennett was posted to No 29 Squadron at North Weald to fly Siskin fighters, although shortly afterwards he moved on to No 210 Squadron at Pembroke Dock and the Supermarine Southampton flying-boat. He quickly established a reputation for skills in navigation; he joined Imperial Airways in 1935 and this skill was of great value for his job of operating flying-boats around the Mediterranean.

When war broke out, Bennett was captain of a mail-carrying flying-boat operating between Southampton and New York; once again his navigation skills proving of great value. He rejoined the RAF in the summer of 1941 and was given command of No 77 Squadron at Leeming, equipped with Whitleys. The following April he was appointed CO of No 10 Squadron with its Halifax bombers. Later that month (28/29 April 1942) he led a raid against *Tirpitz* as she lay hidden in a Norwegian fjord. His aircraft was hit several times and the crew were forced to bale out. With Norwegian help they evaded the Germans and returned to England via Sweden. Bennett was awarded the DSO as a result of this raid.

Soon after his return he was called to see Harris at HQ Bomber Command. After months of argument it had been decided, against the wishes of Harris, to form a specialist target-finding force. Harris chose Bennett to be its leader. Promoted to Group Captain and armed with a store of energy and enthusiasm, he set about the task of creating this force from nothing—and in the face of much official hindrance. That the PFF was so successful was in no small part due to the personal efforts of Don Bennett. The initial lack of success made him fight harder for the equipment and personnel he knew to be essential. By the end of 1942 the PFF was proving its worth time after time, but at a heavy cost in crews. Early in 1943 the PFF was renamed No 8 Group and Bennett was promoted to Air Commodore. As the war progressed so did No 8 Group, not only with marking targets but with a range of other activities. For his outstanding leadership of the Pathfinder Force, Bennett was made a Companion of the Order of the Bath and a Commander of the British Empire.

USAAF B-17 Fortresses during a daylight attack on Lorient. The combined bomber offensive of daylight raids by the Americans and night raids by the RAF provided a double blow to the German defences.

bombed what they thought was the German town but actually hit parts of Denmark. Among the four aircraft lost was a PFF Halifax from No 35 Squadron. The second PFF-led raid, Frankfurt on 24/25 August, was no more successful, cloud obscuring the target. The raid to Kassel on 27/28 August was much better; weather conditions were good and the PFF aircraft were able to illuminate the area and bomb the aiming points. The results of these three raids should have come as no surprise, as the PFF squadrons were using the same equipment and facing the same difficulties of weather and unserviceability as the Main Force squadrons. Also, it was still early days and tactics had yet to be worked out to suit the conditions for each sortie. Bennett had identified many of the difficulties he was likely to face and had, even before operations commenced, starting 'banging desks' to get the equipment he knew was needed.

The need for a true blind-bombing aid was paramount. The 'Oboe' system, which had been tested in late 1941, held great promise and should be ready for operational service soon. Equally promising was the H2S radar system.

While pushing for the essential equipment, the PFF

staff also developed techniques to get the best out of the target-finding/marking concept. The three standard techniques developed were 'Parramatta', 'Newhaven', and 'Wanganui' (the names coming from the home towns of Bennett, his PA and Squadron Leader Ashworth respectively).

August 1942 saw a development of major significance. On the 17th twelve B-17 Fortresses of the USAAF's 97th Bombardment Group (BG) attacked the marshalling yards at Sotteville-les-Rouen. All the aircraft claimed to have bombed the target, and all returned safely. It was a small but significant beginning, the start of the combined bomber offensive. This book deals with the 'Six-Year Offensive' of Bomber Command and there is insufficient space to include consideration of the US 8th Air Force's contribution. However, it would be impossible to ignore this aspect of the strategic offensive in toto. Throughout the remainder of this account reference will be made to the US operations, and involvement in strategic planning, where and when they have a direct relevance to Bomber Command.

The first real PFF success came on 28/29 August with a raid on Nuremberg. It was, by recent Bomber Command standards, a small raid of only 159 aircraft. The PFF aircraft marked the aiming point with a new device—'Red Blob Fire'. This was a converted 250lb incendiary filled with a benzol-rubber-phosphorus mixture, its main advantage being that it burned brightly for some time. The bombers claimed good results, the markers being easy to see and aim at. It was however a costly raid with 23 aircraft lost, including 25 per cent of the 41 Wellingtons. An attack scheduled for Saarbrucken on 1/2 September in fact fell on Saarlouis some 13 miles away. The major problem for Bomber Command was still that of finding the target.

During August the PFF flew 175 sorties, losing sixteen aircraft, PFF losses were to remain higher than average (except for the Mosquitoes whose loss rate was remarkably low). As the first aircraft over the target they received the full weight of the defences, especially if the German ground control had guessed the correct target and had fighters waiting, before the benefit of numbers, and thus saturation, appeared with the Main Force.

The Air Ministry directive of 3 September was of the type for which Harris had an intense dislike. It stated that the Joint Intelligence Committee Technical Sub-Committee had decided that the Axis oil situation was critical, a statement which had been made on more than one previous occasion. It then went on to state that the hydrogenation plant at Pölitz was of prime importance in the production of aviation and motor fuels, and diesel fuel, the loss of which would be of major significance, especially in view of operations on the Russian Front. For once Harris did not go into vehement print against this instruction; he simply ignored it.

Unfortunately, with improvements for the attackers came improvements in the defences—ever the case in the 'swings and roundabouts' of military developments—and the German night fighters continued to take a heavy toll of bombers. To try to redress the balance the latter part of 1942 saw many developments: bombers flew in compact streams to swamp small areas of the defences, diversionary raids were mounted, deception plans were instigated, and the 'electronic' war began in earnest. Some of these elements had already been tried; from now on they became ingredients in a series of complex tactical plans.

Minelaying remained an important element of Bomber Command's anti-naval campaign. By mid-1942 the vast majority of all minelaying in European waters was being carried out by Bomber Command. Most 'Gardening' sorties were still notable only for their lack of event—long, trying sorties with no spectacular result at the end. There were exceptions, as this report from a No 61 Squadron crew highlights:

'The aircraft was engaged in minelaying operations in the Baltic when it unexpectedly came across an enemy convoy. Evasive action was taken and no serious

'Bomber' Harris on one of his rare visits to a flying unit, with A/Cdre Gus Walker inspecting a Halifax.

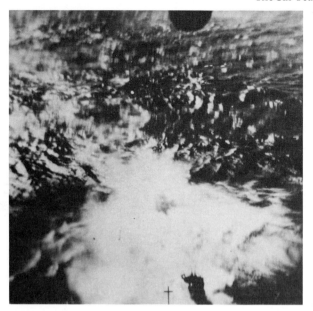

An unsung role of many Bomber Command units, especially the Whitley squadrons, was that of anti-U-boat operations. Hours of searching were rarely rewarded with the opportunity to attack a U-boat. Note the tail wheel of the No 58 Squadron aircraft at the top of the photo and the U-boat at the bottom.

consequences resulted from the anti-aircraft fire. After crossing the coast of Jutland at 6,000 feet we hit heavy flak. The first shot hit us full in the bomb doors and started a very serious fire as the flares and distress signals, hydraulic oil and fuselage immediately burst into flames. At the same time another shot hit the nose of the aircraft, bursting the bomb-aimer's window and blowing him straight up beside me. It also blew out most of the glass from my cockpit. Then two fighters, one of which we had seen previously, fired at us and wounded the rear-turret gunner in the leg. They also put a cannon shell into the mid-upper turret which burned the gunner and started off his ammunition. The plane filled with dense black smoke which nearly choked all of us and as I was unable to see my instruments I stalled the aircraft. Only when the smoke cleared could I regain control, by which time we were flying at 4,000 feet. I then dived immediately for some clouds and lost the fighters and flak.'

After this very trying experience the crew managed to get back to England and belly-land.

Minelaying sorties were frequently tasked to areas around the U-boat bases and the Baltic training area as part of the continuing war against this potent threat.

It is often forgotten just how involved Bomber Command was in the war against the U-boats, not only with minelaying and the attacks on U-boat-related industry and ports, but also with direct anti-submarine

patrols. From May 1942 to the end of the year the Command flew 1,100 day sorties on such patrols over the Bay of Biscay, operations being undertaken by Nos 51, 77, 61 and 405 Squadrons, No 10 OTU, and also No 304 (Polish) and No 311 (Czech) Squadrons which were transferred to Coastal Command. During this period the aircraft spotted 70 U-boats and carried out attacks on 50 of them. The *Bomber Command Quarterly Review* carried details of such an attack by a No 405 Squadron aircraft which sighted a U-boat off the coast of northern Spain:

'As our aircraft altered course to attack down sun from the U-boat's starboard beam, the escort vessels fell back on the U-boat's quarter and opened up with intense flak. The Halifax came in at right angles to the track and released six torpex depth-charges from 200ft while the submarine was fully surfaced. Immediately before release the U-boat turned away and the stick fell towards its stern. The Halifax turned and made a second attack from the port side, releasing three depth-charges from 50ft, the stick fell across the conning tower. Meanwhile the bomber was avoiding flak from the escorts, the trailing aerial was shot away before cloud-cover was gained.'

A small but accurate attack on Karlsruhe on 2/3 September was followed two nights later by an equally effective raid on Bremen when 251 PFF-led bombers caused heavy damage. On this attack a new tactic was employed, having its origins in the 'Shaker' technique, whereby a force of 'illuminators' used flares to allow the 'visual markers' to identify and mark the aiming point. To consolidate this mark a force of 'backers-up' then dropped incendiaries on the markers. Attacks on Duisburg (6/7 September) and Frankfurt (8/9 September) were not so successful, because of poor weather, but the basic tactical plan had been proved. The attack on Düsseldorf (10/11 September) saw the PFF employ a new improvised marker, the 'Pink Pansy'. It was also the most complex marking to date. PFF aircraft dropped red flares to mark the western edge of the town and green flares to mark the eastern edge. 'Pink Pansies' were then used to mark the actual aiming point. This was the first use of 'Pink Pansies' (so called because they ignited with a pink flash), modified 4,000lb incendiaries which actually weighed 2,700lb. The idea was for the Main Force bombers to fly between the two sets of flares and drop on the markers. It was a good raid by 479 aircraft, causing serious damage, but with heavy losses as 33 aircraft were declared missing, including five out of thirteen Wellingtons sent by No 16 OTU.

Stirling W7564 of No 7 Squadron was one of the PFF marker force. Its crew reported:

'Bombed across aiming point—saw own flares in town. Hit often by flak over target, starboard petrol tank holed and port oil pipes severed. Port inner prop and gear sheared off. Port outer engine fell off. Captain and

Hampdens of No 408 Squadron, RCAF. [Peter Green]

WOP held control, Engineer turned off useless pipe lines. Height 100 to 200 feet over Dutch coast, all movable objects jettisoned. Crossing English coast, starboard inner engine cut out and Captain crash-landed in field near Weeley, Essex. Captain and WOP unconscious, nav extracted them. Aircraft burst into flames with rear-gunner still aboard. Sgts Thorpe and Mallott re-entered the aircraft to rescue him but petrol tanks blew up and they were killed. Rear-gunner badly burnt but rescued by F/S Jenner.' (Captain—F/O Trench awarded DSO, Nav—P/O Selman awarded DFC, WOP—Sgt Edwards awarded DFM.)

Two nights later a heavy raid caused severe damage in Bremen, a city which had felt many blows from Bomber Command during 1942. The following night (14/15 September) a force of 202 bombers attacked Wilhelmshaven, this being the last operational use by Bomber Command of the Hampden—aircraft of No 408 Squadron having the honour of closing this chapter of endeavour. The Hampden had never been a great success as a bomber but it had shouldered the mine-laying task for over two years.

While the night attacks by Main Force continued to spread increasingly accurate destruction to such places as Essen, Saabrucken, Munich, Wismar, Krefeld, Aachen, Kiel, Cologne and Osnabruck, the squadrons of No 2 Group were still occupied with small-scale but daring daylight low-level attacks throughout Europe. It is impossible in this account to cover every aspect of this work, yet it remained an important element of the overall Bomber Command effort, albeit small in comparison with the nightly Main Force attacks. Some raids stand out as even more spectacular than the norm; one

such was that by four Mosquitoes of No 105 Squadron against the Gestapo HQ in Oslo, which was timed to coincide with a rally of Norwegian Nazis. On 25 September the four aircraft set out from Leuchars. One was shot down during the target run by a Focke-Wulf Fw 190 but the rest pressed home their attacks; three bombs went through the building without exploding, the fourth stayed inside, but was a dud. Nevertheless, it had been a spectacular raid of pinpoint accuracy and yet another blow to Nazi pride.

LE CREUSOT

On 20 July a series of additional targets in France had been issued by the Air Staff, three being singled out for mention: Le Creusot (the Schneider Armament and Locomotive works), Paris (Citroen) and Gien (ordnance depot). However, it was October before any of

The Mosquito attack on the Gestapo HQ in Oslo, Norway.

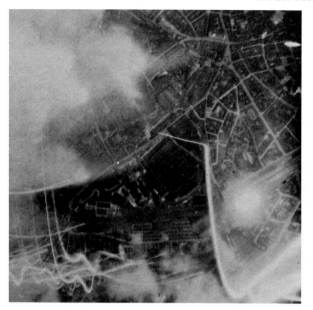

F/L Smythe in his Lancaster of No 97 Squadron over Krupps, Essen, 16/17 September 1942—the best aiming-point photo of Krupps yet taken. [97 Sqn records]

these was scheduled for attack. On 17 October one of the most famous raids of the war took place. It had been decided that the only way to achieve success, and prevent French casualties, was to go in at low level by day. The task of bombing Le Creusot was given to the Lancasters of No 5 Group and low-level practice flights around England gave the crews time to get used to the problems of low-level operations. On the afternoon of 17 October 94 Lancasters took off, flew low-level over the Channel and sped on into France—'At the height we were flying we disturbed the cattle in the fields and numbers of them stampeded. At one place we saw oxen

bolt, dragging their plough after them. Many of the French peasants in the fields waved to us as we swept over'. It was certainly an exciting change from the normal night missions, but there was an element of trepidation—after all, the last such daylight mission (Augsburg) had involved heavy casualties. In the event, the bombers met no opposition other than light flak over the target, causing minor damage to two of the Lancasters. Crews reported accurate bombing, a total of 140 tons being dropped. Six Lancasters from the force had been tasked to attack a nearby power-station; one of these aircraft crashed into the building. The only other casualty from the raid was an aircraft of No 207 Squadron which had turned back with an engine failure. As it was flying at 40 feet off Brest it was attacked by three Arado Ar 196 seaplanes: in the ensuing battle the Lancaster shot down two of the attackers but was hit by at least one burst of fire, which killed the flight engineer. The Lancaster returned safely.

Despite the tonnage of bombs dropped, the lack of opposition, and the optimistic reports of the crews, post-attack reconnaissance showed only moderate damage to the main industrial buildings.

A PFF and No 5 Group raid on Genoa on 22/23 October opened a week of Main Force operations against targets in Italy; this initial raid was followed by another trip to Genoa and two to Milan. The first attack on Milan was a daring daylight raid by 88 Lancasters from No 5 Group. The aircraft flew individual routes across France to a rendezvous at Lake Annecy before crossing the Alps. The raid came as a total surprise to the Italian defences and only one aircraft was shot down, although two more were lost over France.

Below left: Group ops boards for the Le Creusot raid.

Below: Lancasters of No 97 Squadron en route, low-level over France.

These raids were followed by two weeks of very little tasking for the night bombers, until a force of Lancasters raided Genoa on 6/7 November, a raid repeated by 175 aircraft the following night. The campaign against Italy continued (as well as attacks against Hamburg and Stuttgart) to the end of the month, with two further attacks on Genoa and four on Turin. The Turin raid of 28/29 November, by 228 aircraft, brought yet another VC for Bomber Command, this highest of all awards going to an Australian pilot of No 149 Squadron, Flight Sergeant Rawdon Middleton.

A significant meeting of the War Cabinet Chiefs of Staff Committee took place in November, which included 'an estimate of the effects of an Anglo-American bomber offensive against Germany'. This meeting took a wide-ranging view of the whole question of air bombardment in the strategic sense and had as its starting premise: 'A heavy bomber force rising from 4,000 to 6,000 heavy bombers in 1944 could shatter the industrial and economic structure of Germany to a point where an Anglo-American force of reasonable strength could enter the Continent from the West.' Considering that 1942 had been a year of immense struggle for Bomber Command, despite the first signs of a growing capability in accuracy and bomb tonnage delivered, this was a forward-looking document. One of its major purposes, however, was to put a strong case for the bomber forces to be given the share of the overall resources that would be needed for the plan to be effective.

The paper started with an analysis of the damage caused by the German raids on Britain between June 1940 and June 1941, it being considered that this gave a better assessment of the effects of bombing than anything that could be obtained from intelligence sources

Above: Damage to the factories at Le Creusot.

Below: Le Creusot target area – damage plot.

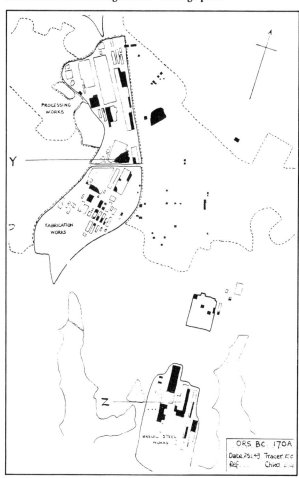

The crew of a No 44 Squadron Lancaster 'pose' to examine a map. [44 Sqn records]

regarding the effect of the RAF's bombing campaign to date. The conclusion was that the German offensive had created major problems and that if it had been more concentrated, and not been subject to diversion of effort, it would have had a serious impact on British war industry and civilian morale. The important aspects of concentration of effort and dedication of resources to the primary aim were therefore included as key elements of the plan. Using the assumed increase in the size of the Anglo-American bomber force, the paper estimated that by the end of 1943 some 50,000 tons of bombs would be dropped every month, rising to 90,000 tons in late 1944 when the total of 6,000 heavy bombers would be available. (It is interesting to note that the total German tonnage dropped in the twelve months from June 1940 was only 55,000 tons.)

To achieve its aim the plan considered the destruction of 58 German towns with populations of over 50,000, the top eighteen having populations of over 250,000. Alongside each town were listed the activities which made it a suitable target, industrial and administrative.

Among the general conclusions were a number of statements as to why this plan would be effective: 'Germany is in no condition to withstand an onslaught of this nature, her strength has passed its peak and is diminishing.' ... 'It is difficult to estimate the moral consequences of a scale of bombardment which would far transcend anything within human experience. But I have no doubt that against a background of growing casualties, increasing privations and dying hopes it would be profound indeed.' ... 'As resources were destroyed the Germans would have three options— 1. Reduce level of civil resources below that needed to maintain the national economy. 2. Divert effort of armed forces and munitions industry to defensive measures to hold off the bombers. 3. Divert resources into civil industries.'

Although signed by Portal as CAS, this document had the support of the Combined Chiefs of Staff. The conclusions it reached seemed quite reasonable, but they were an accurate summary of the effect such a campaign would have had on Britain. However, it was still not appreciated how different the German industrial, economic and administrative system was from Britain's (Germany did not fully transfer to a war economy until late 1943).

In its overall approach the document was an extension of the campaign already being undertaken by Bomber Command. By adding the American bomber forces into the total, and continuing to expand both, the prerequisite of weakening Germany before the invasion of the Continent would thereby be achieved. It was this plan that was to form the basis of the British arguments at the forthcoming Casablanca Conference.

November also brought renewed calls from the MEW for concentration of effort against the German ball-bearing industry. This was translated into a forthright directive to Harris on 21 November: 'The destruction of the Schweinfurt factories would result in a loss to the Germans of considerably more than half their requirements in ball-bearings for the production of armaments ... I require that you now reconsider your plans to attack Schweinfurt and the associated ball-bearing factories on the principle that their destruction should be regarded as of critical importance to our strategy, and that the objective now to be obtained is the complete devastation of the factories and town in one overwhelming operation.' An annexe to the directive gave details of a suggested plan of attack. Harris replied two days later objecting to the suggested plan for a large-scale attack, there being too many contradictory ele-

Right: Genoa, 22/23 October 1942. [97 Sqn records]

Below: No 2 Group Boston 'OM-D' of No 107 Squadron, November 1942.

Above: A Halifax of No 77 Squadron touches down at Elvington. [Tom Treadwell]

Above right: The all-important collection of in-flight rations.

Right: Waiting for the green.

ments. His basic premise was for a night incendiary attack, but delivered at low level to ensure accuracy and thus a more limited effort because of the need to use experienced crews. However, he went on to object to the attack in general as he did not believe that loss of the Schweinfurt factories would cause the level of disruption implied by the Air Staff; furthermore, he considered the suggested 'acceptable' loss rate of 200 crews for just one operation ridiculous as it would have 'a crippling material and morale effect on the squadrons taking part'.

A few days later (24 November) a revised CoS memo stated future policy as:

1. Render material assistance to Russians.
2. Prepare for the invasion of Europe.
3. Soften-up NW Europe by bombing—'From now on we must strike with ever-increasing strength at the German industrial and economic system, submarine construction, sources of air power, and morale of the German people'.

Regardless of this, Italy remained top of the target list into December, although Main Force also went to

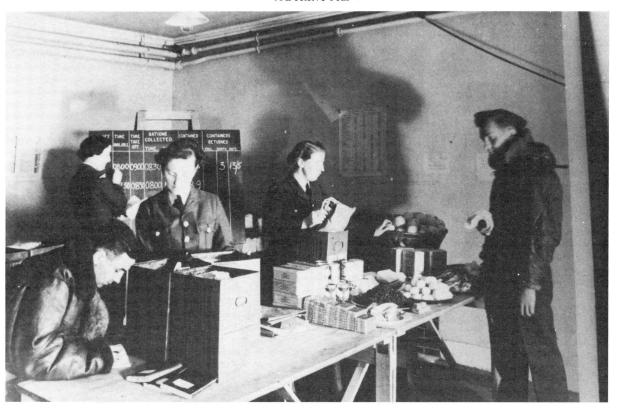

Frankfurt and Mannheim, with a further three attacks on Turin. Meanwhile the squadrons of No 2 Group carried out yet another spectacular raid: 93 aircraft (Bostons, Venturas and Mosquitoes) were tasked against the Philips factories at Eindhoven. The attack was delivered from ultra-low level in good weather and the factories were badly damaged, but, as with so many daylight raids, there was a heavy price—fourteen aircraft were lost.

On 3 December some aircraft began using 'Tinsel', a device designed to blot out the German night fighter communications and so make the GCI task even more difficult. The operator would search for the relevant control frequency (in the 3–6MHz band) and then switch on the transmitter, whereupon a microphone in the engine sent noise out over the control frequency.

As the Italian campaign closed, Bomber Command returned to Germany. On 20/21 December 232 aircraft attacked Duisburg. On the same night six Mosquitoes of No 109 Squadron went after the power-station at Lutterade as an operational trial of 'Oboe'. Crews reported a good attack but subsequent PR could not distinguish the new bomb craters from the old. Further small-scale 'Oboe' raids were flown on subsequent nights to test the system and evaluate the best method of employment. These culminated in 'Oboe' being used by two aircraft as a marker force over Düsseldorf on the night of 31 December, although only one of the aircraft could make use of the 'Oboe' signals. However, the results from this small raid by two Mosquitoes and eight Lancasters looked promising. Was this, at last, the blind-bombing aid so badly needed by Bomber Command?

The *Bomber Command Quarterly Review* carried an analysis of the effect of the bombing campaign upon the Ruhr during 1942: 'Throughout 1942 our blows became increasingly severe, the German High Command could do nothing but apportion a still greater number of much-needed guns and, above all, fighter aircraft to the defence of their western front. Meanwhile the Press and radio referred to a great "industrial migration", giving the impression that a wholesale transfer of industries mainly to the eastern Reich, was actually in progress. Some individual factories certainly were transferred eastwards, and the other industrial areas, e.g Silesia, Austria and Saxony, had inevitably expanded during the war. But geography had pre-determined that the Ruhr would remain indispensable to the German war

One hour after the Eindhoven raid, 6 December 1942.

machine.' The bottom line was that although a great deal had been achieved, there was still much to do in this region. 'Happy Valley', as the crews called the Ruhr, would stay high on the target list.

The statistics showed a huge increase in effort over 1941, approaching 800–900 per cent in some instances. Of the 60 squadrons, 53 per cent were 'heavies' (giving an average daily availability of 262 aircraft); this was reflected in the total tonnage dropped (45,560 tons), and the use of over 4,000 heavy (4000lb) bombs. Incendiaries made up 42 per cent of the total (it had been 12 per cent in 1941), an important change in bombing tactics. Mining statistics are even more impressive: an increase of 807 per cent to 9,574 mines in 4,743 sorties.

And so Bomber Command approached Year 4.

CHAPTER FIVE

The Storm Breaks over Germany

I T IS NOTEWORTHY that by 1 January 1943, 37 per cent of all Bomber Command pilots were from the Commonwealth (Canada, Australia and New Zealand), including an entire Canadian Group; plus, of course, all the Commonwealth aircrew other than pilots. To this must be added the volunteer aircrew from other nations, and it becomes apparent what a truly cosmopolitan organization Bomber Command was. By 1945 the proportion of Canadian, Australian and New Zealand pilots had risen to 46 per cent. It was not quite the same with the groundcrew, although as 'national' squadrons were formed in RAF Bomber Command these did contain national groundcrew.

While 1942 had been a critical year for Bomber Command's survival, 1943 was to be the first year in which it began to deliver the long promised destructive power—and with previously unheard of accuracy. A Bomber Command analysis put forward the hopes for 1943: 'Prior to the winter victories of the Soviet armies,

Bomber Command was contributing an essential element to the failure of the enemy's campaign in Russia by drawing off the German fighter force, reducing the productivity of German industry by bombing, and hampering it further by locking up very large manpower resources in flak and civil defence measures. Now the Germans are in retreat and everywhere on the defensive . . . in these circumstances the bomber offensive if concentrated on Germany will, in the immediate future, be not merely important, but decisive in crushing the German power to wage war.'

After a week of small-scale raids against Essen, Harris was keen to return to the heavy poundings of German towns which had rounded off 1942. Instead he received

Most bomber squadrons were cosmopolitan, shoulder flashes of many nations being evident. Here a crew form at No 1657 HCU, Stradishall—note Canada and Netherlands flashes. [Peter Rowland]

A Stirling of No 218 Squadron.

a new directive from the Air Ministry (14 January) calling for a renewed offensive against the U-boat bases in France. The War Cabinet, after considerable pressure from the Air Staff, had agreed to the 'area bombing' of these installations 'with the object of effectively devastating the whole area in which are located the submarines, their maintenance facilities and the services, power, water, light, communications and other resources upon which their operations depend'. Bomber Command was instructed to attack Lorient at the earliest opportunity and then to analyze the results of this attack before proceeding with the destruction of St Nazaire, Brest and La Pallice. This directive was little more than the realization that pinpoint attacks on these targets were not possible by night and not viable by day; and yet they were of such importance that they simply must be attacked. If the individual U-boats could not be destroyed, then surely the destruction of the associated facilities would, at the very least, reduce their effectiveness. It was a bold decision in that it called into question an area attack on a French target and the likely civilian casualties that would result.

The Bomber Command view was that 'if the number of operational U-boats is to be substantially reduced, the menace must also be powerfully attacked at earlier stages in its career and the continued flow of reinforcements decisively choked. The achievement of a decision is hastened by strategic bombing of the factories employed on the construction of component parts and by the bombing of the U-boat building yards.' It was estimated that German output was 20 boats a month from eighteen main yards, although 80 per cent came from just five ports. Added to this were 110 component

factories, 63 of which were located in 21 key towns (which also had other significant industrial targets within their area). The Command plan was to attack those 'areas' containing such targets; it had become the standard argument for the effectiveness of area attacks against industrial towns.

A rider to the directive stated that these attacks were not, however, to prejudice concentrated raids on Berlin or on other important objectives in Germany and Italy.

The new directive was not well received by Harris, partly because he saw it as yet another diversion of effort away from the real battle to be fought over Germany, and partly, as he so rightly said, because it was a waste of time as the critical areas of the U-boat bases were well protected and immune from air attack by the current weapons (it was to be a very different story at the end of 1944 when Bomber Command had the equipment to deal with such targets). Nevertheless, the first large raid of the year was tasked against Lorient, 122 aircraft carrying out an unsuccessful raid on the U-boat base on 14/15 January. Among the bombers operating that night were aircraft from the new No 6 (RCAF) Group, making their operational debut as a Group. The attack was repeated the following night by 157 aircraft.

A raid on Berlin, in accordance with the directive, provided the opportunity to try out a new device, one which was to have great significance throughout the rest of the war. On the night of 16/17 January a force of 201 bombers, all four-engined types and mainly from No 5 Group, took part in the first raid to make use of purpose-designed target indicators (TIs). The modified incendiaries which had previously been used as TIs had revealed severe limitations, and Bennett had fought for many months to acquire purpose-designed ones. How-

A North American Mitchell II of No 98 Squadron. [98 Sqn records]

ever, bad weather meant scattered bombing, despite the TIs, and a poor result. Following this raid it was back to smaller-scale operations against Essen. In the meantime another new type entered service with Bomber Command, the North American Mitchell. On 22 January twelve Mitchells from Nos 98 and 180 Squadrons joined Bostons and Venturas attacking airfields in France.

When the Allied leaders met at Casablanca in January, the long and complex agenda included the prosecution of the combined bomber offensive by the American bomber units and Bomber Command, as part of the 'Germany first' policy—i.e., before Japan. Various plans had been considered at Staff level, including Portal's paper outlining the proposition that a heavy bomber force of 6,000 aircraft could end the war, and these were the bases for the discussions. The outcome was a broad statement of the intent behind the Combined Offensive for 1943: 'Your primary object will be the progressive destruction and dislocation of the German military, industrial and economic system, and the undermining of the morale of the German people to a point where their capacity for armed resistance is fatally weakened.'

The directive issued by the Combined Chiefs of Staff on 21 January went on to detail five main target systems for attack, none of which were new and all of which had, at one time or another, been scheduled for attack by Bomber Command: submarine construction yards, aircraft industry, transportation, oil plants and 'others in the war industry'. This kind of broad instruction suited Harris admirably as it meant that he was not tied down to using his resources against what he termed 'unprofitable and unsuitable' targets.

The last week of the month saw a concentration of effort against the U-boat targets, with three raids on Lorient. There was also an attack on Düsseldorf (27/28 January) which included 'Oboe' Mosquitoes carrying out the ground marking technique. The 'Oboe' Mosquito ground marking combination was to prove the most accurate technique until dive marking was introduced by No 5 Group later in the war.

As part of a rationalization of Bomber Command's organization the PFF was granted Group status, becoming No 8 (Pathfinder) Group on 25 January.

At the end of January the latest in a series of technical additions went into operation, a raid on 30/31 January to Hamburg being the operational debut for the H2S radar system. A great deal was expected from this device. At long last here was a system that did not depend on ground stations; it could be used anywhere and with no limit on the numbers of aircraft. The theory was good, the practice not so promising. The raid was not a great success, bombing being quite scattered. But one thing that could not be denied was the increased bomb tonnage now being dropped by Bomber Command, although this was mainly due to an increase in the percentage of heavy bombers rather than any overall increase in the Order of Battle (ORBAT). By early February the Command had a notional strength of 1,091 bombers, of which 642 were 'heavies' (119 Stirlings, 228 Halifaxes and 295 Lancasters). By the middle of the year the monthly tonnage being dropped had reached 20,149, three times that of the same period in 1942.

One result of all the changes that had been taking place was that there was now a plethora of new ideas and tactical concepts. Almost monthly someone came up with a new way to attack a particular type of target, the best way to use TIs and so on. The PFF was often at the forefront of invention, although the Groups were not short of ideas. This situation became even more evident in the months that followed and at times it was hard for the ordinary crews to keep up with new developments.

February brought a call from the Air Staff for Bomber Command to attack Berlin in order to 'rub in the recent Russian victory', by which they meant the surrender of the German 6th Army at Stalingrad on 31 January, the worst defeat yet suffered by the Germans. Despite this call to attack Berlin no Main Force raid was launched against the 'Big City' until March, the main effort

throughout February being devoted to Italy (Turin, La Spezia and Milan being attacked), Lorient (four large raids) and various targets in Germany (Cologne, Hamburg, Wilhelmshaven, Bremen and Nuremberg). Although much experience was gained in the use of H2S, few of the attacks were very successful. It had rapidly become obvious that the key to success with H2S was experience and practice; only the trained eye could interpret the confused mass of responses on the screen. It was all too easy for an operator to convince himself that he recognized a particular feature.

The raid on Berlin on 1/2 March was also a partial

H2S

'On night operations it has become necessary for Command to prohibit anyone using H2S before a certain position it reached. To disobey radar silence is not only suicidal as far as you are concerned but is a criminal betrayal of the rest of Bomber Command. The sole reason for radar silence is to deny the enemy a means of knowing there is a raid on the way until our aircraft have climbed to a height where ordinary sound location or radar on the ground can plot them.'

The desire to equip Bomber Command with accurate navigation aids had been given great impetus by the findings of the Butt Report of 1941. Among the many devices considered was the use of an airborne radar system, the principle of which had been proved by ASV (Air to Surface Vessel) and AI devices. There was no technical reason why a reasonable ground image should not be possible from such systems. In October 1941 a meeting held at TRE put forward the advantages of an AI-type system: it would be independent of ground stations and thus have unlimited range (a major consideration), and it would be impossible to jam (not so). Trials with a 9cm AI set in a Blenheim proved the principles of ground mapping; all that was needed now was a better set to give greater definition of ground features.

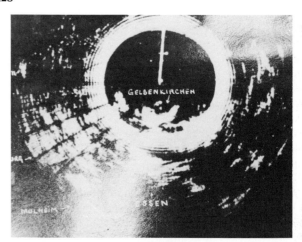

Above: H2S screen showing Gelsenkirchen.

Left: Section of H2S map showing the Ruhr area. [Tom Treadwell]

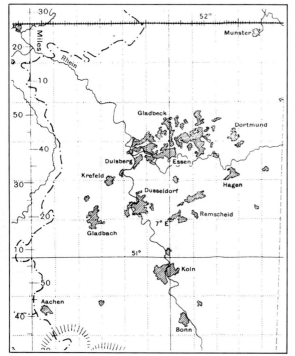

TRE conducted further trials using Halifaxes equipped with a rotating scanner, to give 360-degree cover, and a PPI (Plan Position Indicator) display to make interpretation easier. Development continued with the magnetron being used instead of the klystron, giving greater range. In August 1942 Bennett saw the system and was impressed with its possibilities for the PFF; he threw his support behind the concept. There were many problems to overcome, including stabilization of the picture during manoeuvres, discrimination of features from the general clutter, and reliability. By December a number of sets had been delivered to Nos 7 and 35 Squadrons, the Halifax being the most suitable aircraft regarding scanner position. It soon became obvious that here was an excellent navaid; coastal features and towns were easy to identify and so general navigation (i.e., aircraft position) was fairly simple. However, its employment as a bombing aid was more problematical as it was often difficult to make out an accurate aiming point unless ground features were unique and distinguishable. Using predictions and overlays, the operator could analyze the picture and interpet what he was seeing, but it took practice to make sense of the often confused series of blobs. Although the H2S system had great advantages over the land-based radio aids, it was not able to achieve the same accuracy for blind-bombing.

As the introductory comment states, it did not take the Germans long to devise systems to listen out for H2S and thus discover the position of the aircraft, including use of a homing device by the night fighters. Nevertheless, H2S was a superb technical achievement and was developed into an excellent radar in the post-war period.

failure; damage was caused in various parts of the city but not the concentration of bombing that had been expected. Berlin was a particularly difficult target on H2S, the response being confusing, but refining the picture to determine the aiming points was an altogether different matter. An attack on Hamburg two nights later was the last raid before Harris changed his strategy.

The Casablanca Directive was a clear call to the advocates of strategic bombing to prove their case. In March 1943 Bomber Command launched a sustained attack on Germany. The first part was the 'Battle of the Ruhr', from March to July, aimed at destroying the vital war industries of that region.

THE BATTLE OF THE RUHR

Harris saw the Essen raid of 5/6 March 1943 as a turning point. Led by an 'Oboe'-equipped PFF force, 442 bombers attacked the industrial city of Essen and this elusive target received heavy damage for the loss of only fourteen aircraft—'Years of endeavour, of experiment, and of training in new methods have at last provided the weapons and the force capable of destroying the heart of the enemy's armament industry'. This raid was the opening move in the new offensive aimed at flattening the Ruhr and its vital industries.

While Bomber Command was taking the offensive to Germany, the U-boats were having another very successful season in the Atlantic. In March another 500,000 tons of Allied shipping was sunk, leading to Admiralty calls for Bomber Command help and implementation of the January directive, although, as has been noted, Bomber Command had already been attacking some of the designated targets.

In the middle of this new offensive and with his forces now heavily engaged, Harris was even less inclined to divert any effort to the French U-boat bases. He repeated his arguments of previous weeks that it simply was not worth the effort expended and that it was much better to attack the sources—i.e., construction yards and component factories. Although Portal supported the case, the Admiralty remained firm in their request for Bomber Command's attacks on these targets. Harris then argued that this would mean a 25 per cent diversion of effort for at least two months, a critical period for his main offensive. Reluctantly the Admiralty agreed to suspend its request; in a directive dated 6 April the Air Staff instructed Harris to discontinue these area attacks in order to concentrate on the offensive over Germany. However, it was suggested that harassing attacks should be maintained, perhaps by 'fresher' crews.

An analysis of the effectiveness of the PFF during its first nine months of operation (to March 1943) showed two distinct phases: Phase I (August–December 1942), when no radio aids were available and no special target-marking devices had been developed, showed little improvement over pre-PFF accuracy, results still being very dependent on weather and the strength of the defences; Phase II (January–March 1943) looked much better, with the use of 'Oboe' and H2S. With 'Oboe' ground-marking it was estimated that bombing results were three times better. One of the great improvements was the introduction of purpose-designed target indicators. The prospects for the rest of the year, as the

Lancaster 'Q' of No 97 Squadron in a sad state after a photoflash exploded. [97 Sqn records]

PFF grew more experienced in the use of the various devices, looked promising indeed.

One of the routine series of operational analyses undertaken concerned the use of the bombers' guns for self-defence. The whole question of a 'policy' for air gunners had been examined on previous occasions, with no firm conclusions, and it was still very much a matter of crew tactics. Some gunners never fired their guns in anger during an entire tour of operations; some never even saw a night fighter. In some crews it was policy not to open fire unless the fighter came into the attack; a quick glimpse of a fighter in the darkness did not always mean that he had seen you, and to open fire would certainly have given the aircraft away. Among other crews—and this was somewhat more in line with the general guidance given—the policy was to fire at anything that moved as this showed that the bomber crew was awake and ready, so perhaps the fighter would be better advised to go away and pick on somebody else!

Statistics showed that the rear turret was most frequently in action; for example, in the period November 1942 to February 1943, of 139 instances of heavy bomber gunners engaging targets, no fewer than 123 had been by the rear gunners. The average number of bullets fired was 235, the maximum 1,000, and this from a total available of 6,000 rounds for a Lancaster rear turret (4,800 for a Stirling and 3,000 for a Halifax). The

A Lockheed Ventura over Ijmuiden, Holland, 13 February

ORS contended that a limit of 3,000 rounds be imposed, thus giving an appreciable weight-saving, and associated improvement in performance. At other times it was argued that the removal of the front and mid-upper turrets, with the associated weight-saving and improved aerodynamics, would give the aircraft an improved

No 619 Squadron Lancaster; note H2S blister. [F. Slater]

performance that would far outweigh the loss of fire-power. The arguments had been ranging for some time concerning the problems of the 0.303in guns with which the RAF bombers were equipped. The guns were certainly reliable and they pushed out a high rate of fire, but their effective range was limited. The 'wise' enemy fighter pilot could stand away from the range of the gunners and take shots at a bomber with its highly destructive cannon.

The AOC-in-C of No 5 Group, Cochrane, among others, argued that the air gunners should fire more often, letting loose at the faintest shadow; the additional 'own goals' which might result from this would, he suggested, be far outweighed by the gains. Others including Bennett argued strongly against this idea. In the event it was individual crew choice as to which technique they thought gave them the best chance of survival. By the end of the year most had worked out that their chances of completing an operational tour were slim—about 3 in 10.

A 'typical' encounter between a Halifax of No 51 Squadron and a number of German fighters was reported as follows: 'The rear-gunner was on his first operational sortie. Just before reaching the target area special signals gave warning of an approaching aircraft. This proved to be a Fw 190, which came in to attack but made off without firing when the rear-gunner opened fire at 600 yards. Twelve minutes later, after leaving the target, another Fw 190 was sighted 500 yards away on

the starboard quarter. The rear-gunner at once opened fire while the Halifax turned in towards the direction of attack. The third fighter, encountered 20 minutes later, was most determined. This was a Ju 88 and was first sighted about 1,000 yards away on the port quarter. It passed astern of the Halifax and came in on the starboard quarter. The Halifax turned to starboard, at 400 yards both rear and mid-upper gunners fired at the same time as the Halifax corkscrewed. The rear-gunner gave the orders for evasive action and remained throughout complete master of the situation. The Halifax returned to base without damage of any kind.'

The 'special signals' mentioned above refer to one of the first warning devices fitted to Bomber Command aircraft. In the latter months of 1942 Stirlings of No 7 Squadron had been fitted with 'Boozer', a piece of equipment designed to pick up enemy radar signals and display their type to the bomber crew. It was a simple system using a series of coloured lights to indicate which type of radar was looking at the aircraft. By early 1943 it was a triple-channel system and the intention was to fit the device to all the Command's aircraft. For various reasons this did not take place and distribution remained limited.

In the period from the start of the 'Battle of the Ruhr' to mid-May, about 60 per cent of Bomber Command

The Renault factory at Le Mans after Mosquito attack, 9 March 1943.

The Mosquito was able to carry a heavy bomb load and yet maintain its performance.

Main Force effort was tasked against targets in the Ruhr, Duisburg being the most frequently visited. Other large raids went to Essen, Bochum, Mannheim, Dortmund, Nuremberg, Munich, Stuttgart, Berlin, Frankfurt, Stettin and, farther afield, the Skoda Works at Pilsen. The same period brought a number of new developments, such as the first sorties by No 1409 (Met) Flight, a specialist unit tasked to provide weather reconnaissance for the Command. Also, on 13/14 April, Mosquitoes began night harassing raids, the idea being to keep the sirens going throughout Germany—a foretaste of the much larger and effective raids by the Light Night Striking Force.

At the height of the Ruhr offensive yet another directive landed on Harris's desk. The Allied Conference held in Washington during May 1943 took yet another look at the progress of and future plans for the Combined Bomber Offensive. One of the plans under consideration was that presented by the American bomber Commander, General Eaker. The so-called 'Eaker Plan' had been outlined in April, its central argument being that it is 'better to cause a high degree of destruction in a few really essential industries than to cause a small degree of destruction in many industries'. The key target systems outlined in the Casablanca Directive were turned into 76 precise targets, the destruction of which was seen as an essential pre-requisite to the Allied invasion of the Continent. Eaker stressed that this could only work if there was an adequate bomber force and so suggested that the two bomber arms should work together to this general plan. The Washington Conference was in general agreement with this proposal but disagreed with a number of the target systems and allowed for greater flexibility of action by increasing the number of targets (at the request of the Air Staff).

The directive that emerged from all this (3 June 1943) brought into effect a Combined Bombing Strategy, code-named 'Pointblank', which was to remain in force for nearly a year. Despite the desire to keep the targets fairly broad, the final directive, issued on 14 May, contained details of 76 'precise targets' covering the six main target systems. Figures were given as to the expected impact the destruction of these specific targets would have; for example, if the targets listed under the submarine construction yards and U-boats bases were destroyed it would reduce construction by 89 per cent. The four primary target systems were to be the submarine construction yards and U-boat bases, the German aircraft industry, ball-bearing production, and oil installations.

The attacks on the German aircraft industry were singled out for special mention: 'If the growth of the German fighter strength is not arrested quickly it may become literally impossible to carry out the destruction planned and thus to create the conditions necessary for ultimate decisive action by our combined forces on the Continent.' The overall strategic plan called for the US VIII Bomber Command to attack the stated targets by day and for RAF Bomber Command to hit the same area by night—truly a combined offensive. In the event, this very rarely happened.

The early months of 1943 had brought realization to the American Bomber chiefs that their hoped-for ability to strike at Germany by day was proving to be an expensive failure, a point which Bomber Command had been trying to impress on them ever since the suggestion was first made. It was a hard-learned lesson and there was much pain yet to suffer before a solution was found. It was hardly much better for Bomber Command as losses continued to rise, and all too often were above the 'acceptable' 4–5 per cent long-term average. A series of Bomber Command Tactical Notes (issued later in 1943) expressed the problems by outlining the state of the German defences and discussing tactical solutions.

The notes paid great attention to the need for sound planning, the aim being 'to launch as many bombs as possible towards the target, and to do so without heavy casualties. The maximum destruction for a certain tonnage of bombs results from concentration because the civil defence system is overwhelmed, especially by the concentration of incendiary bombs. The cumulative effect of many conflagrations, between which the fire-fighting service has to be distributed, and the damage to water-mains, multiplies the area of devastation.' There was also the added benefit of swamping the defences through concentration in time and space; although the risk of collision and damage from the bombs of other aircraft was increased, it was considered that both of these were kept to the minimum if crews flew parallel attack courses.

One of the greatest danger periods was the climb away from base after take-off and the forming of the bomber stream. How many times bombers came close to each other in cloud as they climbed to their initial cruising levels does not bear thinking about, and it is amazing that so few mid-air collisions took place as hundreds of aircraft left airfields only a few miles apart and all began to head in the same direction. The crew had to stay alert for the merest glimpse of a dark shape sliding towards them; on countless occasions the skipper had to make a sudden lunge at the controls to avoid another bomber as it slid by in the recently vacated space a few feet above. To witness a mid-air collision was horrific: darkness suddenly rent by a huge fireball as the two bombers met—bombs, fuel and

Well-wishers wave the Lancasters away. [44 Sqn records]

oxygen combining to form a terrible funeral pyre, from which very few escaped.

Once over the target there was the very real risk of being on the receiving end of bombs from a friendly aircraft above. In a report looking at the instances of aircraft being hit by incendiaries, it was concluded that the risk was small: an average of six per 800 aircraft, with an expected two hits per aircraft affected. Two examples from the Düsseldorf raid of 25/26 May 1943 illustrate the problem: Lancaster R5609 of No 106 Squadron was hit by a single 4lb bomb which passed through the rear fuselage causing little damage; Stirling EH879 of No 149 Squadron had a much rougher time when it was hit by five 30lb bombs, the results of which were:

1. Through cockpit roof, floor and out through bomb doors just missing the controls.
2. Through fuselage and bomb bay severing bomb fusing and release cables.
3. Through wing root into fuselage; destroyed three batteries, damaged cables.
4. Tore away corner of No 2 tank, went into under-carriage bay, tore and punctured one tyre.
5. Hit starboard outer engine, tore away corner of oil tank causing engine to seize through lack of oil.

The Stirling managed to return to base safely! It survived the war and was eventually disposed of in February 1946.

The danger was not only from the small incendiaries; larger bombs as well rained down all around and a few hit friendly bombers lower down in the bombing stack. For those who chose to fly low over the target, the danger was particularly extreme.

Left: Halifax flight engineer's panel.

Below left: Ammunition runs in the fuselage of a Halifax.

As soon as the German ground control organization had worked out which town was the target, the fighters would gather for the kill. The bomber, heavy, cumbersome (although often thrown around like a fighter during evasion), laden with fuel and bombs, was always at a disadvantage against the nimble, heavily armed night fighter. June brought the operational debut of 'Monica', another piece of electronic kit designed to help counter the German defences. Unlike the previous warning device, 'Boozer', this was an active system developed by the Royal Aircraft Establishment in 1942. The concept was to provide a warning device for the rear gunners as most attacks came from the rear quarter. The transmitter sent out a signal which reflected off any object behind the aircraft. The signal was translated into a series of pips audible on the intercomm; the nearer the contact then the more rapid the pips. The Mk III version of 'Monica' became operational in June 1943 and had a minimum range of 1,000 yards and a maximum range of four miles. There was no IFF (Identification Friend or Foe) and while in the bomber stream the equipment picked up signals almost constantly, the result being a most annoying constant bleep on the intercomm. It was considered to be a nuisance. The modified Mk IIIA had a visual rather than audio signal, but the problem of too many signals remained. The theory was good in that a signal should indicate a fighter closing to effective range, at which point the bomber could go into an evasive manoeuvre. Without doubt the system saved a few lives, but it also increased the collision risk as aircraft took violent evasion in the bomber stream. Worse was to follow as the Germans developed their 'Flensburg' system to home onto the signals from the 'Monica' warning device. By mid-1944 'Monica' had been withdrawn from Main Force use but was retained by the RCM squadrons of No 100 Group.

An alternative to avoiding the enemy night fighter was to shoot him down, or at least persuade him to go and find someone else to bother. The air gunners needed to maintain a constant vigil, searching the night sky, not daring to relax for even a moment. A glimpse of movement, a slightly darker patch of sky—was that a fighter trying to sneak in? A burst from the guns to show that this bomber is awake and not an easy prey (the arguments for and against which have been outlined above).

Another method of getting back at the enemy fighters was to include one's own fighters in and around the bomber stream, not in the same style as escorts for day formations but rather as free-roaming fighters. As early as October 1942 Harris had proposed to Fighter Command that they put a few Mosquito fighters into the

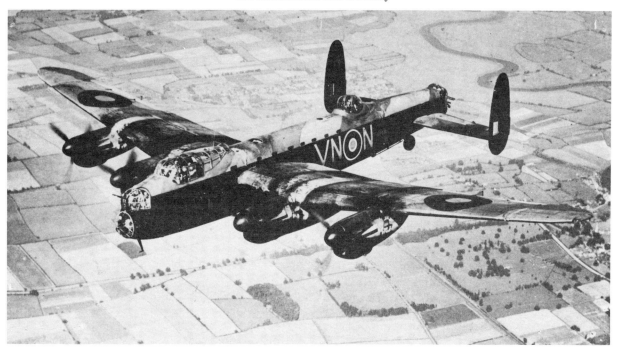

bomber stream as escort. This concept only became practicable with the introduction of an electronic aid to enable the enemy to be located. Standard AI (air interception radar) was all very well for its intended purpose but it did not distinguish the threat aircraft from the bomber stream. The introduction of 'Serrate' provided a solution to the problem. This device was developed by the Telecommunications Research Establishment (TRE) to provide bearings on a range of German AI radars (FuG 202, 212 and 220), with a maximum range of 50 miles. The idea was that the roaming fighter would pick up a 'Serrate' contact and fly towards it; when in range the target would appear on,

Two views of the much-photographed Lancaster R5689, of No 50 Squadron.

for example, a Beaufighter's own AI and an interception would be completed. In June the Beaufighter VIs of No 141 Squadron were equipped with the new kit and began training, being tasked with the first operational mission on the 14/15th of the month. A Main Force of 197 Lancasters and six Mosquitoes were tasked to attack Oberhausen; it was an accurate raid despite bad weather, but seventeen Lancasters (8.4 per cent) were lost.

At last realization had dawned that air superiority was a basic prerequisite for successful bombing operations. The 1920s belief that the 'bomber will always get through' had been modified by the proviso 'as long as the enemy fighter forces have been destroyed'.

Central planning for the invasion of the Continent, an event now postponed until 1944, involved a major reorganization of force. As part of this reshuffle, Bomber Command said farewell to No 2 Group in May when that organization was transferred to the newly created Tactical Air Force. The contribution of the crews of No 2 Group had been tremendous. They had been conducting a daylight war against some of the most heavily defended parts of Europe; the years had brought spectacular achievements, and heavy losses. Many histories of Bomber Command ignore the part played by this Group, the attitude being that Bomber Command meant 'heavies' and so No 2 Group did not count! During this final period of their time with Bomber Command, the Group's squadrons had been very active, attacking a wide range of targets throughout Germany and Occupied Europe. Losses had been reasonably low (about 2 per cent), but when eleven Venturas of No 487 Squadron, RNZAF, attacked a power station near Amsterdam on 3 May they were bounced by German fighters and lost nine of their number; a tenth aircraft limped back to England, Flight Lieutenant Duffill landing at Feltwell. The final aircraft, piloted by Squadron Leader Leonard Trent, went on to and attacked the target, but was shot down. Only when the full tale was told after the war was this act granted recognition—Trent was awarded the VC. The Squadron Operational Diary recorded: 'A very black day in the squadron history ... a better set of boys could not be met in 30 years, everybody is feeling dazed by the news'. It left No 487 Squadron with only six operational crews.

The final sorties by No 2 Group while under Bomber Command were flown on 31 May when 54 aircraft were sent to five different targets, the only casualty being a Mitchell from No 180 Squadron.

May also saw the most famous of all Bomber Command's exploits, a raid which fired the imagination of the people of Britain, and one which has been the subject of more argument, and publications, than almost any other—the 'Dams Raid'.

THE DAMS RAID—OPERATION 'CHASTISE'

The concept of causing industrial disruption and destruction by attacking certain critical dams had been in the British bombing plans for some time (back to the WA plans of the pre-war period). However, it was only with the advent of a suitable weapon that the raid became practicable. The weapon, and the impetus for the raid, came from one of Britain's greatest inventor/designers, Dr Barnes Wallis at Vickers. As one of his many weapons developments he addressed the question

Wing Commander Guy Gibson, VC, DSO, DFC, signing a photo of the shattered Möhne dam after the spectacular and highly successful Dams Raid.

of how to breach the great concrete and earth dams of Germany. After countless experiments he concluded that the only effective method was to explode a charge against the lower part of the wall, relying on water pressure from the explosion to destroy the structure. The bomb would need a special delivery technique and would call for extreme accuracy in the attack. It needed a specialist squadron. Wing Commander Guy Gibson had just completed a tour of operations with No 106 Squadron, bringing his total to an incredible 174 missions. He was summoned to HQ No 5 Group and asked to carry out one more, very special mission, for which he would form and lead a special squadron. Having agreed, he then set about creating the unit, choosing the crews and forming No 617 Squadron. The Lancasters had to be modified to take the new weapon. Although this weapon is usually referred to as the 'bouncing bomb', it was in reality a mine—which bounced. Early trials with 'Upkeep', the dams variant of this weapon, were unsuccessful, but by early May the problems had been overcome and the squadron training was well advanced. It was only just in time as it was essential to attack the dams while the water level was still high.

The attack plan, code-named Operation 'Chastise', was for nineteen aircraft to attack in three waves. The first wave of nine aircraft, led by Gibson, was to attack the Möhne Dam and then, if successful, would fly on to attack the Eder Dam. The second wave of five aircraft would attack the Sorpe Dam; and the third wave, also of five aircraft, would act as an airborne reserve, to attack any of the dams not already breached.

At 2130 on 16 May the first wave took off, rapidly followed by the other sections. Soon after crossing the Rhine one aircraft was shot down by flak, crashing near

Dorsten. Gibson's section arrived unscathed over the Möhne Dam just after midnight. Gibson went into the attack, placing his mine well and scoring a hit. As soon as the water had settled again, Flight Lieutenant Hopgood made his run, but, hit by flak, he dropped late and the mine went over the target. His aircraft crashed soon afterwards, but two of the crew survived. Having seen that the German gunners had identified the attack pattern, Gibson decided to escort the next aircraft into the target. Flight Lieutenant Martin made his run but the mine went short. When Squadron Leader Young ran in he was escorted by Gibson and Martin; the mine was accurate and great cascades of water shot over the dam wall—but still it held. The fifth mine, dropped by Flight Lieutenant Maltby, did the trick and the dam gave way. As the circling Lancasters watched, the wall collapsed and a great torrent of foaming water burst into the valley. Gibson took part of the force on to the Eder Dam; the others returned to base.

They found the target undefended and so the attack runs could be flown without interference. Flight Lieutenant Shannon hit the dam, causing a slight breach. Squadron Leader Maudslay dropped late and was hit by the force of the explosion; his aircraft survived this but was shot down on the return flight. Pilot Officer Knight put in a good attack and the wall cracked and fell apart. Yet another Lancaster was lost on the return flight, Squadron Leader Young falling to a coastal flak site in Holland. Of the first wave, only five aircraft returned to Scampton.

Of the second wave, two were forced to return early.

Two others were lost on the outbound route, both probably falling to flak. The sole remaining aircraft, flown by Flight Lieutenant McCarthy, went on to the target and carried out an attack; although the weapon hit the dam it did not cause a breach. The third wave also lost two aircraft to flak, while a third had to abort the mission. The other two Lancasters continued, one (Flight Sergeant Brown) attacking the Sorpe, and the other (Flight Sergeant Townsend) attacking the Ennepe. Although both attacks were accurate, neither dam was breached.

Undoubtedly, 'Chastise' had been a great success. Two of the primary targets had been breached, resulting in widespread damage from flooding; the overall effect of the torrents of water has been the subject of much debate ever since the raid took place. However, losses had been high: eight of the fourteen Lancasters failed to return and 53 aircrew lost their lives.

The Press reported: 'Tonight walls of water swept down the Ruhr and Eder valleys in Germany, destroying everything before them, after the RAF had attacked and breached two dams. The raids, by specially fitted Lancaster bombers using new "bouncing" bombs, were planned to cripple Germany's vital industrial heartland.'

Many gallantry awards were made to survivors of the raid. Wing Commander Gibson was awarded the VC for his 'outstanding bravery and leadership during the raid'. The other surviving pilots, Knight, McCarthy, Maltby, Martin and Shannon, were each awarded the DSO, with Brown and Townsend receiving the CGM. The other awards consisted of fifteen DFCs and twelve DFMs.

CHAPTER SIX

The Bombing Offensive Gathers Pace

A NEW DIRECTIVE of 10 June continued the general precepts of 'Pointblank' but with a somewhat different slant on the target systems to be attacked. In draft form on 3 June, it had listed the priorities as: 1. German fighter aircraft strength; 2. submarine yards and bases; 3. aircraft industry; 4. ball-bearing industry; 5. oil installations; 6. synethetic rubber and tyre plants; and 7. military motor transport. To confirm the pre-eminent nature of the task against the German fighter forces, it went on to state four areas in which this policy could be effective:

1. The destruction of airframe, engine and component factories, and the ball-bearing industry on which the strength of the German fighter force depends.

2. The general disorganization of those industrial areas associated with the above industries.

3. The destruction of those aircraft repair depots and storage parks within range, and on which the enemy fighter force is largely dependent.

4. The destruction of enemy fighters in the air and on the ground.

A week later, on 10 June, the draft directive was confirmed. Once again much of the wording had been left vague, partly at the suggestion of the Air Staff in order to give Harris a greater degree of flexibility in the selection of targets. There was certainly nothing in the directive to deflect Bomber Command from its now well-established programme of attacks against key industrial cities, all of which contained at least some element covered by the target systems listed in the directive. Meanwhile the Battle of the Ruhr had been continuing. Following the Dams Raid there had been a one-week lull in Bomber Command operations. The offensive reopened on 23/24 May when 826 aircraft attacked Dortmund in what was an accurate and destructive raid, but with the loss of 38 aircraft. During the next four weeks Main Force attacks, by up to 800 aircraft, were tasked against Düsseldorf, Cologne, Essen, Bochum, Wuppertal, Munster, Oberhausen, and, in an attempt to try low-level visual bombing, the Schneider factory and Breuil steelworks at Le Creusot (on 19/20 June).

At last the production of heavy bombers was reaching reasonable levels and the expansion of the Command was taking effect. The previous year had seen only slow expansion in terms of numbers of squadrons but generally increased capability, with a higher percentage of 'heavies'. By mid-1943 both elements were coming together; furthermore, Bomber Command was now hitting what it was trying to hit. Starting in June, Fighter Command instituted offensive patrols ('Flower') against German night fighter airfields to coincide with the period that the bomber stream was crossing the enemy coast. Two months later this was further developed to include AI aircraft patrolling around these bases ('Mahmoud' patrols).

The night of 20/21 June brought a highly successful raid, and one that was the first of its kind in that the bombers flew on to land in North Africa instead of returning to England. This was the first of the so-called 'Shuttle' raids. The force, mainly from No 5 Group, comprised 60 Lancasters and the target was the ex-Zeppelin works at Friedrichshafen on the shores of Lake Constance. The factory was an important centre for the manufacture of 'Würzburg' radars and the destruction of this target would help Bomber Command's own offensive by reducing the supply of these excellent radars. A crew member's account follows:

'Approaching the French coast at 19,000 feet, we encountered heavy cloud and electric storms up to 24,000 feet. We therefore decided to come down below the front and lost height to 5,000 feet. We were suddenly engaged by the defences of Caen or the outer defences of Le Havre—owing to technical difficulties with navigation instruments we were then uncertain of our exact position. Four 4-gun heavy flak positions engaged us for about 4 minutes. During this time we altered course by about 30 degrees every 8 seconds, alternately losing and gaining height by 1,000 feet. The flak bursts were mainly 300–500 feet behind and about the same distance above us. It was noticed that the rate of fire of the guns was extremely high! We flew on below cloud at 2,500–3,000 feet across France and encountered no further opposition.

'Three-quarters of an hour's flying time from Lake Constance it was necessary to feather the port-inner engine, which was emitting showers of sparks, so we continued on three engines until we sighted the Lake. By that time we had increased height to 6,000 feet. As the port-inner engine is essential for the Mk XIV bombsight, it was unfeathered and allowed to windmill, but shortly afterwards the engine caught fire. We were unable to feather it or extinguish the fire, which grew in intensity. The Captain then jettisoned his bombs, told the Deputy Leader to take over and gave the order to prepare to abandon aircraft, first diving across the lake into Switzerland, and subsequently turning the aircraft towards Germany. We were about to bale out, expecting the petrol tanks to explode, when the engine seized and the fire went out. By this time we had descended to 4,000 feet but were able to maintain height.

'We stayed over Lake Constance for 13 minutes and had an excellent view of the attack. There were approximately 16–20 heavy flak guns and 18–20 light flak guns, and 25 searchlights, within a radius of 6–8 miles of the target. Several aircraft were coned but not for any length of time. Heavy guns were firing both predictor-control and unseen. As the defences were heavier than expected, the Deputy Leader gave the order for all aircraft to increase height by 5,000 feet, so that the attack was actually delivered from 10,000 to 15,000 feet.

'Leaving the target area, we commenced to fly over the Alps. By skirting the peaks we eventually crossed, gradually gaining height to 14,000 feet. The 600-mile flight over the Mediterranean was slow, as we had to fly at 140mph to prevent over-heating. Eventually we sighted the Algerian coast and landed safely at Maison Blanche at 0752, after a flight of 10 hours and 13 minutes.'

The attack had been in two parts, the first bombs falling on TIs provided by the small PFF force; the second attack was a 'timed run' from a visual point on the shores of the Lake (a technique being developed by

No 5 Group). The factories received numerous hits and were heavily damaged. No aircraft were lost. The attack had been controlled by Wing Commander G. L. Gomm (taking over from Group Captain Slee), the first use of a 'directed attack' (later known as Master Bomber), although the basic technique had been used by Gibson during the Dams Raid.

Three nights later, on 23/24 June, 52 of the Lancasters flew back to England, bombing targets at La Spezia on the way. The final four weeks of the Battle of the Ruhr saw attacks on Cologne, Gelsenkirchen, Krefeld, Mulheim, Aachen and Wuppertal, plus a return to Turin and a special operation to destroy the Peugeot factory at Montbeliard. The nights were getting shorter as summer progressed and so only the nearer targets could be attacked; but increasing losses had imposed a growing strain on the Command. The majority of losses were put down to the growing strength and efficiency of the German night fighter defences, which included the operational debut on 3/4 July of JG 300 operating single-engined fighters in the 'Wilde Sau' (Wild Boar) tactic.

Bomber Command's Operational Research Section (ORS) continued its investigations into a wide range of tactical matters. One of the regular series of reports was that which concerned the German defences, their composition and strength, and the relevance of various tactical methods. The work of the ORS has often been ignored by historians. It was known to very few of the crews during the war itself, but it played an essential part in the creation of new ideas and tactics—'a fruitful alliance between the air force and the scientists which enabled Bomber Command to evade the German air force and, with increasing accuracy, to find and hit its targets'.

A Halifax of No 77 Squadron being serviced at Elvington. The part played by the Halifax squadrons has often been ignored, the aircraft living in the shadow of the Lancaster. [Tom Treadwell]

THE BATTLE OF HAMBURG—
OPERATION 'GOMORRAH'

Next it was the turn of Hamburg and in late July and early August this city received four very heavy and accurate attacks.

On the night of 24/25 July, after much delay and heated discussion at the highest levels, the bomber stream starting using 'Window'. This device was simplicity itself but proved to be one of the most significant developments introduced during this critical period.

The Hamburg raid was the subject of a report by the ORS: 'The very low casualties incurred in the first two attacks were largely due to the temporary disorganization of the German fighter defences by a new counter-measure which precluded the vectoring of controlled night fighters. The final attack was ruined by unexpected deterioration of weather conditions over the target. Eighty-seven aircraft is a high price in itself, but in comparison with the loss sustained by Germany in the almost complete annihilation of her second city, it can only be regarded as minute. Hamburg was indeed a great city by any standards. It was the second city and maritime centre of Germany. The "Hafen" with its imposing array of shipbuilding yards, docks, warehouses and administrative buildings was the basis of Hamburg's contribution to German economic life.

'The destruction of Hamburg by bombing was thus far the stiffest task yet undertaken in air warfare. It was not until 1 August that smoke from the conflagrations cleared sufficiently to make reconnaissance possible. The heavily damaged areas covered 6,200 out of the 8,380 acres which comprise Hamburg's closely built-up residential areas. All parts of the city and dock were shattered—all four main shipbuilding yards were hit, five floating docks were sunk or badly damaged, 150 industrial plants were destroyed or badly damaged, plus massive distortion of communications and power.'

German reports were equally candid about the extent of the destruction: 'The port was severely hit, the damage was gigantic. The failing of the water system, and the fighting of fires which remained from earlier attacks, hampered all work severely. The whole of Hamburg was on fire. Rescue, evacuation, clearing of vital roads, fire fighting, etc, asked the impossible from the available LS forces. Economically, Hamburg was knocked out, as even the undamaged parts had to stop work on account of the destruction of water, gas and electricity supplies'—after the raid of 29/30 July.

In between the attacks on Hamburg, Main Force had been to Essen and Remscheid. It had been a very successful campaign against the second city of Germany, causing Goebbels to comment on the resulting damage as a 'catastrophe, the extent of which simply staggers the imagination'. It was the fulfilment in many ways of what the bomber chiefs had said for a long time: a concentrated and accurate raid(s) on an industrial city would remove it from the war. Speer expressed the opinion that if another six big German cities were similarly destroyed he would not be able to maintain armaments production. These are very significant comments, worthy of consideration over the question of the validity of the bombing campaign.

An important aspect that is often overlooked, especially when considering loss rates, is the number of aircraft damaged by enemy defences (rather than shot down). The instances of aircraft returning after being shot up by a fighter were outweighed many times over by those that returned with varying degrees of flak damage. In some cases the crew could achieve no more than a crash-landing, and the bomber was written off. Others were put down safely but on inspection of the damage were considered to be 'beyond economical repair' and went for spares and scrap. With many others the long-suffering and hard-pressed groundcrew worked miracles and put the aircraft back together again; in some cases this was literally a question of 'sticking' two, or more, aircraft together to make one good one. The net result of such damaged aircraft was to

---

'WINDOW'

One of the most simple yet effective devices to be producing during the war was 'Window'. The basic principle still forms an essential counter-measure used by current front-line aircraft (as 'Chaff'), although the idea of dropping metallic strips to create spurious radar responses was first outlined in 1938. Development was slow but by 1941 the TRE was carrying out trials with oblong strips of aluminium foil which, it was thought, would look like an aircraft response, thus presenting more 'targets' to the radar. This had a twofold benefit: it could confuse the real target response by hiding it among many others; or it could be used to simulate a much larger force of aircraft than was actually present. By early 1942 the system was ready for use. Fighter Command objected on the grounds that the Germans might employ the same device.

The argument continued, with Harris claiming that use of 'Window' might reduce bomber losses by 30 per cent. Agreement came on 23 July and 'Window' went into use with the short offensive against Hamburg. It was an immediate success, throwing the German defences into confusion. Bundles of 'Window' were thrown out of the bombers as they crossed a 'line' 60 miles from the target, the rate being one bundle a minute right up to the time that the 'line' was crossed on the return leg. It was hard work but considered well worth the effort if it helped the chances of survival.

The German defences soon developed various counters to the use of 'Window' but they could never solve the problem. 'Window' continued to be used, and developed to match the frequencies of other German radars. By 1944 the monthly production was three million bundles for use against 'Würzburg', 1.5 million bundles for SN-2, and half a million bundles for 'Freya'—the scale of the operation was enormous. It was not only the individual bombers of Main Force that carried 'Window'; it was often employed for specialist purposes, the aircraft of No 100 Group playing a vital part in this area, including three squadrons contributing to the Special 'Window' Force from July 1944 onwards. The main aim of the SWF was to create a false bombing force as part of the spoof tactics. A similar spoof was worked during D-Day, but this time the aircraft dropped 'Window' to simulate a fleet!

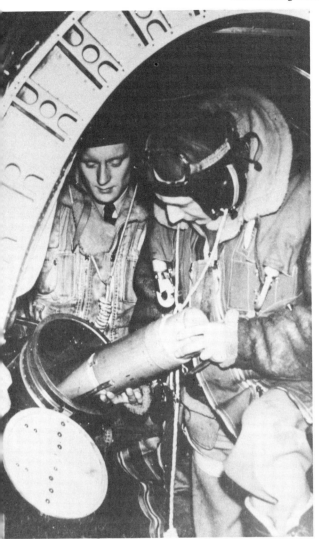

Wellington flare chute.

reduce the daily availability. If a crew had managed to stagger back in their aircraft—to which deep attachments were often formed, especially if it was considered to be a 'lucky' aircraft—they were determined to try to get it back again. If it was one of the more unpopular machines, eliciting comments such as 'no loss, best shot of it', then few tears were shed. At certain periods the level of flak damage, and thus the loss of aircraft availability, caused great concern at Bomber Command. The introduction of 'Window' not only saved aircraft from being shot down but it also improved the flak-damage statistics. The level had been running at around 15 per cent but post-'Window' this fell to 5 per cent.

Early August brought a large-scale return to Italy, mainly as an 'encouragement' to that country to leave the war. Main Force raids had a major impact on Italian public opinion and without doubt contributed to the Italian decision to seek an Armistice in early September. Genoa, Milan and Turin were attacked on a number of nights. Following the Turin attack of 12/13 August, Flight Sergeant Arthur Aaron was awarded the VC for his part in the raid.

PEENEMÜNDE

On 17/18 August Bomber Command launched Operation 'Hydra', the attack on the German research installation at Peenemünde. There had been growing evidence all year that the Germans were working on rocket weapons, and that one of the most important installations was at Peenemünde on the Baltic coast. By late June the War Cabinet had decided that the site must be destroyed by bombing and called on Bomber Command to mount a large-scale attack at the earliest opportunity. Harris requested a delay so that the longer autumn nights would favour the bombers, and also give the Command time to work out a suitable plan. In the event, this plan was to be one of the most complex yet devised and it was to include a number of novel features, including the use of a Master Bomber, the role being performed by Group Captain John Searby of No 83 Squadron.

A force of 596 bombers, over half being Lancasters, converged on Peenemünde on this moonlit night, their routeing having been devised to confuse the German defences as to the true nature of the target. It was essential that the target be destroyed; without the Master Bomber and the use of backers-up it is doubtful if this would have been achieved. The original markers went down a little off the aiming points but this was soon corrected and the factory and experimental station received the brunt of the attack. Flight Lieutenant Shaw was skipper of Lancaster DS677 of No 426 Squadron: 'Excellent visibility and green TI markers guided this aircraft to the target. Ruden Island turning point was plainly marked with green TIs and bombing was done with green TIs in the bombsight. The whole peninsula wall appeared ablaze and smoke was rising to 4,000 feet. Bombed at 0036 from 8,000 feet, diverted to Newmarket on return.'

Forty aircraft were lost, most of them from the final wave which was hit by night fighters racing to the area once the bombing had started. This is often recorded as the first operational use by the night fighters of the upward-firing cannon known as 'schräge Musik' (jazz music), although ORS had been discussing the existence of these weapons for some time. It was certainly a devastating method of attacking the bombers. The night fighter would slide into position in the blind spot below the bomber and close in; the upward-firing cannon would then rip into the belly and wings causing mayhem and often setting the fuel tanks ablaze. Unless the first burst was badly aimed, there would be little chance of escape.

The 'battle' of the decoys continued, the German defence forces devising ever more innovative ways, including imitation TIs, to persuade the Allied bombers to drop their bombs in the middle of nowhere. In theory, these fake TIs were obvious from the colour (although 'they never quite got the red right'), the way they burnt and the pattern; but, in the heat of the moment and the confusion in the target area, some crews did bomb the decoys. If enough bombs fell on the decoys, then that attack would start to take on the visual appearance of a genuine target. The problem of decoy sites and techniques was highlighted at briefing, and Bomb Leaders made a point of ensuring that their boys would not make any mistakes. The Master Bomber technique was one way of countering the decoy problem and ensuring accurate, concentrated bombing even if the TIs were slightly off the aiming point.

As raids increased in scale and accuracy so the problem of 'creepback' also increased. The basic situation was such that a tail up to 8 miles long would form from the aiming point down along the line of approach, the cause of which was bombs going short of the aiming point. It was put down to bomb-aimers not taking enough care in identifying the aiming point (or marker) and dropping their bombs only when this was in the correct position in the bombsight. Estimation of range was very difficult when approaching the target, which was soon a huge blazing mass, and looked much closer than it really was. There was an attitude of mind, not universal and by no means on every sortie, which said that any part of the target was good enough. It seems that most crews at least thought this at one time or another, but for the vast majority it was no more than a passing thought. The determination to identify the aiming point and get the bombs smack on target comes through time after time in crew reports; many flew the target run two or three times until the bomb-aimer was happy that the target was just right—with the added dangers not only of lingering over the defences but also

No 44 Squadron boys, 1943.

Above: Bombs go down on Nuremberg, 27/28 August 1943. [97 Sqn records]

going against the stream of bombers while repositioning.

The recent series of attacks had certainly had an impact on some authoritative German opinion. On 25 August Milch declared: '. . . must decide on priorities . . . only the [Messerschmitt] 110 in sufficient numbers can give us the necessary relief at night . . . our fighters have to hit the enemy hard day and night to force him to abandon the policy of destruction of our arms production. Germany is the real front-line and the mass of fighters must go for home defence . . . the only chance to defeat day and night bombers'.

Others, such as Jeschonnek (Chief of General Staff of the Luftwaffe), were of a different opinion: 'Every four-engined bomber the Western Allies build makes me happy, for we will bring these down just as we brought down the two-engined ones, and the destruction of a four-engined bomber constitutes a much greater loss to the enemy.' It was a view that was shared later by some Western experts (with hindsight) who postulated that an all-Mosquito force would have been more effective, cheaper, and would have suffered far fewer casualties. Goering could see the sense of the argument put forward by Milch and took it to Hitler, in what was probably his last stance against the Führer and in support of his Luftwaffe. Hitler was furious and declared that it was only the offensive that mattered; all effort should be put into offensive systems.

Yet another Allied Commanders' Conference, this time at Quebec in August 1943, brought renewed discussion on the best way to pursue the air offensive. In essence there was nothing new from the Quadrant Conference, the directive which was issued on 3 September: 'The progressive destruction of the German military, industrial and economic system, the disruption of vital elements of lines of communication, and the material reduction of German air combat strength by the successful prosecution of the Combined Bomber Offensive from all convenient bases is a pre-requisite to "Overlord". This operation must therefore continue to have the highest strategic priority.'

To Bomber Command this meant business as usual. The problem was that business as usual was becoming harder and harder, and the rising toll of casualties was having a serious effect on the front-line strength and experience level of the Command; even Bennett was complaining that the experience level of the crews being sent to the PFF had dropped in recent months. An attack on Berlin on the night of 23/24 August cost 56 aircraft from the 727 taking part, a loss rate of 7.9 per cent. The Halifax units had suffered particularly badly, losing nearly 10 per cent of their number, including six out of 34 PFF aircraft. The 121 Stirlings of the third wave lost sixteen of their number (13 per cent loss). It was estimated that at least 33 of the bombers were shot down by fighters, 20 of them over the target area itself, most of the others being lost on the inbound route. The German fighters were ordered to land just after midnight because of fog at their bases and this probably reduced the number of losses among the last wave of attackers (2.5 per cent loss as against an average of 7 per cent for the other waves). Many of the flak losses were put down to aircraft straying off course and falling foul of defended areas such as Bremen. The fighters were being given a running commentary by ground control:

2133—Bombers approaching Amsterdam
2155—Bombers flying east; orbit searchlight beacons
2217—Bombers approaching Bremen
2238—Berlin is possible target
2304—All fighters proceed to Berlin
2332—Bombers over Berlin

In this way the controller could keep his options open. All the fighters would know where the bomber stream was at any given time and could keep pace with it. As soon as a fighter found the bomber stream, often aided by other fighters dropping flares or markers, it could use either its electronic aids or glare (searchlight, moonlight, target fire) to pick up individual bombers. Multiple kills became quite common, three or more bombers falling to the same fighter in a single night. The bomber stream was so concentrated that once the fighter had found it there was a plethora of targets.

It was a similar story a few nights later, on 31 August, when 7.6 per cent of the 622 bombers were lost, the Stirlings suffering a staggering 16 per cent from their 106 aircraft. A third raid on the 'Big City' three nights after that confirmed that the German defences were simply too strong, 22 of the 316 Lancasters falling to the defences. Attacks on Leverkusen (1.1 per cent loss), Nuremberg (4.9 per cent) and Monchengladbach (3.8 per cent) indicated that Berlin was a particularly tough nut.

It had been a severe lesson. True, losses against other targets in Germany had been somewhat lower, nearer to the 'acceptable' average of 4 per cent, but the overall conclusion was the same—the defenders were starting to win the battle. Bomber Command would have to develop new tactics and ideas or would simply bleed away. The experiment with the 'Serrate'-equipped Beaufighters appeared to have been a failure. By September 233 sorties had been flown, giving rise to 1,180 'Serrate' contacts of which 108 were converted to AI which led to 30 visual sightings resulting in 20 combats. Total claims were for thirteen enemy aircraft destroyed, for the loss of three Beaufighters. However, it was made clear in all the reports that the problem did not lie with the equipment or tactic but in the Beaufighter's lack of performance.

Extract from logbook of Tom Treadwell, a bomb-aimer with No 77 Squadron.

As before, there were two distinct areas for consideration: improve the tactical plan to avoid the defences or counteract the defences by passive (electronic deception) or active (shoot down the fighters) methods. Planning for raids had always been a complex business, especially since 1942 with the adoption of concentration in time and space, and attempts to keep the enemy guessing until the last moment. This whole area of tactical planning was revised again and ever greater and more complex deception plans were included in the schedule for an operation. If the fighters could be drawn away to the wrong target, then perhaps losses could be kept down. Unfortunately, Main Force strength was not sufficient to make splitting of the bomber stream a truly viable option, although small-scale feints and 'spoof' (diversionary) raids might prove successful. In September the 'Bullseye' exercise was introduced whereby training units undertook flights which would appear to the enemy early warning radar controllers like the start of a bombing raids. As the tracks developed, but at a very late stage, the aircraft would turn around and go back towards Britain, but by that time, hopefully, the damage had been done. The 'Bullseyes' were also simulated missions since they gave the trainee crew all

Date	Hour.	Aircraft Type and No.	Pilot.	Duty.	REMARKS (including results of bombing, gunnery exercises, etc.).	Flying Times. Day.	Night.
					Time carried forward :—	114.540	114.15
2.8.43	23.35	HALIFAX II JB 963	F/SGT DAFFEY	BOMB AIMER	OPS HAMBURG		5.20
12.8.43	21.00	HALIFAX II JB 839	F/SGT DAFFEY	BOMB AIMER	OPS MILAN LANDED ODIHAM		8.45
13.8.43	15.25	HALIFAX II JB 839	F/SGT DAFFEY	BOMB AIMER	ODIHAM - BASE	1.15	
17.8.43	20.55	HALIFAX II JB 963	F/SGT DAFFEY	BOMB AIMER	OPS. PEENEMUNDE LANDED WELLSBOURNE		7.40
18.8.43	11.45	HALIFAX II JB 963	F/SGT DAFFEY	BOMB AIMER	WELLSBOURNE - BASE	1.0	
22.8.43	20.55	HALIFAX II JB 963	F/SGT DAFFEY	BOMB AIMER	OPS. LEVERKUSEN		5.20
23.8.43	20.15	HALIFAX II JB 963	F/SGT DAFFEY	BOMB AIMER	OPS. BERLIN 3 ENGINES. DAFFEY - D.F.M.		7.45
26.8.43	13.45	HALIFAX II JB 963	F/SGT DAFFEY	BOMB AIMER	AIR TEST	30	
26.8.43	22.30	HALIFAX II JD 371	F/SGT DAFFEY	BOMB AIMER	CIRCUITS AND BUMPS		1.05
27.8.43	21.00	HALIFAX II DT643	F/SGT DAFFEY	BOMB AIMER	OPS. NUREMBURG LANDED WING		7.15
					TOTAL TIME	148.25	157.25

'THE 100 SQUADRON BOYS'

Squadron life, and squadron songs, were an essential part of the picture; they bound everyone together with a sense of purpose and belonging. This No 100 Squadron song was fairly typical of the many 'created' by Bomber Command units:

[Air: 'McNamara's Band']

1. We are 100 Squadron—we're the boys who know the score,
If anyone denies it we will spread him on the floor,
At bombing and beer and billiards and all the Cleethorpe's Hops,
We have got the gen—we're the leading men—we certainly are
the tops.

CHORUS
While the bombs go bang and the flak bursts clang and the
searchlights blaze away,
We weave all over the starlit sky
And wish we'd gone by day.
Pattison, Pattison save us now
We can't abide the noise.
A credit to Butch Harris, the 100 Squadron boys.

2. Oh we love to nip in smartly to a little buzz bomb site,
And smartly nip off home again and get to bed at night.
We're saving our night vision up for other earthly joys,
And now we're safely in the Mess, meet the 100 Squadron boys.

3. My name is William Irving, and I'm from the Middle East
And what you think about me here, I don't care in the least
I'm in command of 'A' Flight though you may no think it so,
There is not a pub in Lincolnshire or a WAAF that I don't know.

4. My name is Harry Hamilton, I'm an unpretentious Scot,
And although in a way I have little to say I sometimes think a lot.
If you ask my crew if I have any faults, they'll tell you in accents
sweet
You can see the ants as I stooge over France at altitude *zero feet*.

5. My name is Traff and I joined the RAF—well pretty near the start,
My trade is navigation, but I'm a bit of a wolf at heart.
I've a popsy here and a popsy there and I don't care if they're wed
So long as their husbands don't come home and find me still
in bed.

[6, 7, 8: more of the same!]

9. I'm Otto (Bang on the Target) Towers, and many an aiming point
Was chalked up to my credit over many a Nazi joint.
But now I'm in semi-retirement and whenever the red light blinks
I set off on my bike on a local strike—and will till the lifeboat
sinks.'

the planning and flying tasks of a typical mission; many of these exercises were just that and not part of the operational plan, simply being simulated operations involving friendly searchlight and fighter opposition.

Late summer saw Bomber Command operating at high intensity with major attacks throughout Germany, plus 'one-off' missions such as that of 8/9 September against the long-range gun batteries at Boulogne. This latter mission included participation, in the night attack, by American B-17s. Since the Dams Raid, No 617 Squadron had been something of a specialist unit, undertaking precision attacks and experimental work. On 14/15 September the squadron was tasked to attack the Dortmund–Ems canal with the new 12,000lb bomb. On this particular occasion they were recalled because of weather, but went again the following night, only to lose five out of eight aircraft without causing significant damage to the target.

Despite the heavy losses morale on the squadrons remained high. In many ways the life of a Bomber Command aircrew member was a strange one. Unlike the soldier in the field (or desert or jungle), he went to war from the peace, security and relative comfort of a well-established airfield to face danger and hardship for a few hours; then to return to England, with perhaps a trip down to the squadron's pub or a night at a local dance—but always with the knowledge that the skies of Germany would soon call again. And next time, would *his* aircraft be the one that 'Failed to Return', would it be *his* personal effects that were quickly and quietly removed from the room, a new face then to appear in his place? So many faces did not reappear, they were gone—so what! Pass another beer and sing another song. It was an attitude of mind that few other than operational aircrew could understand; it made them appear hard and indifferent, yet it was the only defence against mental collapse. It would always happen to the other fellow, and if it did not—well, enjoy it while you can. By no means all Bomber Command airfields were well equipped and comfortable, although the pre-war permanent stations were usually quite good. Many of the airfields built during the war were far more basic and elicited a variety of uncomplimentary statements from aircrew and groundcrew. Conditions at the dispersal points were often harsh, and the winters in the early 1940s were some of the most severe on record.

The most frequently visited target during this period was Hannover. The raid of 22/23 September saw the introduction of a new tactic. In an effort to reduce losses a 'spoof' raid was mounted to confuse the defences and allow the main attack a free run. The 'spoof' raid by 21 Lancasters and eight Mosquitoes, all from No 8 Group, used 'Window' and flares in an attack on Oldenburg—to try to make themselves look like the Main Force. Meanwhile, 711 aircraft went to Hannover. The raid was not a great success but the loss rate of 3.7 per cent was an improvement over previous weeks. A raid on the same target a few weeks later, on 8/9 October, saw the final departure from Main Force attacks of the work-horse of Bomber Command—the Wellington. The previous night the target had been Stuttgart and included in the force of 343 Lancasters were aircraft from No 101 Squadron with their highly secret ABC ('Airborne Cigar') equipment to jam the German night fighter frequencies. These aircraft carried an additional crew member, a fluent German-speaker whose job was to listen to the German night fighter frequencies and select those to jam using the transmitters carried on the

THE WILL TO GO ON?

Throughout the war there were instances of aircrew who had lost their nerve and had to be withdrawn from flying. This was usually referred to as LMF (Lack of Morale Fibre), but was often a much more complex problem—'Fear was a subject that was never talked about except perhaps in a jocular manner after a few beers, yet it was present to a varying extent in each one of us. Normally the feeling was just bottled up.'

In May 1941 there was an attempt to codify the procedure to be taken in respect of these 'W' (Waverer) cases of individuals, 'whose conduct may cause them to forfeit the confidence of their Commanding Officer in their determination and reliability in the face of danger'. There were seen to be two categories of individual: those who maintained a show of carrying out their duties, and those who simply refused to. It was no light matter to declare that you were not able to go back on another operation. The first feeling was that the crew was being let down; this thought alone was enough to make many think again and once more hide their individual fear. If the feeling was too strong, or the 'powers that be' became aware of it, then the situation was still kept at an informal level within the squadron, with the Flight Commander and Squadron Commander trying to persuade, in some cases cajole, the individual into carrying on. Once it became obvious that nothing would change the decision, then it became imperative to remove the individual from the squadron and his usual circle of contacts—to prevent 'contamination'. The Medical Officer would become involved and made his report as the matter was referred to Group and the individual posted away as soon as possible. From mid-1941 loss of the flying brevet became automatic.

It may seem a harsh system but in truth it was not. Every effort was made to try to persuade the man to return to flying, with no stigma attached. Only when this was of no avail did the system take harder action, with the intention of protecting the rest of the squadron and preventing a general collapse—although such an event seems unlikely to have resulted, even in the darkest days of winter 1943/44. Considering the many thousands of young men who flew on these hazardous missions, in full knowledge of their chances of survival, the problem was very small-scale. Certainly, all were afraid at times; it is remarkable that so many had the will to go on—and on.

aircraft. This jamming of the VHF control frequencies was very effective and remained an essential element in the RCM conflict. Prior to the employment of ABC most RCM work had been conducted by ground-based stations in Britain with associated problems of range, the main devices used being 'Ground Grocer' (April 1943), 'Ground Cigar' (July 1943) and 'Corona' (October 1943). Airborne equipments such as 'Mandrel', to interfere with early warning radars, and 'Tinsel' (and 'Special Tinsel'), to disrupt radio transmissions, had been employed with mixed success since late 1942.

Throughout the summer various new electronic aids, mainly for jamming elements of the German defence network, had been introduced. This electronic war had become so complex, and so vital, that the decision was taken to incorporate the main effort within a specialized force. On 23 November No 100 (Special Duties) Group came into being, under the command of Air Vice-Marshal Addison of No 80 Wing. The new Group was given four main tasks:

Below left: Aircrew of No 77 Squadron smile after the op has been scrubbed! [Tom Treadwell]

Above and below: Wellingtons of No 30 OTU being prepared for a leaflet-dropping sortie, September 1943.

1. Give direct support to night bombing and other operations by attacks on enemy night fighter aircraft in the air or by attacks on ground installations.

2. Employ airborne and ground RCM equipment to deceive or jam enemy radio navigation aids, enemy radar systems and certain wireless signals.

3. Examine all intelligence on the offensive and defensive radar, radio and signalling systems of the enemy, with a view of future action within the scope of the above.

4. Provide immediate information, additional to normal intelligence information, as to the movements and employment of enemy fighter aircraft to enable the tactics of the bomber force to be modified to meet any changes.

In November the Beaufighter-equipped No 141 Squadron moved to West Raynham to become part of the new Group. As a 'Serrate'-equipped unit it was to continue the roving fighter role it had been performing since the summer. Trouble was still being experienced with the special equipment and the crews had doubts as

Lucky charms played an important part for many aircrew. [51 Sqn records]

to the effectiveness of their aircraft. On 19 November Beaufighter V8799 (Flight Lieutenant Macandrew and Flying Officer Wilk) were tasked to patrol Bonn-Hangelar: 'Two distant "Serrate" contacts to the NE were ignored; one contact followed by AI contact at 19,000 feet near Aachen but enemy aircraft worked into a stern position and a 30-minute dogfight ensued. Followed enemy aircraft down to 3,000 feet before

Servicing a Lancaster. Groundcrew took great pride in looking after 'their' aircraft. Note the Goering quote 'No enemy aircraft will fly over the Reich territory', painted above the bomb doors.

THE ELECTRONIC WAR

The electronic aspects of the Bomber Command offensive were both complex and fascinating. The main period of RCM (Radio Counter-Measures) was from 1943 onwards with the formation of the specialist No 100 (Bomber Support) Group, but various aspects of the electronic war had been in place from the early months of the war. It was very much a game of move and counter-move and it was new, there being no previous experience to build on.

Up until 1941 the major British use of RCM had been to counter German bombing beams, with little thought being given to 'offensive' uses of electronic warfare. With the seizing of a 'Freya' radar in the daring Bruneval raid of February 1942, the British scientists had more solid data with which to proceed towards a true jamming system to disrupt the German radars. At the same time, Bomber Command was becoming concerned as to increasing losses and any system to reduce these losses would receive its support. 1942 saw a number of developments with the introduction of jamming systems such as 'Mandrel' and 'Tinsel'. An important element of RCM was discovering what the enemy was doing and ELINT (Electronic Intelligence) requirements expanded.

Throughout 1943 new systems were introduced to jam/spoof air and ground radars and ground-to-air communications (especially night fighter control frequencies); most of the ground-based systems were under the control of No 80 Wing. With the introduction of an AI-homer to the Beaufighter, active RCM could begin—hunting down the enemy fighters. For some time the bombers had carried warning systems to indicate the presence of enemy aircraft; it was a mixed blessing as the Germans developed a homer. The formation of No 100 Group in November 1943 at last provided a co-ordinated effort that played a significant part in the Bomber Command offensive, albeit a contribution that is hard to quantify. Throughout the remainder of the war the RCM battle became ever more complex as more systems entered service and No 100 Group acquired a wider range of tasks, and an increasing number of squadrons. One

commentator concluded that 'the combination of jamming and deception allowed Bomber Command to continue its offensive when a head-on battle of attrition would have destroyed it'.

PRINCIPAL SYSTEMS

'Airborne Cigar' (ABC): To jam R/T control frequencies
'Ground Cigar': As above
'Airborne Grocer': To jam FuG 202 and 212 AI radars
'Ground Grocer': To jam AI
'American Mandrel': To jam early warning radars such as 'Freya'
'Carpet': To jam 'Würzburg' GCI and gun-laying radars
'Corona': Ground voice jam of nightfighter R/T control
'Dartboard': Similar to above
'Drumstick': Ground jam HF W/T
'Jostle': To jam R/T
'Big Ben Jostle': To jam V-2 control beam
'Mandrel': To jam EW radars such as 'Freya'
'Piperack': Radar jammer
'Shiver': To jam GCI and gun-laying radars
'Tinsel': To jam night fighter R/T
'Tuba': To jam EW
'Boozer': Warning system to indicate illumination by enemy radars: e.g., three-light system: dull red = 'Würzburg' GCI, bright red = 'Würzburg' gun-laying, yellow = AI
'Monica': Warning system
'Fishpond': Warning system (also known as 'Mousetrap')
'Perfectos': Homing on to German IFF
'Serrate': Homing on to German AI

No 101 Squadron Lancaster ME590 after the Augsburg raid, 26 February 1944. Note ABC aerials. [101 Sqn records]

abandoning the chase near Eindhoven. During the descent the enemy aircraft was able to get into stern position three times and Beaufighter evaded only with difficulty.'

Another of the new aids to enter service around this time was 'G–H', which had its operational debut against factories in Düsseldorf on the night of 3/4 November. Post-raid photography showed that 90 per cent of the bombs, all of which had been dropped blind using the system, had fallen within the target area, exceeding the accuracy predictions made for 'G–H'. The system was not new in that it had been proposed at the same time that 'Gee' was being looked at; this 'H' system would, in theory, have better accuracy than 'Gee' but would be limited, like 'Oboe', in the number of aircraft which could use it at any one time. What transpired, therefore, was in effect a 'reverse Oboe' whereby an aircraft transmitted to mobile stations to get its information for fixes. More aircraft could use the system in a given time, but it depended heavily on the aircrew for accuracy.

On the same night a Lancaster pilot of No 61 Squadron, Flight Lieutenant Bill Reid, won the VC for his courage and leadership during the Düsseldorf raid.

November also saw the opening moves in what was to turn out to be the greatest concerted strategic air offensive yet mounted by Bomber Command—the Battle of Berlin. The winter of struggle was about to begin.

Above: No 199 Squadron Stirling III. Just visible around the airframe are some of the various aerials which made this an effective radio counter-measures (RCM) aircraft. [Peter Green]

Below: Les Bartlett with his No 50 Squadron Lancaster. Note the 'Monica' aerial below the rear turret. [Les Bartlett]

CHAPTER SEVEN

A Winter of Struggle

BY LATE 1943 Bomber Command was a force capable of causing massive destruction deep into the heart of Nazi Germany. However, the last months of the year proved to be the most difficult phase of bombing yet carried out.

The winter of 1943–44 provided the first opportunity consistently to operate large forces over distant targets in central Germany, including Berlin. This was a very different proposition from attacking targets in the Ruhr and western Germany. For these raids to be successful, two conditions had to be fulfilled. First, the bomb load had to be concentrated around selected aiming points and, second, the loss rate had to be maintained at an economical level.

Harris believed that the war might be brought to a close by one final onslaught from the air. He felt that if the US 8th Army Air Force were to join with Bomber Command in one major offensive, then it would bring about the downfall of Nazi Germany, thus saving a prolonged land offensive. In a minute to Winston Churchill on 3 November Harris wrote: 'We can wreck Berlin from end to end if the USAAF will come in on it. It will cost between 400–500 aircraft. It will cost Germany the war.' However, none of his expectations actually occurred. First, the Americans were not interested in bombing Berlin by day as it would have proved too heavy in casualties in the absence of long-range fighter escort. Secondly, the actual loss rate proved higher than anticipated—over 500 aircraft from Bomber Command alone. Finally, the offensive did not destroy Berlin, nor did it bring about the defeat of Germany.

THE BATTLE OF BERLIN

Three attacks against the German capital had taken place in August and September 1943, causing widespread damage and evacuation. The raids served many purposes, including testing the reaction time and co-ordination of the German night fighter force. During the next few weeks, Harris decided that the time was right for an all-out offensive. German morale was supposedly low, the war against Russia was not going well and, in the south, Italy had turned against the Germans.

The Battle of Berlin began in earnest in November 1943. From early Bomber Command studies, it is clear that a long and arduous fight was expected and, in view of the importance of the target and strengthened enemy defences, an increasing loss rate as the battle continued

was not considered unreasonable. From the studies, this is evident from the continued build-up of German home defences. The information stated was based on known numbers of German Air Force units deployed in Germany and in Occupied Territories: heavy guns—7,941; light/medium guns—12,684; searchlights—6,880; barrage balloons—2,256. At that time no detailed information of Army and Naval flak units was available, but in view of opposition to strategic air attack it was estimated that 15 per cent should be added to figures in respect of heavy and light guns and 10 per cent in respect of searchlights.

Phase I: 18 November–3 December
At the beginning of the offensive, Bomber Command was divided into six Groups comprising 57 heavy-bomber squadrons. Over half of the squadrons were equipped with the Halifax or Stirling, both types with performance limitations. This resulted in heavy losses and several squadrons were withdrawn, leaving the Lancaster squadrons to bear the brunt of the battle in its later stages.

18/19 November: More than 400 Lancasters were detailed to attack Berlin, with a second force tasked to attack Ludwigshafen. The Berlin force flew out over the North Sea and across the Dutch coast; the weather was not as clear as expected and the forecast winds proved unreliable. A combination of poor H2S sets and bad weather led to most of the Pathfinders failing to drop their markers. The Main Force bombed the general area of the city but bombs were scattered and damage was virtually impossible to assess. Fighter opposition over the target was slight, but flak was very heavy. The long return route was south from Berlin, then south of the heavily defended area of the Ruhr, across Belgium and northern France and across the Channel. The result of the first night of the new offensive was, generally, a failure due mainly to problems associated with the weather and the technique of blind marking.

22/23 November: The weather forecast was almost perfect for the operation. Harris decided to make the most of the advantages and ordered a maximum effort. The total of 764 aircraft detailed for Berlin that night was a record for this phase of the offensive. The route was near-direct, allowing for increased bomb loads. The weather proved to be worse than expected, although this resulted in many German night fighters being grounded. Initial assessment of the raid was difficult, due to the cloud cover, but the raid later proved to be an outstanding success. The return route was around the city to the south and straight back home. This raid was the first real success of the offensive, due largely to excellent marking by the Pathfinders and accurate bombing by the Main Force. However, the Stirlings suffered heavy losses in both serviceability and casualty rate. Harris therefore ordered the withdrawal of the Stirlings from bombing raids over Germany.

23/24 November: In view of the success of the previous night, Harris ordered another raid by a force mainly of Lancasters. There were problems, however, in preparing a force which had only just returned from the previous night and fewer than 400 aircraft were dispatched. The rush in preparing aircraft for the raid led to a large number of technical problems. The target was again covered by cloud; nevertheless accurate blind marking by the Pathfinders and accurate bombing by the Main Force led to a successful result.

26/27 November: This night 443 Lancasters were dispatched, with a second force detailed to attack Stuttgart as a diversionary raid. The route taken to Berlin was across the Channel and Belgium and, once past Frankfurt, the bomber stream divided north-east for Berlin and south for Stuttgart. The weather over Berlin was generally clear. Accurate marking led to accurate bombing by the Main Force and resulted in a successful raid. The route home was direct across Germany and Holland, but the bombers faced further problems on arriving back over England. Everywhere south of Yorkshire was covered in mist and fog, causing most aircraft to be diverted to bases in Yorkshire or even further afield. Many were forced to attempt landings in fog further south due to being short of fuel. Nearly 30 Lancasters crashed or crash-landed, resulting in several crews being killed. The result of the night's effort was mixed. The diversionary raid against Stuttgart had proved to be successful, causing confusion among the German defences and probably reducing the number of casualties on the Berlin raid. However, 28 Lancasters were lost, plus many more on returning home, demonstrating a continuing rise in losses during the offensive.

2/3 December: This raid was planned to be a maximum effort. However, fog at the Yorkshire airfields meant that most of the Halifax units did not take part. 458 aircraft were dispatched, but many turned back due to

A hard winter made it even more difficult to keep aircraft availability rates up.

severe icing encountered over the North Sea. The bad weather continued all the way to the target, causing the bombers to become scattered. Also, German fighters were up in strength. All this led to the raid being a failure. More bombers were lost on the return journey, ending a miserable night for Bomber Command. The official result of the raid was very disappointing and damage to Berlin was slight.

Berlin was well protected not only with active defences of searchlights, flak and nearby night fighters, but also by a comprehensive series of decoy sites. One of the main sites at Nauen (15 miles north-west of the city) covered an area of over 9 square miles and was fully equipped with buildings, industrial complexes and an array of pyrotechnic devices to simulate all aspects of the Berlin defences—and the various stages of an attack. This site, and others around the city, comprised a complex and effective deception that took much of the bombing weight from the Bomber Command raids. These decoy sites were not always successful and they never fooled all the crews, but every bomb load wasted on a site was a victory to the defenders. Few crews recall much about these decoy sites, other than the fact that they were mentioned at briefing and 'did not appear to be effective as they were too obviously fakes'. Statistics do not quite agree with this statement (see Table 1).

As the initial phase of the battle came to an end many questions were being raised. The Allied Commander

By late 1943 the Lancaster was becoming a major element within Main Force. Shown here is an aircraft of No 50 Squadron.

conferences at Teheran and Cairo at the end of 1943 had proposed changes in the offensive, including a complete reorganization of the American strategic bomber forces, although maintaining the 'Germany first' principle. Harris and Eaker had feared a reduction in the impetus of their campaigns but both were determined to persist with their policies; for Harris this meant that the campaign against Berlin had to be successful. The initial analysis was not good and the arguments raged as to the best way forward.

Harris had no doubts and outlined his views in a letter of 7 December. In this he ran through Bomber Command's recent achievements in terms of the destruction, by percentage of area, of certain German industrial cities. From this he concluded that his Command could achieve, by April 1944, 'a state of devastation in which surrender is inevitable'. The consideration for this victory was that he should be given priority of production in certain areas, such as Lancaster production, and equipment to make No 100 Group fully operational. As a final comment he added that 'any delay, against the ever-increasing defences of Germany, is likely to prove fatal'. The idea of victory without a costly invasion of Europe had great appeal. This suggestion caused uproar in certain circles. Bottomley sent a strongly worded reply on 23 December, concluding: 'I am to emphasize the fact that your night bombing forces would make the greatest contribution by completely destroying those vital centres which can be reached by day only at heavy cost; examples are Schweinfurt, Leipzig and centres of the twin-engined fighter industry'. Harris was not impressed by such 'intervention'.

Phase II: 16 December–3 January

Following the last disappointment, there were no further raids to Berlin for two weeks.

16/17 December: Harris ordered a further attack on the city to make the most of a favourable weather forecast which predicted fog over the German night fighter airfields. The fog did in fact keep many of the German fighters on the ground, but not all, and several bombers

The Battle of Berlin was fought mainly by the Lancasters, although some raids included major participation by Halifax units.

were shot down en route to the target. Having reached the target, conditions were favourable for the bombers and the bombing by the Main Force proved successful. The return route was north of Berlin, across Denmark and the North Sea. Unfortunately, weather at many of the bomber bases was not good and several aircraft either crashed or were abandoned by their crews. Records show that this raid was a success, although a total of 54 aircraft were lost out of the 493 dispatched.

23/24 December: A longer more southerly route was planned, with fewer bombers than normal dispatched. This resulted in the smallest tonnage of bombs dropped since the offensive began. The German night fighters scored little success and the Main Force arrived over Berlin in favourable conditions. Unfortunately, the favourable conditions were not taken advantage of. Damage to the target area was slight. This raid was not considered one of Bomber Command's most effective attacks against Berlin.

29/30 December: Harris, once again, ordered a max-

Above: Halifax I L9530 of No 76 Squadron. [76 Sqn records]

**Below: The daily struggle to keep aircraft serviceable—
Halifax overhaul.**

imum effort against Berlin. Over 700 aircraft were dispatched including over 250 Halifaxes, the first time that a large force of Halifaxes had been used against Berlin for over a month. The route was across the North Sea and Holland, towards Leipzig and north-east to Berlin. The route and diversionary raids confused the German defences and the bombers reached Berlin with relative ease. Conditions were generally near-perfect although, for reasons unknown, bombing was scattered and relatively unsuccessful. Perhaps the trepidation of the crews at the prospect of yet another trip to the 'Big City' was having an increasingly adverse effect on their results.

1/2 January 1944: The first night of 1944 began with

Berlin again chosen as the target. It was an all-Lancaster raid of over 400 aircraft, and the route was the familiar direct line across Holland. The bombers were soon engaged by the night fighters, resulted in several aircraft being shot down before reaching the target. Cloud and a strong wind over the target made marking difficult, resulting in scattered and relatively ineffective bombing.

2/3 January: There was no rest for the Lancaster crews as Harris ordered a further attack on Berlin. The route

Left: The intensity of the campaign kept the armourers busy! [RAF Scampton records]

Above: Two 500lb bombs (with comments!) are loaded on to a Stirling, August 1943.

Below: An 8,000lb blast bomb. Note the WAAF driver, carrying out one of the many tasks allotted to women at bomber stations. [83 Sqn records]

TABLE 1: THE BATTLE OF BERLIN*

Date	Aircraft Dispatched		Lancaster		Halifax		Mosquito		Stirling		Bomb tonnage
Phase I											
18/19 November	444	(9)	440	(9)	–		4		–		1,594
22/23 November	764	(26)	469	(11)	234	(10)	11		50	(5)	2,465
23/24 November	383	(20)	365	(20)	10		8		–		1,335
26/27 November	450	(28)	443	(28)	–		7		–		1,576
2/3 December	458	(40)	425	(37)	15	(2)	18	(1)	–		1,686
Totals	**2,499**	**(123)**	**2,142**	**(105)**	**259**	**(12)**	**48**	**(1)**	**50**	**(5)**	**8,656**
Phase II											
16/17 December	493	(25)	483	(25)	–		10		–		1,815
23/24 December	379	(16)	364	(16)	?		8		–		1,288
29/30 December	712	(20)	457	(11)	252	(9)	3		–		2,315
1/2 January	421	(28)	421	(28)	–		–		–		1,401
2/3 January	383	(27)	362	(27)	9		12		–		1,116
Totals	**2,388**	**(116)**	**2,087**	**(107)**	**268**	**(9)**	**33**		**–**		**7,935**
Phase III											
20/21 January	769	(35)	495	(13)	264	(22)	10		–		2,401
27/28 January	530	(33)	515	(33)	–		15		–		1,761
28/29 January	677	(46)	432	(20)	241	(26)	4		–		1,954
30/31 January	534	(33)	440	(32)	82	(1)	12		–		1,961
Totals	**2,510**	**(147)**	**1,882**	**(98)**	**587**	**(49)**	**41**		**–**		**8,077**
Phase IV											
15/16 February	891	(43)	561	(26)	314	(17)	16		–		2,643
24/25 March	811	(72)	577	(44)	216	(28)	18		–		2,493
Totals	**1,702**	**(115)**	**1,138**	**(70)**	**530**	**(45)**	**34**		**–**		**5,136**
Grand totals	**9,099**	**(501)**	**7,249**	**(380)**	**1,644**	**(115)**	**156**	**(1)**	**50**	**(5)**	**29,804**

*Losses are shown in parentheses.

was, once again, virtually direct. Several night fighters scored early successes and by the time the force reached Berlin nearly one-third of the Pathfinders dispatched had either returned to base early or been shot down. For the remainder, marking proved difficult. The result was scattered bombing with no specific damage. This was an even more disappointing raid than the previous one in terms of losses and damage inflicted on Berlin.

This brought to a close a series of unsuccessful raids against Berlin. The reasons for the lack of success are not particularly obvious, although the long transits in severe weather conditions in the middle of winter must have been a factor. Also, to have little rest between operations would have pushed the bomber crews to the limits of their capabilities. Although German defences proved to be strong on occasion, they were no stronger than during earlier raids on Berlin; so they alone could not have been a major factor. Weather over the target was not favourable on many occasions and made marking difficult. The fact that the Pathfinders suffered heavy casualties had two major effects on results achieved during this phase of the offensive. First, fewer Pathfinders actually reached the target area; therefore fewer markers were dropped, making the task of the Main Force much more difficult. Second, the experi-

enced crews lost were not always being replaced by crews with the same amount of experience.

The decision by Harris to withdraw the Halifaxes from all but one of the raids during this phase led to fewer bombs being dropped on the target. It was also noticeable that the number of aircraft dispatched for each raid, apart from one maximum effort, reduced steadily during this phase of operations. Finally, morale among the crews of Bomber Command had begun to suffer in the face of high losses for little positive result.

Phase III: 20–31 January

From Bomber Command studies, it is apparent that by this stage of the offensive less than 25 per cent of Berlin was estimated to have been devastated. This figure compares less favourably with other major cities at that time: Hamburg—70 per cent devastated; Wuppertal—70 per cent; Mannheim—55 per cent; Hannover—55 per cent; Düsseldorf—40 per cent; Essen—40 per cent; and Dortmund—33 per cent. To increase the pressure on Berlin, Harris clearly had to bring more aircraft into his plans; the Halifax squadrons had to rejoin the offensive. He also had more Mosquitoes available and more Pathfinder Lancasters were equipped with H2S Mk III sets.

20/21 January: This new phase began with Harris ordering a maximum effort of 769 aircraft. With the lessons learnt from the last unsuccessful raids on Berlin, the decision was made to do away with the direct-line approach to the target. Due to cloud cover over the target area, it was virtually impossible to assess the raid. German night fighters achieved much success during the outbound and return transits. Of the 35 bombers lost on this raid, 22 were Halifaxes.

27/28 January: In view of the losses suffered by the Halifaxes during the previous raid, Harris decided to leave them out for this next raid. 515 Lancasters were dispatched and, once again, took an indirect route to the target. Night fighter activity was slight on the way to the target and the bombers reached Berlin without serious mishap. The target was covered by cloud but marking was observed to be fairly accurate with the Main Force producing good results. Unfortunately, several losses resulted during the return flight. The raid was assessed to have caused reasonable damage to Berlin.

28/29 January: There was no rest for the crews as Harris ordered another maximum effort raid with more diversionary raids and support operations. The route was a long northerly transit across Denmark and south-east to Berlin, returning the same way. The route proved to be too far north for many of the night fighters. Several

combats, however, took place when the Main Force reached Berlin. Despite the fierce air activity, the Pathfinders carried out very accurate marking, bringing, generally, very good results. The long return flight against strengthening headwinds, in severe icing conditions, resulted in several aircraft being lost on the way home. This raid, without doubt, was a success although losses to Bomber Command were heavy; no fewer than 46 aircraft were lost, with several more crashing on returning home.

30/31 January: After just one night of rest, the crews of Bomber Command prepared themselves for another onslaught. This was the third raid in four nights against Berlin. The route was the familiar northern one across Denmark, but the return flight was direct, allowing a greater bomb load to be carried. The weather was thick cloud with severe icing which caused problems for the German night fighters, although combats did take place

Below: A No 75 Squadron Stirling crew pose with bombs and aircraft; note the 'V' on the nearest bomb.

Right: OTU Wellingtons continued the leaflet-dropping role as part of their operational training.

Below right: Mosquitoes of the Light Night Striking Force gave the German defences a major problem.

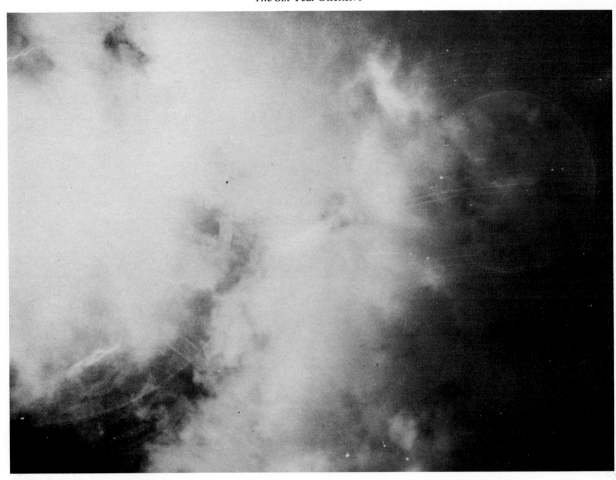

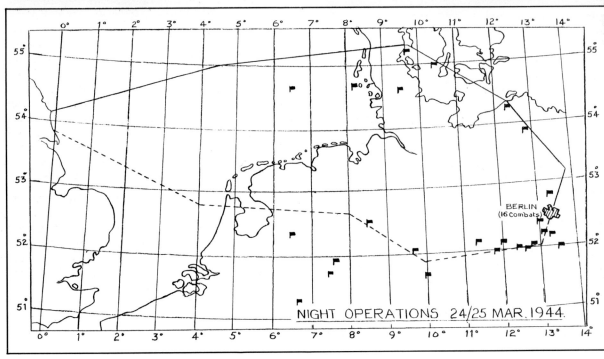

NIGHT OPERATIONS 24/25 MAR.1944.

BERLIN
(16 Combats)

Left: Over Berlin, 24/25 March 1944.

Right: F/O Cowling in his Lancaster of No 619 Squadron, 1944. [F. Slater]

as the bombers neared the target, resulting in several bombers being shot down. Thick cloud over the target area made raid assessment difficult although it is believed that severe damage was caused to the city. Again the losses proved to be high with 33 aircraft lost.

Despite these losses, the damage to Berlin was now significant and the effect on the population must have been devastating. The weather during this period was very cold and the scattered bombing left large areas of Berlin in ruins. The four raids during this phase of the offensive can be assessed as, generally, very successful. The fact that the Halifaxes had been brought back into the offensive for three of these raids is significant, as it meant that a greater tonnage was dropped on the city. With the moon making conditions unsuitable for several nights, the crews of Bomber Command were given a well-earned rest.

Phase IV: 15 February–25 March
This period marked the final phase of the Berlin offensive with just two more raids on the city. With a long lay-off from operations, due to the moon and weather, the squadrons had a good opportunity to recover their strength.

15/16 February: The offensive resumed with Harris ordering a maximum effort. Nearly 900 aircraft were dispatched—a record number of aircraft and a record tonnage during the offensive. The route taken was the northern route across Denmark and south-east to Berlin. Numerous combats took place resulting in several bombers being shot down. The target area was covered by cloud making marking difficult, although the concentration of numbers ensured reasonable success by the Main Force. The return journey was virtually direct across the North Sea. It was the heaviest raid on Berlin during the war.

There were several more attempts to continue the offensive against Berlin during the following nights of February, but these were cancelled due to the weather. Other raids were made over the next few weeks against major German cities, but it was more than a month before Harris decided to have one more attempt against Berlin. With the planned Allied invasion of Normandy getting closer, he probably realized that he would be able to have just one final attempt at the city before his forces were diverted to other tasks.

24/25 March: A maximum effort was ordered for this final onslaught. More than 800 aircraft were dispatched by the northern route to the target. The Main Force flew north and then east across Denmark. Unfortunately, wind forecasts had been grossly inaccurate, resulting in the Main Force becoming scattered. The bombers arrived over Berlin at different time intervals instead of being one stream. Those of the Main Force managed to bomb Berlin, but many who had been blown well south had no option other than to release their bombs and turn for home. The route home was mainly direct except for avoiding the Ruhr. It was during the return transit that the majority of the losses for that night were suffered. This raid proved to be a disaster for Bomber Command. No fewer than 72 aircraft (8.9 per cent) were lost, the heaviest proportion during the offensive.

So, the Battle of Berlin was over. Harris's belief that Germany would be defeated by sustained bombing alone against Berlin and other major cities had proved to be inaccurate. Over 9,000 sorties had been flown against Berlin during the offensive. At no stage of the war was a bombing campaign against a single target carried out to the same extent.

Whether or not the Battle of Berlin was successful has been argued ever since. It certainly cost Bomber Command heavier losses than anticipated—more than 500 aircraft during the sixteen raids. However, Berlin was in virtual ruins and the effect that the campaign had on local industry and the morale of the German people may never be known. Statistics alone should not determine the success or failure of the campaign. It had forced Germany into giving yet another boost to the anti-aircraft defences at a time when steel was desperately needed for armour, and had weakened the Luftwaffe in both aircraft and experienced pilots.

The fact that the objectives were never achieved could lead to the assumption that the campaign was not a success. It could also be suggested that the disaster of the final raid led to the campaign ending abruptly for fear of not being able to sustain any further losses on such a large scale. This should not be considered the case as, first, nights were becoming shorter, meaning that bombing targets as far away as Berlin was considered too risky; and, second, Harris realized that Bomber Command's main efforts from then on would be in direct support of preparations for the forthcoming Allied invasion of Normandy.

TIs fall on the Rhône aero-engine works.

Although the Battle of Berlin took much priority throughout the winter, other directives were issued in early 1944. A directive from DCAS to Harris on 14 January stated: 'Attack, as far as practicable, those industrial centres associated with German fighter airframe factories and ball-bearing industry, especially Schweinfurt . . .continue to attack it until it is destroyed or until alternative directions are issued'.

The 'failure' of Bomber Command to mount an immediate raid on any of these targets was a source of irritation to some in the Air Staff, especially Bottomley. Following a heavy raid against Magdeburg on 21/22 January, he asked why the target had not been Brunswick or Leipzig, commenting . . . 'As conditions at these two targets were equally favourable last night, it now appears that the Command is operating to a policy of its own and is disregarding both the policy and the precise instructions for its implementation which have been laid down by the Air Staff'.

This was followed on 28 January by a reinforced directive from the Air Ministry to Bomber Command which stated: 'Maximum effort of strategic bomber forces is to be concentrated upon key installations in the German fighter aircraft industry and ball-bearing industry, and the towns associated with these key installations. For Bomber Command: 1. Schweinfurt. 2. Leipzig. 3. Brunswick. 4. Regensburg. 5. Augsburg. 6. Gotha. For "Oboe" and "Gee-H" attacks—Ja_ger ball-bearing factory, Wuppertal.' It also allowed for 'Crossbow' targets (V-1 launching sites) when weather conditions were unsuited to 'Pointblank' targets. Berlin was given as a final weather option.

Despite these directives aimed at German aircraft manufacturing, it was towards the end of February before Bomber Command attacked any of the targets specifically mentioned in the second directive. Reasons for this are unclear, but it is interesting to note that, from the time the first directive was issued, five out of the next six major efforts were against Berlin, and not against targets specified. Much of the reason lies in the character of Harris, his determination to pursue a primary aim (a sound military precept) and his dislike of certain individuals (such as Bottomley). However, smaller raids of vital importance did take place. On the night of 8/9 February twelve Lancasters of No 617 Squadron attacked an aero-engine factory at Limoges, resulting in a major loss in production at the factory.

A further directive issued from the Air Ministry to Bomber Command on 17 February revised target priorities. It stated: 'Revision of target priorities. Overall mission stays the same. Primary objective stays the same. Other objectives: 1. "Crossbow". 2. Berlin and other important industrial areas.'

Despite the fact that Schweinfurt was listed top priority of the reinforced directive (28 January), it was not until the night of 24/25 February that Harris elected to attack this very important target. Germany's main ball-bearing factories were located in Schweinfurt and had been attacked the previous day by American B-17s. Bomber Command's force of 734 aircraft was divided into two raids separated by two hours. The first wave suffered 22 aircraft lost due mainly to night fighters, but the second wave lost just eleven machines, of which just four were lost to night fighters. The exact success of the raid is unclear as bombing is believed to have been mainly short and Schweinfurt recorded only 'nominal damage'. Incidentally, Leipzig, listed as second priority, had only just been attacked a few nights earlier, on 19/20 February, but with limited success.

As a result of the directive issued on 17 February, listing the revision of target priorities, it was several weeks before large raids were dispatched to attack the V-weapon sites, although minor operations began almost immediately. Attacks against Berlin and other important industrial areas continued for the time being.

A further directive from ACAS (Ops) to Harris on 4 March included: 'Attack the following marshalling

Lancaster crews getting ready to go to Frankfurt on 18 March 1944. 620 'Lancs' were part of the total force of 846 aircraft.

yards using ground markers—to provide planning data and help "Overlord": Trappes, Aulnoye, Le Mans, Amiens/Longeau, Courtrai, Laon.' This directive provided an immediate change of emphasis for Bomber Command in the preparation for the Allied invasion. On the night of 6/7 March marshalling yards at Trappes were attacked, followed, the next night, by a successful attack against rail yards at Le Mans. During the remainder of March several more raids were carried out against marshalling yards at Le Mans (13/14th), Amiens (15/16th and 16/17th), Laon (23/24th), Aulnoye (25/26th), and Courtrai (26/27th).

Other than Berlin, several thousands of tons of bombs were dropped on German cities throughout the winter. Details of the major cities, total aircraft dispatched and total tonnage of bombs dropped in the period December 1943–March 1944 are listed in Table 2.

THE NUREMBERG RAID

For the target on the night of 30/31 March, Harris chose the city of Nuremberg. This choice was an interesting one, as it was an ancient city not known as being of major industrial importance. There were however several small factories around the city and it was a

Target	Dates of raids	Aircraft dispatched	Aircraft losses	Bomb tonnage
Frankfurt	20/21 December, 18/19 and 22/23 March	2,312	96	8,701
Stuttgart	20/21 February, 1/2 and 15/16 March	2,018	50	6,576
Leipzig	3/4 December, 19/20 February	1,350	102	4,006
Schweinfurt	24/25 February	734	33	2,262
Essen	26/27 March	705	9	2,834
Magdeburg	21/22 January	648	57	2,240
Brunswick	14/15 January	498	38	2,226

TABLE 2: BOMBER COMMAND RAIDS, DECEMBER 1943–MARCH 1944

central link in rail and water communications. But any route taken to get to Nuremberg involved passing close to very heavily defended areas. Perhaps one explanation of Harris's choice was to destroy, in one single blow, the shrine of Nazism.

That night, 795 aircraft (572 Lancasters, 214 Halifaxes and 9 Mosquitoes) took off from bases all over England, many never to return. Pilot Officer Les Bartlett, a bomb-aimer with No 50 Squadron at Skellingthorpe, kept a diary throughout his tour of operations. He had just been awarded the Distinguished Flying Medal, and Nuremberg was his 21st 'Op'. The entry for Thursday, 30 March 1944 reads:

'Such a nice day today, little did we know what was in store for us. Briefing was getting later each day as the days grew longer, and today it was at 5 p.m., so we all had an afternoon nap. The target was Nuremberg. Where was that? "Oh, this should be a nice quiet stooge," someone said, but that remained to be seen.

'At 2200 we taxied out and were first airborne. Everything was quiet during the climb to 20,000 feet over the Channel. We crossed the enemy coast and it was eyes wide open. As we drew level with the south of the Ruhr Valley, things began to happen. Enemy night fighters were all around us and, in no time at all,

combats were taking place and aircraft were going down in flames on all sides. So serious was the situation, that I remember looking at the other poor blighters going down and thinking to myself that it must be our turn next, just a question of time. A Lancaster appeared on our port beam converging, so we dropped 100 feet or so to let him cross. He was only about 200 yards or so on our starboard beam when a string of cannon shells hit him and down he went.

'We altered course for Nuremberg, and I looked down at the area over which we had just passed. It looked like a battlefield. There were kites burning on the deck all over the place—bombs going off where they had been jettisoned by bombers damaged in combat, and fires from their incendiaries across the whole area. Such a picture of aerial disaster I had never seen before and hope to never see again.

'On the way into the target, the winds became changeable and we almost ran into the defences of Schweinfurt but we altered course in time. The defences of Nuremberg were nothing to speak of, a modest amount of heavy flak which did not prevent us doing a normal approach, and we were able to get the target indicators dropped by the Pathfinder Force in our bombsight to score direct hits with our 4,000lb "Cookie" and our 1,000lb bombs and incendiaries. We were able to get out of the target area, always a dodgy business, and set course for home. To reach the coast was a binding two-hour stooge. The varying winds were

No 50 Squadron Lancaster R5546, 'VN-T', went missing on the Nuremberg raid on 30/31 March 1944.

PFF casualties were high. Among losses on 22/23 April 1944 was No 7 Squadron Lancaster 'J', shot down by a night fighter. All the crew were killed. Leon Noakes (3rd from right) was on his 95th op.

leading us a dance. We found ourselves approaching Calais instead of being 80 miles further south, so we had a slight detour to avoid their defences. Once near the enemy coast, it was nose down for home at 300 knots. Even then, we saw some poor blokes "buy it" over the Channel. What a relief it was to be flying over Lincoln Cathedral once more. Back in debriefing, we heard the full story of the Squadron's effort. It was the worst night for the Squadron.'

It was, in fact, the worst night for Bomber Command. Of the 795 aircraft dispatched, 95 failed to return—64 Lancasters and 31 Halifaxes. Ten more were totally written off after returning—five Lancasters and five Halifaxes, and another 59 aircraft damaged. This represented a loss rate of 12.1 per cent of the Lancaster force and 16.8 per cent of the Halifax force, with the loss of 535 lives and a further 180 wounded or taken prisoner-of-war.

It appears that the weather forecast had been wrong. Also, several wind-finding errors had been made, causing the Main Force to become so scattered that one-fifth of the force did not pass within 30 miles of one

turning point. This led to a 'straggling' force of more than 100 bombers bombing the town of Schweinfurt by mistake. Finally, the Luftwaffe night fighters scored a considerable success. The first fighters had appeared before the bombers reached the Belgian border and constantly harassed the force for the next hour. By the time the Main Force reached Nuremberg, some 80 bombers had been shot down, with a further 55 aircraft having aborted for technical reasons. The main raid at Nuremberg was considered a failure. The city was covered by thick cloud and little damage was done to the target area. The only evidence that bombs fell on Nuremberg came from German radio reports. It later appeared, from German sources, that most of the damage done at Nuremberg was to residential areas, with only slight damage to industry.

For Bomber Command, the cost of the Nuremberg raid was disastrous and proved to be the most severe blow in its history, bringing to an end the long-employed tactic of massed attacks against major targets. It would be later in the war before these tactics were to be used again.

With the nights becoming shorter and preparations for the Allied invasion of Europe taking more effect, Harris knew that his bombing offensive against the German cities was over and, for the time being, turned his attention to the support of Operation 'Overlord'.

CHAPTER EIGHT

'Overlord' and Beyond

IN THE EARLY months of 1944 it became apparent that those who were planning Operation 'Overlord' were expecting a massive campaign of air preparation and subsequently of direct air support for the armies. The plan for the Allied invasion of Europe had rapidly developed from a distant, and sometimes even doubtful, project to that of an imminent operation. Following the long and strenuous bombing campaign against Berlin throughout the previous winter, it had become apparent that the war would only finally end in the defeat of the Germans in the field.

The Nuremberg raid was temporarily the last of Bomber Command's all-out offensives against the German homeland. In preparation for 'Overlord' the emphasis was switched to targets in Occupied Europe and the transportation system in western Germany, although occasionally further raids were carried out on the German cities in an effort to keep the German night fighter force well to the east. The change in the allocation of targets to support preparations for the invasion was not particularly well received by Harris although, it must be said, he gave his full support to all directives received.

Operational control of Bomber Command was passed to SHAEF on 14 April and on the 17th a directive issued by Air Chief Marshal Sir Arthur Tedder, Deputy Supreme Allied Commander, to Bomber Command included the intended role of the Command throughout the operation: (a) To deplete the German fighter forces. (b) To destroy and disrupt rail communications, particularly those affecting the movement towards the 'Overlord' lodgement area. The directive continued: 'In view of the tactical difficulties of destroying precise targets by night, Bomber Command will continue to be employed in accordance with their main aim of disorganizing German industry.' It also stated that these operations were to be, as far as possible, complementary to those of the United States Strategic Air Forces.

This date marked the official change in Bomber Command's priorities on targets, although Harris had already made a start earlier in the month with two major raids on 9/10 April against railway yards at Lille and Villeneuve-St-Georges, followed the next night by raids against more railway yards at Tours, Tergnier, Laon, Aulnoye and Ghent. On those two nights some 1,600 sorties had been flown, causing widespread damage to the railway network. As well as the new offensive against the railway network, Bomber Command continued attacks against German industry. Following one such raid, on the night of 26/27 April against Schweinfurt, Sergeant Norman Jackson of No 106 Squadron was awarded the Victoria Cross for outstanding bravery after he had tried to save his burning Lancaster by climbing onto the wing to extinguish a fire. Unable to hold on, he was swept through the flames and over the edge of the wing, dragging his parachute behind, only partly inflated and burning in several places. Amazingly, Jackson survived despite appalling injuries.

By the end of spring, the Luftwaffe night fighter force was at its peak of effectiveness. Production had been rationalized by reducing the number of aircraft types. At the same time, airframe production was being dispersed out of the 27 main complexes into ten times that number of small factories distributed throughout the country. There was a similar dispersal of aero-engine production, thus making the industry far less vulnerable to air attack than previously.

Maintaining its offensive against the railway network and German industry throughout the build-up to 'Overlord', Bomber Command also took part in deception raids against targets further north from the planned invasion area of Normandy. Finally, when not involved in operations supporting the invasion build-up, raids were made on major German cities and other targets. On the night of 12/13 May special minelaying operations were carried out by 22 Mosquitoes of No 8 Group to block the Kiel Canal.

In preparation for 'Overlord', Bomber Command began a new campaign, one that was different from anything else it had previously attempted on a large scale. At the end of the Berlin offensive, about 70 per cent effort had been directed against targets in Germany. During April 1944 less than half the bombs dropped were against targets in Germany, and in May over 75 per cent of Bomber Command sorties were against targets in France and other occupied territory outside Germany. In June less than 9 per cent of bombs dropped were against targets in Germany. The effort devoted by Bomber Command in these months to the French railway system and many other objectives outside Germany was not part of the strategic air offensive against Germany, but it did have a profound bearing on it.

During the final weeks before the invasion, Bomber

Command had concentrated much of its effort on destroying the German lines of communication in France and, in the final two weeks, attempted to destroy the German coastal batteries covering the approaches to the French Channel ports. These attacks were carried out with great determination by crews who were not to know that they were just part of the overall diversionary plan. Only when the invasion was imminent did the attacks switch to the coastal batteries overlooking the planned British landing beaches.

JUNE–SEPTEMBER

The successful Allied invasion of the Normandy beachheads in June, and the following break-outs in late June and July, did not permit Bomber Command to resume a full-scale strategic air offensive against Germany. However, many supporting operations by the heavy bombers were still needed, notably against the V-weapons which at times were given top priority. The targets which the heavy bombers were dispatched against during this period can be categorized as follows: V-weapon launch sites; road and rail communications; fuel depots; troop and armour concentrations/battlefield targets.

During the first week after the D-Day landings, Bomber Command flew nearly 2,700 operational sorties at night in support of the landings, of which two-thirds were against road and rail communications. Pilot Officer Andrew Mynarski of No 419 Squadron, RCAF, was posthumously awarded the Victoria Cross following one such raid, on the night of 12/13 June, against railyards at Cambrai after he tried to save the rear gunner in his burning aircraft.

On 14 June Bomber Command was able to resume daylight raids, the first for over a year. That such operations were now possible was due mainly to the fact that the Main Force could be protected by Allied fighters for short penetration raids. This first raid involved over 200 Lancasters and was targeted against German naval forces opposing Allied shipping off the Normandy beaches. Despite the protection of fighter escort, daylight operations still exposed the bombers to enemy fighter activity and, in poor weather and cloudy conditions, made accurate bombing difficult and increasing the risk of French civilian casualties. These two reasons led to a reluctance to dispatch more daylight raids than necessary. Throughout the remainder of June many raids, diversionary raids and support operations were carried out by Bomber Command in support of 'Overlord'. Brief details of the larger raids are listed in Table 3.

In support of the British 2nd Army's breakout from the Normandy beachhead in July, code-named Operation 'Goodwood', two major raids were dispatched on 7 and 18 July to bomb fortified villages in the area of Caen. The first raid consisted of over 450 aircraft but, although reducing areas to rubble, it failed to destroy the German defences. This led to the second raid, with

April 1944: a No 149 Squadron crew pose with their Stirling at Methwold prior to an SOE supply drop. [Peter Rowland]

TABLE 3: MAJOR RAIDS CONDUCTED BY BOMBER COMMAND, JUNE 1944*

Date	Targets	Aircraft dispatched	Lancaster	Halifax	Mosquito	Stirling
5/6	Coastal batteries	1.012 (3)	551 (1)	412 (2)	49	–
6/7	Communications	1.065 (11)	589 (10)	418 (1)	58	–
7/8	Communications	337 (28)	122 (17)	195 (11)	20	–
8/9	Communications	483 (4)	286 (3)	169	28 (1)	–
9/10	Airfields	401 (2)	206	175 (2)	20	–
10/11	Railways	432 (18)	323 (15)	90 (3)	19	–
11/12	Railways	329 (4)	225 (3)	86 (1)	18	–
12/13	Communications	671 (23)	285 (6)	348 (17)	38	–
14	Le Havre	234 (1)	221 (1)	–	13	–
14/15	Troop positions, railways	667 (4)	284 (1)	355 (3)	28	–
15	Boulogne	297 (1)	155	130 (1)	12	–
15/16	Ammo fuel dumps, railways	451 (11)	303 (11)	99	19	30
17/18	Railways	317 (1)	196 (1)	90	19	12
22/23	Railways	221 (8)	111 (4)	–	9	–
27/28	Railways	223 (4)	214 (4)	–	9	–
28/29	Railways	230 (20)	28 (2)	202 (18)	–	–
30	Villers-Bocage	266 (2)	151 (1)	105 (1)	10	–

*Losses are shown in parentheses.

more than twice the effort of the first raid, and resulted in the Germans being driven from the area. These two raids were followed by a third major raid, when on 30 July a force of nearly 700 bombers was dispatched to the Normandy area in support of a mainly American ground attack. Quickly the Allies advanced through northern France, giving the Germans little time to create an effective line of defence.

Throughout the summer, raids had continued against the V-weapon sites. These raids, often carried out in daylight, were pressed home with great determination. Many pilots distinguished themselves during this period of operations—none more than Squadron Leader Ian Bazalgette of No 635 Squadron, who was posthumously awarded the Victoria Cross following a raid, in which he was Master Bomber, against a V-1 storage depot at Trossy St Maximin on 4 August.

Two more significant raids took place in the second week of August in support of the Allied advances in Normandy. On the night of the 7/8th, over 1,000 bombers were dispatched to attack positions ahead of the Allied ground troops. Understandably, total precision was needed to ensure that damage was inflicted on enemy positions only. A week later, on the 14th, more than 800 aircraft were dispatched to attack German positions facing the 3rd Canadian Division advancing on Falaise. Harris reckoned that a Main Force attack was the equivalent of a 4,000-gun barrage.

The following day, over 1,000 aircraft were dispatched to attack several German night fighter airfields in the Low Countries in preparation for a renewed offensive against targets in Germany. The air assault, including the part played by Bomber Command, had a major impact on the course of the campaign. As the German commander Von Runstedt stated: 'The main

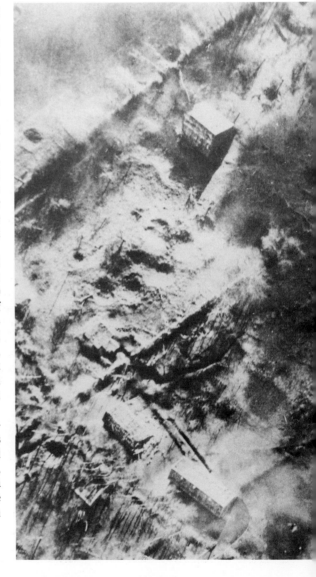

The end of a flying-bomb site after a 'Crossbow' raid; V-1 launching ramps and buildings smashed.

AIR CHIEF MARSHAL SIR RALPH COCHRANE, GBE, KCB, AFC

Ralph Cochrane was born, the third son of Baron Cochrane of Cults, at Cults in Fifeshire on 24 February 1895. He joined the Royal Navy in 1912 and three years later transferred to the Royal Naval Air Service airship branch. In 1918 he transferred to the newly formed Royal Air Force when his work in testing the first airship mooring mast brought him the award of the Air Force Cross later that year.

Throughout the early 1920s, Cochrane served with the RAF in Egypt and Iraq and, as a flight commander with No 45 Squadron, was mentioned in despatches for operations in Kurdistan in 1923. Following a tour in Aden, he returned to England in 1930. During the early 1930s, Cochrane was Director of the Staff College and served at the Air Ministry and the Imperial Defence College before he became defence adviser to the New Zealand Government. Between 1936 and 1939 he was Chief of the Air Staff of the Royal New Zealand Air Force.

In 1939, Cochrane became Aide-de-Camp to King George VI and then commanded RAF Abingdon. In February 1942 he was promoted to Air Vice-Marshal and appointed AOC No 3 Group, Bomber Command, before being appointed AOC No 5 Group the following year.

Cochrane's first task was to work closely with Wing Commander Guy Gibson in planning the Dams Raid, carried out by No 617 Squadron in May 1943. His close liaison with the squadron continued and helped to plan other specialist raids. With the new Commanding Officer, Wing Commander Leonard Cheshire, he worked on the idea of developing the Mosquito for target marking, a theory put into practice on 5 April 1944 when Cheshire himself flew a Mosquito to mark an aircraft factory at Toulouse, which Lancasters of No 5 Group then destroyed. Soon afterwards, Harris told Cochrane that No 5 Group could operate on its own. Throughout the remainder of the war No 5 Group continued attacks against Germany and other major targets, using heavier bombs such as 'Tallboy' and 'Grand Slam'.

Cochrane was described as a strict but fair man. Harris himself described him as 'a most brilliant, enthusiastic and hard working leader of men'. Cochrane commanded No 5 Group until January 1945 when, soon after, he was knighted and became AOC-in-C Transport Command until 1947. He commanded Flying Training Command until 1950 and was then appointed Vice-Chief of Air Staff until his retirement from the RAF in 1952.

---

difficulties which arose for us at the time of the invasion were the systematic preparation by your air force, the smashing of the main lines of communication, particularly the rail junctions, and the third thing was the carpet bombing. Those were the main things which caused the general collapse.'

Between June and August 1944, over 180,000 tons of bombs were dropped, but only some 30,000 tons were against targets in Germany. This fact indicates the extent to which, for Bomber Command, the strategic air offensive against Germany had become a secondary effort. Instead, much effort had been placed on the continuation of attacks against the French railways, V-weapon sites and oil plants. For Bomber Command the oil offensive proved to be a marginal and haphazard affair, partly through the intransigence of Harris who saw this target type as the classic 'panacea' upon which so much wasted effort had been expended in the past. However, the American strategic bombers had achieved somewhat better results and so the argument between the supporters of the oil offensive and those of the transportation/communications offensive unabated. The oil-versus-transportation debate was long and

heated—and it continues to this day, both sides producing volumes of statistics and predictions to support their particular case. However, the situation had, by late 1944, become somewhat confused in that the overall effect of the two 'campaigns' had become interlinked. The direct impact of a reduction in oil production was heightened by the problems of transporting the available fuel to where it was needed; it was all very well to be producing aviation fuel, but this fuel was of no value if it could not be delivered to the fighter units. This important aspect has all too often been ignored in the past by those seeking to identify a single source for the German collapse of early 1945. The overall situation certainly worried Speer, who, in a memo of May 1944 to Hitler, wrote: 'With the attacks on the hydrogenation plants, systematic bombing raids on economic targets have started at the most dangerous point'. However, these decisive results depended upon a concentrated and sustained effort by the heavy bombers, for it was evident from photographic reconnaissance that the Germans were not abandoning even their most heavily damaged oil plants. The efficiency of the Germans' repair organization, and their flair for improvisation,

---

TABLE 4: MAJOR RAIDS CONDUCTED AGAINST V-WEAPON SITES BY BOMBER COMMAND, 16 JUNE–31 AUGUST 1944*

Date	Dispatched	Lancaster	Halifax	Mosquito	Stirling
16/17 June	405	236	149	20	–
23/24 June	412 (5)	226 (5)	164	22	–
24/25 June	739 (22)	535 (22)	165	39	–
27/28 June	721 (3)	477 (3)	207	37	–
2 July	384	374	–	10	–
5/6 July	542 (4)	321 (4)	201	20	–
6 July	551 (1)	210	314 (1)	26	–
20 July	369 (1)	174 (1)	165	30	–
1 August	777	385	324	67	–
2 August†	394 (2)	234 (2)	99	40	20
3 August	1,114 (6)	601 (6)	492	21	–
5 August	742 (1)	257	469 (1)	16	–
31 August	601 (6)	418 (6)	147	36	–

*Losses are shown in parentheses. †One P-38 Lightning also took part in this raid.

By ....No. 7 Squadron......

For the Month of ....JULY........ 19 44.

DATE	AIRCRAFT TYPE & NUMBER	CREW	DUTY	TIME Up	TIME Down	DETAILS OF SORTIE OR FLIGHT
28.7.44.	LANCASTER III ND.387 "Q"	F/L. P.A. PHILLIES (RAAF) AUS.409939.	CAPTAIN	22.33	04.59	STUTTGART. Visual Centerer. 4 T.I. Green L.B. 4 T.I. Green
		F/L. D.G. GOODWIN (RNZAF) NZ.40584.	NAVIGATOR			1 x 4000 H.C. 2 x 1000 U.S.A. G.P.T.D.025. Red and Green
		F/L. H.O. THURSTON (RNZAF) NZ.416555.	AIR BOMBER			T.I's scattered. Concentration of Reds to N.W. and Greens
		P/O. S. WILLIAMSON (RAAF) AUS.42844.	WIRELESS OP.			to S.E. of target. 2 lots Visual Markers, Red/Green T.I's
		F/S. P.J. JONES	ENGINEER			ignited 01.46 hrs. First lot between glows of Red and Green
		F/S. R. RYDER	MID-UPPER			concentrations and second lot near Greens. Unidentified
		F/S. J.W. NAYLOR	REAR GUNNER			river seen. Master Bomber instructed to bomb Green glow but
		W/O. A.J. HARPER	VISUAL A/B.			much R/T interference. No results seen.
"	JA.677 "U"	S/L. A.J.L. CRAIG	CAPTAIN	22.34	05.24	STUTTGART. Master Bomber and Primary Visual Marker. 3 T.I.
		P/O. G. GRAHAM	NAVIGATOR			Red B.16. 3 T.I. Green B.16. 8 Flares hooded. 8 x 500 G.P.
		F/L. S. BAXTER (RAAF) AUS.40709.	AIR BOMBER			T.D.025. 3 Red and 3 Green T.I's surrounded by Red T.I's.
		F/S. R.F. RICHARDSON	WIRELESS OP.			Instructed Main Force to bomb Green T.I's adjacent to Reds.
		F/O. W.N. BINGHAM	ENGINEER			Told Visual Centerers to back up Greens and Secondary Blind
		P/O. J.R. MORRISON	MID-UPPER			Markers to drop Wanganuis, but only one seen at beginning
		S/L. R. DIXON	REAR GUNNER			and end. Left target at 02.00 hrs. broadcasting till 02.04
		F/L. C.E. BERRY	VISUAL A/B.			Attack at end was 7 miles by 3 miles, N.W. to S.E. main
						branch of Red and Green T.I's to S.E. of this line. Brought
						back 3 Red T.I's, 3 Green T.I's. 8 Flares hooded. (could not
						identify target visually). Fighter destroyed.

were most significant factors. The V-weapon and storage sites took much of Bomber Command's efforts throughout the summer of 1944. Brief details of the larger raids, too numerous to mention each site, between June and August are listed in Table 4.

For some time No 5 Group had been unhappy with various aspects of the new PFF techniques and the employment of the Main Force. Under the forceful leadership of Cochrane and with men like Cheshire, Gibson and Martin, the Group had developed its own ideas. Harris later summed up this period of mid-1944 thus: 'No 5 Group operated largely as an independent unit and developed its own techniques, including the original Master Bomber concept, also offset skymarking continued to develop e.g. "5 Group Newhaven" using offset techniques 1,000–2,000 yards from the aiming point, any error in the red TIs being cancelled by

yellows from the Master Bomber. Other techniques developed, including "sector bombing" with each aircraft given a heading and overshoot setting. This gave a good bomb distribution but needed very accurate low-level marking.'

It was this latter aspect that became the No 5 Group trademark—going in at low level to put the TIs within feet of the aiming point. Although the Group continued to take part in the Main Force operations it also undertook many raids of its own. From spring 1944 onwards there was a trend towards more Group individuality; in April three PFF squadrons (Nos 83, 97 and 627) had been transferred to No 5 Group. While No 5 Group started to go its own way, most of the others were content with the service provided by the PFF, although it is recorded that there were more grumbles from No 4 Group than anywhere else—particularly if the Master Bomber had been critical of the bombing!

Left top: Extract from No 7 Squadron log, July 1944.

Left bottom: Halifax over the Pas de Calais, July 1944.

Below: 12,000lb bombs burst on the U-boat pens at Brest, August 1944.

Below right: The U-boat pens were shattered by these weapons.

OPERATION 'PARAVANE'
In September 1944 the Admiralty believed that the German battleship *Tirpitz*, then anchored in Kaa Fjord in northern Norway, was about to put to sea. This ship remained a major concern for Churchill, who was determined to achieve her destruction. Unfortunately, when armed with a 12,000lb 'Tallboy' bomb, the

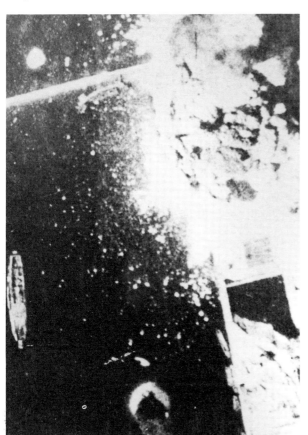

Lancaster did not have the range to reach the fjord from a British base. However, the Russians agreed to allow the Lancasters to land at Yagodnik airfield near Archangel, and so the raid was planned to be carried out by twenty Lancasters of No 617 Squadron, led by Wing Commander J. B. 'Willie' Tait, and eighteen Lancasters of No 9 Squadron, led by Wing Commander James Bazin.

Operation 'Paravane' was undertaken in accordance with Headquarters No 5 Group Operation Order B.393 dated 7 September 1944. The original plan to take off from Scotland, attack *Tirpitz* and fly on to Yagodnik was abandoned on the morning of 11 September; so the alternative plan to fly direct to Russia and operate from there was adopted. The squadrons were ordered to take off at 1700 in order to land at Yagodnik soon after dawn

on the 12th, and carry out the raid later that day. Weather conditions were as forecast until the Russo-Finnish frontier. From there on, some 200 miles, conditions were extremely bad—cloud base some 150–300 feet with visibility in heavy rain squalls down to 600 yards. This was certainly not the weather that had been forecast and, combined with the fact that no navigational aids were available, meant that the arrival in the vicinity of Archangel was as difficult as one could imagine. The force had become quite scattered, but most managed to land at various airfields undamaged, although six aircraft crashed. One Lancaster which crash-landed was flown by Flying Officer Ross of No 617 Squadron. His report reads:

'We had been circling for 2 hours 45 minutes, so I looked for a likely spot to land the aircraft, the

Above: Briefing to attack one of Churchill's favourite targets, the battleship *Tirpitz* which was holed up in Trondheim Fjord, Norway. Note the poster on the wall.

Left: Oil storage depot at Bec d'Ambes under attack, 4 August 1944. [514 Sqn records]

surrounding ground appeared to be waterlogged. Finally, I selected a long stretch of wooden road void of telegraph poles for a distance of about 1,100 yards. The cloud base was at 200 feet in patches and two approaches were made. The first was too far to the right, the second was O.K., but a lorry load of troops had stopped on it. I tried a reciprocal without success. The Engineer reported about 30 gallons of petrol left, so I ordered the crew to crash stations, selected a marshy land, 20 degrees flap, and approached at 115 m.p.h. Aircraft touched down, the crew were all O.K.'

Not all the aircraft that landed undamaged were fit to operate. Many required repairs, the crews were exceptionally tired, and there was no question of operating that day. The immediate aim was to recover all the aircraft to Yagodnik in preparation for the attack, and it was not until 0500 on the 14th that all serviceable machines were ready.

Weather forecasts for the 15th indicated that there would be a chance of a cloudless sky over Kaa Fjord during the afternoon. Following a weather reconnaissance by a Mosquito, the decision was made to attack. Led by Tait, the first of the 28 Lancasters took off at 0630 and the force set course at a very low height. Twenty-one aircraft were armed with 'Tallboys' and the other seven carried 500lb 'Johnny Walker' mines specially designed for attacking ships in shallow water. The operation proceeded as planned until the final run-in to the target. Several 'Tallboy' aircraft did not bomb on the first run because bombs hung up or because the bombing run was not good enough. Eventually, seventeen 'Tallboys' were dropped, two hung up and two were taken back to Yagodnik because, by that time, the target had become obscured under a smoke-screen and could not be identified. All 'Johnny Walker'-equipped aircraft dropped their mines. No fighter opposition was encountered and the flak, although plentiful, was ineffective. All aircraft returned safely to Yagodnik.

Ground crew fitters, No 619 Squadron.

Finally, on 12 November, Tait led the third attack on *Tirpitz*. Thirty-one Lancasters (eighteen from No 617 Squadron and thirteen from No 9 Squadron) took off from Lossiemouth and, this time, arrived to find clear weather over the battleship. Complete surprise had been achieved with no smoke-screen obscuring the target. Several hits were seen, followed by a tremendous explosion as one of the ship's magazines blew up. At 0952 the mighty battleship rolled over and capsized. Just one Lancaster was damaged by flak but managed to land in Sweden. Messages of congratulations arrived at the squadrons from the highest authorities:

From His Majesty The King: 'Please convey my hearty congratulations to all those who took part in the daring and successful attack on the *Tirpitz*.'

From The Prime Minister: 'Heartiest congratulations to all.'

From The War Cabinet: 'The War Cabinet convey to all concerned their congratulations on the brilliant achievement of Bomber Command in sinking the *Tirpitz*. The series of attacks on Germany's most powerful battleship were pressed home with great skill and determination against formidable opposition. The destruction of the *Tirpitz* must rank with the finest feats of Bomber Command.'

Many more messages were received, notably from the CAS and from the C-in-C Bomber Command. Tait was awarded a third bar to his DSO for his outstanding leadership during the three raids on *Tirpitz*, the first time a third bar had been awarded to an RAF officer.

Meanwhile the last Stirling bombing operation of the war occurred when four aircraft of 149 Squadron, based at Methwold, took part in a daylight raid on Le Havre on 8 September.

Operational control of Bomber Command reverted to the Air Staff on 14 September and, just two nights later, on the 16/17th, Bomber Command's operations were in support of the landings by British and American airborne troops at Arnhem and Nijmegen, which took place the following morning, as part of Operation 'Market Garden'. This was followed the next night with further support operations. In total, some 650 sorties were flown by Bomber Command during the first 48 hours of the operation.

On the night of 23/24 September 136 Lancasters and five Mosquitoes of No 5 Group bombed the banks of the Dortmund–Ems Canal, resulting in the canal being

It was difficult to assess the result of the attack from interrogation of crews. Their observations had been hampered by the very effective smoke-screen. Many crews saw a large red flash followed by black smoke from the area of *Tirpitz*, but there was no definite evidence that this was from the battleship. A Mosquito made an attempt to obtain photographs of *Tirpitz* two hours after the attack, but by then low cloud covered the fjord. The pilot managed to sight *Tirpitz* through a gap in the cloud from 9,000 feet, but could only report that the ship was still afloat. It was not until the 20th that photographs were eventually taken by the Mosquito, and from these there was sufficient detail to show that one hit may have been obtained.

After the operation had been completed, all efforts were made to return the aircraft to England as quickly as possible. Unknown to the crews and the Admiralty at the time, the damage had been sufficient to prevent the Germans returning *Tirpitz* to full seaworthiness and she was moved further south near Tromso for use as a heavy artillery battery. This move further south meant that a second attack could be carried out from Scotland.

On 29 October Tait led a force of 40 Lancasters, 20 each from Nos 617 and 9 Squadrons, from Lossiemouth to attack *Tirpitz*. Unfortunately, they arrived to find the fjord covered by cloud. Thirty-two aircraft released their 'Tallboys', but none hit the battleship. Just one aircraft was hit by flak but managed to land in Sweden.

Right top: By late 1944 Bomber Command was involved in intensive day and night operations, the former being made possible by the partial collapse of the German defences and the presence of long-range fighter escort.

Right bottom: The 115 Squadron crew of F/O Rowe and their Lancaster—one of many crews that flew two ops in one day during Operation 'Hurricane'.

breached. Although successful, this raid cost Bomber Command fourteen Lancasters lost (over 10 per cent).

By now the campaign against the French railways was all but at an end. Also, winter was approaching and the deteriorating weather meant that precision bombing was becoming more difficult—added to which, the military campaign in France was rapidly coming to a victorious conclusion. The Allied armies were approaching the Rhine and, on their way, had overrun the V-weapon launching sites. Overall, this presented the opportunity for a final and overwhelming strategic air offensive against Germany.

A plan for renewing the Battle of Berlin had first been considered in a minute from the Chiefs of Staff to the Prime Minister, dated 5 July 1944, when the Chiefs of Staff declared 'that the time might well come in the not too distant future when an all-out attack by every means at our disposal on German civilian morale might be decisive' and suggested to the Prime Minister 'that the method by which such an attack would be carried out should be examined and all preparations made'.

Various means of carrying out such a catastrophic blow were considered. It was pointed out that the previous bombing campaign against Berlin had not

brought the downfall of Germany, and Berlin was indeed capable of sustaining a new offensive, even though in the short term it might bring about a temporary breakdown in the morale of the population. An alternative suggestion was that similar blows might be carried out against other cities such as Hamburg, Cologne, Frankfurt or Munich. This, however, would produce somewhat less effect than a concentration against Berlin, although Bomber Command casualties would be fewer. A final suggestion was therefore put forward: 'Immense devastation could be produced if the entire attack was concentrated on a single big town other than Berlin'. This attack, when it finally came, was against Dresden in February 1945.

The strategic arguments in favour of general area bombing of German towns and cities had therefore been mainly abandoned by the Air Staff. With the campaign in France virtually over, a new directive from DCAS (25 September) to Harris stated that the first priority was, 'subject to weather and tactical feasibility', the oil campaign and that equal second priority was the German rail and waterborne transport systems, tank production plants and depots, ordnance depots, and motor vehicle production plants and depots. Counter-air force action was mentioned but, for the time being, accorded no definite priority. The direct support of land

Left: Photo from F/O Rowe's aircraft during the attack on Heinsberg, 16 November 1944.

Below: No 619 Squadron Lancaster 'Dumbo' in a lonely dispersal.
[F. Slater]

and naval operations was said to be a 'continuing commitment' and bombing of 'important industrial areas' was included. There was, however, no mention of supporting Russian armies in the east. Oil had thus been officially designated as the principal aim of the strategic air offensive and communications had become secondary.

OCTOBER–DECEMBER

With the Allied armies on or near the German frontier, and in some places beyond it, it became increasingly difficult to distinguish between tactical operations against military communications and strategic operations against industrial communications. This difficulty arose from the approach of military forces towards the zones of strategic air operations—not only with communications targets, but also in other cases such as oil plants and cities.

Although supporting the September directive, Harris still believed in a general area bombing offensive. This was reflected in the activities of Bomber Command during October 1944 when a major effort was carried out. Over 17,000 operational sorties were dispatched and more than 13,000 of these were directed against targets in Germany, during which over 50,000 tons of bombs fell on German territory. This weight of attack was more than twice as great as the previous highest tonnage dropped on Germany in a single month. To put this fact into context, during one period of 24 hours against Duisburg Bomber Command dropped about the same weight of bombs as the Germans had dropped on London in the entire war.

TABLE 5: MAJOR RAIDS FLOWN BY BOMBER COMMAND AGAINST GERMAN CITIES, OCTOBER 1944

Target	Date(s)	Aircraft dispatched	Aircraft lost
Cologne	28, 30/31, 31/1	2,131	9
Duisburg	14, 14/15	2,018	21
Essen	23/24, 25	1,826	12
Stuttgart	19/20	583	6
Saarbrucken	5/6	551	3
Dortmund	6/7	523	5
Wilhelmshaven	15/16	506	—

On 13 October a revised directive was issued by DCAS to Harris. It made reference to 'Special Operations', specifying attacks against targets in the Ruhr, and was code-named Operation 'Hurricane'.

OPERATION 'HURRICANE'

Beginning early on 14 October, the Allies launched an all-out air offensive against objectives in the densely populated area of the Ruhr with the intention of demonstrating the Allies' overwhelming air superiority in the area. Operation 'Hurricane' was a maximum effort by Bomber Command and the US 8th Air Force.

Bomber Command's first raid consisted of over 1,000 bombers with RAF fighter escort, resulting in over 4,000 tons of high-explosives and incendiaries being dropped on Duisburg for the loss of fourteen bombers. This was

backed up by the US 8th Air Force dispatching a raid of 2,000 aircraft (including 750 fighters) to the Cologne area.

That night Bomber Command continued the offensive with another raid of more than 1,000 bombers against Duisburg, resulting in a further 4,500 tons of high-explosives and incendiaries being dropped on the city for the loss of seven aircraft.

One pilot who flew on both raids to Duisburg that day was Flying Officer Alan Rowe, a Lancaster pilot with No 115 Squadron based at Witchford. He and his crew flew the first daylight raid (lasting 4 hours 10 minutes), landed back at Witchford, took a few hours' rest and took off again for the night raid (4 hours 25 minutes)—an exhausting day!

In this one period, nearly 9,000 tons of bombs had fallen on Duisburg. These figures give an indication of the extent to which the conditions of the strategic air offensive had been changed by the increased size and efficiency of Bomber Command, by the growth of Allied air superiority and by the Allied reoccupation of France.

Although the versatility of the force was clearly demonstrated, the effectiveness of the September directive was not. About two-thirds of Bomber Command's effort in October was devoted to a resumption of the general area offensive against German towns and cities. There was no great concentration against oil or communications. Indeed, only about 6 per cent of the Command's tonnage for the month was devoted to oil targets. Adverse weather was by no means the only reason why Harris was reluctant to devote a greater part

Halifax III PN167 of No 347 (French) Squadron. Note the blacked-out nose, courtesy of the wartime censor.

of his attack to oil targets. Clearly, his attitude was a factor in the divergence between the pattern of Bomber Command operations during October and the terms of the September directive. Brief details of the large-scale raids against the major cities during October are listed in Table 5.

On 1 November a new directive was issued. It closely followed the lines of its predecessor and oil was again given first priority. Communications, however, became the only second priority; tank and motor transport production plants and depots were omitted. The other important change in the new directive was a reference to 'important industrial areas'. These areas had previously been accorded no priority, but it was now stated

Mustang escort.

that 'as far as operational conditions allow, these area bombing attacks' were 'to be directed so as to contribute maximum destruction of the petroleum industry and the dislocation of the target systems already indicated.'

The clarity of the November directive was undoubted, but this did not mean that the major part of Bomber Command's effort was then devoted to the oil campaign. The problems and difficulties encountered in the oil campaign had indeed grown much greater than they had been in the summer months. As was to be expected, the weather became worse and the chances of making accurate attacks became less. Also, it became increasingly difficult to obtain photographic reconnaissance in bad weather and so know the most appropriate time at which any repeat attacks should be made. Thus there was the danger of wasting bombs on oil plants which had already been put out of action, and not attacking others which had recovered part of their previous production capacity. However, the transparency of these Bomber Command arguments caused many a raised eyebrow.

Despite having been at the peak of effectiveness just six months earlier, the Luftwaffe was now beginning to experience several problems. From the translation of German documents dated 5 November:

'Our numerical inferiority can only be countered by confronting the enemy with temporary and local concentrations of power. It should be added that due to the comparative inexperience of many of our pilots, our losses, not only in actual combat, but also during take-off and landing, are much higher than those of the enemy. A mere increase in aircraft production will not provide a solution to our difficulties at the front.

'As regards our night fighter force, the position is rather more favourable at present. Substantial reinforcements have been received from disbanded bomber and transport units, and striking power has greatly in-

creased. Our total strength of about 1,800 aircraft enabled about 200 fighters to take to the air during each enemy attack. Night fighter crews have achieved considerable success. However, a plan must be devised for the concentration of our forces in western Germany. Since the present fuel shortage only permits the employment of night fighters for a few days each month, our forces, of which one Gruppe should be concentrated in the Ruhr and one Gruppe in the Reich/Main area, should carry out operations at full strength on certain days and times based on previous experience. A further solution would be to convert some night fighter units to Me 262. This would enable us to attack and inflict heavy losses on the Mosquito squadrons which are operating in ever-increasing strength over north-west Europe.'

The activities of the Light Night Striking Force saw

the Mosquito become a scourge of the German defences, achieving results far in excess of the small number of aircraft involved—and with few losses.

The German Ardennes Offensive began on 14 December and, as the year began to draw to a close, the pressure on the crews of Bomber Command continued. The Pathfinders continued to lead the way, but who led the Pathfinders? One gallant young Master Bomber was Squadron Leader Robert Palmer of No 109 Squadron, who was posthumously awarded the Victoria Cross for leading a daylight raid against railways at Cologne on 23 December, his 111th op.

Palmer typified the gallantry of the Bomber Command crews who continued to press home every attack with the utmost determination and skill. The year had begun with Bomber Comand locked in a bitter struggle during the Battle of Berlin, but now ended with victory in sight.

Near the end, Lancasters over Stadtlohn, 21 March 1945.

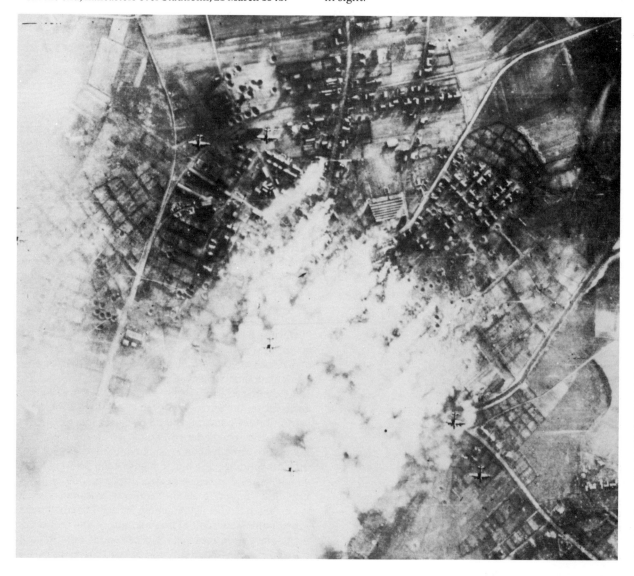

TO FINAL VICTORY

For Bomber Command 1945 began with oil and communications still the first and second priorities. Its Lancaster force had grown to 51 squadrons with some 1,200 aircraft on operational strength. Victory was anticipated in the very near future, but the struggle continued. Despite the relatively low losses, it would be wrong to assume that the last months of the war were carried out without difficulty. Indeed, the very first day of the new year witnessed one of the bravest acts by a young man of Bomber Command. Flight Sergeant George Thompson of No 9 Squadron was posthumously awarded the Victoria Cross following a daylight raid against the Dortmund–Ems Canal.

The offensive in the Ardennes faded with the Germans failing to capture either Brussels or Antwerp, and eventually the German units ran out of supplies. This final gamble by Hitler had failed but nevertheless had held up the Allied advance, and it was to be several weeks before the Allied armies would reach the Rhine.

For some considerable time the Air Ministry had considered a new phase of large raids targeted against major German cities. With the continuous advance by the Russian forces across the eastern frontier of Germany, it was decided that the cities targeted would be the vital supply and communication targets of Berlin, Dresden, Leipzig and Chemnitz. However, any thought of beginning a new offensive against Berlin was considered unwise. A report from the Joint Intelligence Committee dated 25 January stated that: 'The devastation of Berlin, even if it was to coincide with the Russian advance, would be unlikely to break down the German will to continue the war'. It was therefore decided that heavy raids would be carried out against Dresden, Leipzig and Chemnitz as part of Operation 'Thunderclap'.

OPERATION 'THUNDERCLAP'

For Bomber Command, 'Thunderclap' began on the night of 13/14 February when a force of over 800 Lancasters and Mosquitoes attacked the city of Dresden. The result was devastating. Clear conditions led to accurate bombing which caused a firestorm across the city. It also proved the extreme effectiveness of the Bomber Command tactic of 'area bombing', a tactic designed to destroy military targets such as railyards, factories, etc by destroying the area in which these key targets were situated. It is difficult to assess the casualty figure that night in Dresden, but it is believed to have been as high as 50,000.

Much criticism of the raid has been made over the years, not because of the size of force dispatched but because of the widespread destruction in the city and the high number of civilian casualties that resulted, almost suggesting that this could have been the objective for the raid. However, the importance of Dresden as

John Carsons of No 550 Squadron dropping food supplies from his Lancaster during Operation 'Manna', 5 May 1945. 'We crossed the coast at the island of Overflakkee and flew east. We were constantly greeted by countless people waving at us enthusiastically. Next to a smallish village we dropped our "Manna" and the self-written leaflets and after some more sightseeing we turned north-west and returned to North Killingholme.' [John Carsons]

a vital supply route to the German forces in the east facing the Russian army cannot be overstressed. Dresden was attacked for military reasons only. The main post-war 'moral' argument has been the relevance of such a raid when the war was all but won. However, a land offensive through the same area would have seen an even greater number of casualties. The raid cost Bomber Command six Lancasters.

The following night, 'Thunderclap' continued with an attack on Chemnitz by a force of 500 Lancasters and over 200 Halifaxes. This time cloudy conditions over the target area meant that most of the bombing missed the target.

The last Victoria Cross for a member of Bomber Command was posthumously awarded to Captain Edwin Swales, SAAF, of 582 Squadron, who was Master Bomber for a raid against a vital rail junction at Pforzheim on the night of 23/24 February.

With rapidly dwindling fuel supplies, the Luftwaffe faced desperate times. Goebbels wrote in his diary on 1 March: 'The air war has now turned into a crazy orgy. We are totally defenceless against it. The Reich will be gradually turned into a complete desert.' However, the new German jet fighters had begun to appear over the skies of Europe. Designed to counter the main bomber force and, in particular, the escorting Mosquitoes and escort fighters, the Germans achieved extraordinary results during the remaining weeks of the war. As an example of the Luftwaffe's success, during a 48-hour period between 20 and 22 February Bomber Command

Left top: After hostilities many squadrons flew 'Cook's Tours' to look at the damage caused. For the groundcrew this was their first sight of the devastation.

Left bottom: Operation 'Doge', bringing back PoWs from Italy. Lancasters of Nos 106 (ZN), 12 (PH) and 100 (HW) Squadrons at Pomigliano.

lost 62 aircraft, most of them to fighters. On 4 March 100 Luftwaffe night fighters followed the Main Force back to England and attacked 27 Bomber Command bases as part of Operation 'Gisella'. In addition, the night fighters shot down some 20 aircraft, including some on training flights. Although successful, this tactic was never repeated on the same scale. One Luftwaffe night fighter ace was Heinz Schnaufer, who achieved an astonishing total of 121 kills with an exceptional record of multiple kills, including seven in one sortie on 7 March.

March began with two large raids against Mannheim and Cologne, before 'Thunderclap' was resumed on the night of 5/6 March with a further raid on Chemnitz. Extensive damage to the city was caused by large fires, although 22 bombers were lost.

The following week, within the space of 24 hours, Bomber Command twice established new records for the number of bombers sent to a target. On the 11th, 1,079 aircraft attacked Essen, followed the next day by 1,108 aircraft dispatched to Dortmund. These two raids resulted in over 9,500 tons of bombs being dropped. This last raid against Dortmund was to remain a record until the end of the war. Goebbels' diary for 12 March read: 'The morale of the German people, both at home and at the front, is sinking even lower. The air terror which rages uninterruptedly over German home territory makes people thoroughly despondent.'

The result of the oil offensive had by now taken its full effect. From Goebbels' diary (13 March): 'When I call to mind that the amount of petrol available to the Luftwaffe has fallen from 193,000 tons to 8,000 tons, then I realize what can be expected of the Luftwaffe and what cannot. What use is the mass output of new fighters when we have not even the petrol or the crews to put them into action?'

The end of March saw the Allies crossing the Rhine in strength and advancing eastwards. That month also saw the highest tonnage of bombs to be dropped in any single month of the war.

THE FINAL DAYS

Throughout April the major cities of the Ruhr fell into Allied hands. There was no longer 'area bombing' of cities, but more precise attacks against military targets. On the night of 9/10 April a force of nearly 600 Lancasters and Mosquitoes were dispatched to attack German shipping and U-boats at the Baltic naval base at Kiel. This attack resulted in the sinking of the German pocket battleship *Admiral Scheer*. This raid was followed four nights later by a further attack on Kiel which was directed against the U-boats and the port area previously undamaged.

In support of the Russian advance to Berlin, the following night Bomber Command dispatched a large force of 500 Lancasters and Mosquitoes against Potsdam, a suburb to the south-west of the capital. This was the first heavy attack against Berlin since the night of 24/25 March 1944 and proved to be the last major raid of the war against a German city.

Two further major raids took place in four days. Nearly 1,000 heavy bombers and Mosquitoes attacked the island fortress of Heligoland in daylight on the 18th, a highly successful raid with no Bomber Command losses. This was followed on the 22nd by a force of over 750 aircraft which attacked the German port of Bremen in support of the British XXX Corps attack. A few days later Bremen became the first German port to be captured.

The last major raid of the war took place on 25 April when a force of 375 Lancasters and Mosquitoes attacked the Berghof (Hitler's 'Eagle's Nest' chalet) and the SS barracks at Berchtesgaden in the Bavarian Alps. The weather made bombing difficult although considerable damage was apparently caused to the barracks. Later that night, a small force of Lancasters and Mosquitoes was dispatched to attack an oil storage depot in southern Norway. The final offensive operation of the war took place on the night of 2/3 May with a number of attacks on Kiel. During this series of attacks two Halifaxes and one Mosquito were lost—the last Bomber Command casualties.

OPERATIONS 'MANNA', 'EXODUS' AND 'DOGE'

As the war in Europe drew to a close, preparations were made to drop vital food supplies to the civilian population of the Netherlands. On 28 April, Operation 'Manna' commenced. The aircraft to make the first food drop was a Lancaster of No 115 Squadron, followed by further drops from aircraft of Nos 186 and 576 Squadrons. During the next two weeks over 3,000 sorties were flown, dropping some 7,000 tons of food.

With the end of the war in Europe, plans were made for the repatriation of British and Commonwealth prisoners-of-war. Operation 'Exodus' began on 2 May and many Lancasters were converted to carry up to 25 passengers. The first flight back from Europe with PoWs was from Brussels on 4 May. Throughout May a total of some 3,000 round trips took place and returned 74,000 PoWs.

Finally, Operation 'Doge' involved flying home the British 8th Army from Italy and the Central Mediterranean. It was some four months from the end of the war before this operation was completed.

CHAPTER NINE

Conclusions

HAVING LOOKED at the six years of Bomber Command's war it seems logical to attempt a few conclusions. One of the standard ways of summarizing such military effort is to examine the statistics of effort against achievement, and in this case losses. However, this is of limited value since few of the statisticians can agree on the figures; also, for each supporter of a particular case there will be a detractor—both using the same statistics to 'prove' their point. The authors can understand why Harris was so sceptical about many of the facts, figures and assumptions he was given. Some facts however can be stated with confidence. Bomber Command was the only Allied military force engaged on active operations throughout the war; true, there were periods of rest, but these seldom added up to more than a few days. The Command flew 297,663 night sorties and 66,851 day sorties, a total of 364,514 missions—for the loss of 8,325 aircraft. The casualty figures reflected the scale of effort: 47,268 aircrew were killed on operations and 8,090 lost their lives during non-operational flights.

There is great debate as to the percentage of the total British war effort taken up by Bomber Command in terms of resources, and also as to whether these resources could have been better employed elsewhere.

Many heated debates took place throughout the war on the same subject, which was a great source of inter-service rivalry as the military 'cake' was divided up. At the time the only way to have proved the point one way or another would have been to try each one out and see which worked. However, this is an unworkable military precept as equipment, training and planning take a finite time to come together. Bomber Command fought for its very existence; as the aircrew went out night after night to face the dangers over Germany, there were many at home who thought their efforts wasted. What effect did the Allied bombing have on the Axis forces?

Once again this is a much-argued point and individual conclusions depend upon individual opinions. There are few hard and fast facts and figures that can be analyzed with ease. For example, it is true that German aircraft production increased throughout the war despite the attacks on German aircraft factories—from 10,826 aircraft produced in 1940 to 39,807 aircraft in

Right: Essen—a ruined shell like so many German towns. [69 Sqn records]

Below: Lancaster RE740 'KM-O' of No 44 Squadron, July 1942. [44 Sqn records]

1944. It would appear then that all the attacks against these targets were to no avail—but is this so? The problem is that we cannot know what levels of production would have been achieved if the attacks had not taken place. Would the Germans have been able to improve their aircraft production and develop more types? It should be remembered that the German leadership had decided to concentrate on a limited number of aircraft types for ease of production; thus the Bf 109 was still in production well after it was outdated. To continue the same theme, every time an aircraft factory was damaged it was a priority repair demand, thus taking up German resources that could have been used elsewhere. The move to a full war economy in 1943 led to expansion of the German aircraft industry and dispersal of production facilities—yet more drains on the resources of the economy. This argument could be continued to even greater levels and it applies equally well to all aspects of the German economy. Every target that was attacked, unless it was of no value to the Germans, produced a strain on the overall economy.

It is true that this argument only becomes really valid for the period from 1943 onwards when Bomber Command was able to hit most of the targets it aimed at. Pinpoint targets at night remained a very difficult matter, although the Command did achieve some notable successes. The general economic war was fought against area targets, and here we come up against the so-called morality of the bomber offensive. This has been the single most disputed subject since 1945 and has led to the alienation of Bomber Command in the minds of some sections of the public, in similar fashion to that met by the Americans returning from Vietnam— 'It was a mistake so the sooner we forget it the better'. In both instances this snap judgment is unfair.

Twenty-twenty hindsight is an ability we all possess, and it is of no value at all. It is easy to look back at an event and say 'it would have been better to have done X instead of Y'. The only valid approach is to look at an incident in the context in which it took place. Such is the case with the strategic bomber offensive. In 1940 Britain was fighting for her very life and, as perceived at the time, the future of freedom. Defeat followed defeat, German bombs rained down on London, invasion by the victors of Europe might follow at any minute. Only Bomber Command was taking the war to the enemy, showing the Germans that the British people would not give up easily. Every bomb that fell on Berlin was seen as a victory and a just reply to those that were falling on England. It is a small step from one bomb to ten thousand bombs; the principle is the same, all that has changed is the capability.

Gradually the scale of the offensive increased, more bombs fell on German soil than did on British soil— good, victory had to be assured. The British public were behind the offensive, the aircrew had a job to do and all had relatives who were proud that their sons were taking the war to the enemy; most knew of people made homeless or killed by the German attacks. It was never the stated policy of either side to kill as many civilians as possible; both used air power as an economic weapon and as a means of putting pressure to bear for a surrender. Every major city of western Europe contains substantial industrial premises; thus every one could be considered a legitimate military target. Does a tank only become a weapon once it is at the front; is the person who makes the shells involved in the war—or does the shell only count once it is in the gun? The nature of the argument could be continued but the basis should now be clear. It still becomes a matter of individual opinion.

That a great deal of damage was caused to German industrial, including military industrial, installations cannot be doubted. The disruption of the German economy through attacks on communications and power (including oil) had significant effects on various aspects of the war. It is true to say that none of these was decisive in bringing overall victory, but the contribution to that overall victory is beyond doubt—except to a few sceptics. It is impossible to say how the course of the war would have been influenced by a change in priorities. It has been argued that the resources should have gone into naval equipment to prevent the losses to U-boats, but that would have been a defensive strategy—although it was essential to preserve the sea lanes. More tanks might have been built—they were desperately needed in the Middle East—but for the Army at home they could not play a decisive part until the invasion of France. This could be continued to look at many other aspects, but would be of little value. The bottom line is that there was no other offensive system of equal capability.

If the German homeland had not been attacked, Germany's resources and capability would simply have increased, as did those of Britain once the German air attacks became minimal. It is far better to fight over the other man's territory; for one thing, he then has to defend it. The German home defence network was forced to become extensive, complex—and a drain on resources, with over 1 million men engaged on home defence, plus large numbers of aircraft and guns, all of which could have been used for offensive purposes had there been no need to defend Germany. In 1942 could these have made the difference to the German invasion of Russia, and if Russia had fallen then what hope would there have been for the Allies?

This book has attempted to give an accurate account of the basic facts of the offensive (although the important American contribution has been glossed over because of space), while at the same time providing a feeling for various aspects of the life of Bomber Command. The conclusions are left to the individual reader—but with the comments above as guidance.

APPENDIX A: CHRONOLOGY

The aim of this chronology is to provide an easy-to-use guide to the major events/incidents
which involved Bomber Command between September 1939 and May 1945. It is not the intention to list every event,
but most of those listed are covered in detail within the body of the text.

1939

3 Sept.	Britain declares war on Germany
	139 Sqn Blenheim recce of Schillig Roads, the first operational sortie
	51 and 58 Sqn Whitleys drop leaflets over Germany
4 Sept.	Attacks on shipping in Schillig Roads and Kiel Canal
1/2 Oct.	First Bomber Command sorties to Berlin—leaflet-dropping
14 Dec.	99 Sqn lose 6 of 12 Wellingtons attacking German capital ships
18 Dec.	50 per cent losses on shipping attacks in Schillig Roads

1940

16 Mar.	British civilians killed in bombing near Scapa Flow
19/20 Mar.	Sylt attacked in retaliation
3 Apr.	Portal takes over as C-in-C Bomber Command
4 Apr.	Directive
9 Apr.	Germans invade Denmark and Norway
11 Apr.	First raid on mainland Europe—Stavanger airfield
13/14 Apr.	Hampdens commence 'Gardening' operations
10 May	German offensive in West launched
10/11 May	First bombing attacks on German mainland
11/12 May	First raid on German town—Mönchengladbach
15/16 May	99 bombers attack industrial targets in Hamburg and Ruhr (first strategic bombing mission)
4 Jun.	Directive
10 Jun.	Italy declares war on Britain
11/12 Jun.	First Bomber Command raid on Italy—Genoa and Turin
20 Jun.	Directive
22 Jun.	France signs Armistice
1/2 Jul.	First use of 2,000lb bomb—against *Scharnhorst* at Kiel
4 Jul.	Directive
Jul.–Oct.	Battle of Britain anti-invasion campaign
13 Jul.	Directive
12/13 Aug.	First Bomber Command VC—to F/L Learoyd of 49 Sqn—Dortmund–Ems Canal
24 Aug.	Luftwaffe bombs London
25/26 Aug.	First bombs on Berlin, retaliation for attack on London
2/3 Sept.	First raid on U-boat bases—Lorient
15/16 Sept.	VC to Sgt Hannah of 83 Sqn—Antwerp
21 Sept.	Directive: oil/communications, then industrial towns
23/24 Sept.	First true 'Main Force' attack—Berlin
15/16 Oct.	Last operational use of Fairey Battle by Bomber Command
25 Oct.	Peirse takes over as C-in-C Bomber Command
30 Oct.	Directive: adopt 'fire-raising' tactics
16 Nov.	Hamburg attacked using incendiaries to 'mark' target
16/17 Dec.	First 'area attack' (Mannheim), retaliation for attack on Coventry on 14/15 Nov.

1941

10 Jan.	First 'Circus' operation by Blenheims—Forêt de Guines
15 Jan.	Directive: precision bombing of oil targets
10/11 Feb.	Stirling first op (No 7 Sqn) to Rotterdam
24/25 Feb.	Manchester first op (No 207 Sqn) to Brest
9 Mar.	Directive: anti-naval campaign, especially U-boats
10/11 Mar.	Halifax first op (No 35 Sqn) to Le Havre
31 Mar/1 Apr.	First use of 4,000lb bomb—Emden
28 Apr.	Blenheims commence 'Channel Stop' ops
22 Jun.	Germans attack Russia

4 Jul.	VC to W/C Edwards of 105 Sqn—Bremen
7/8 Jul.	VC to Sgt Ward of 75 Sqn—Munster
8 Jul.	First RAF B-17 Fortress op (No 90 Sqn)—Wilhelmshaven
9 Jul.	Directive: mixture of precision and area targets
Jun./Jul.	Cherwell Commission on bombing accuracy
11/12 Aug.	First op trial of 'Gee'—Mönchengladbach (115 Sqn)
25/26 Aug.	Last RAF Bomber Command raid by B-17 Fortress—Emden
29/30 Aug.	First op by Australian sqn (No 455 Sqn)—Frankfurt
29/30 Aug.	First ops in support of Resistance
11 Sept.	Directive
27 Oct.	Directive
7/8 Nov.	37 aircraft lost from 400 on various ops; conservation policy introduced
Dec.	First operational use of 'Oboe', Stirlings to Brest

1942

Jan.	Washington Conference—strategic bombing campaign strategy agreed
12 Feb.	'Channel Dash' by German warships
23 Feb.	Harris takes over as C-in-C Bomber Command
14 Feb.	Directive No 22: maximum effort, area targets against morale
3/4 Mar.	Successful precision attack on Renault factory, Billancourt
3/4 Mar.	First Lancaster op (No 44 Sqn)—minelaying
Mar.	Tour length set at 200 hours
8/9 Mar.	First use of 'Shaker' technique ('Gee')—Essen.
10/11 Mar.	First Lancaster bombing op (No 44 Sqn)—Essen.
27 Mar.	First Bomber Command attack on *Tirpitz*, Trondheim Fjord.
28/29 Mar.	Trial incendiary attack tactic on Lübeck
29 Mar.	Air Council agree to withdraw 2nd pilot from heavy bombers
10/11 Apr.	First 8,000lb bomb dropped—Essen
16 Apr.	Singleton Enquiry into strategic bombing campaign
17 Apr.	Daylight raid on Augsburg by Lancasters; VC to S/L Nettleton of 44 Sqn
23/24 Apr.	Four-day campaign against Rostock started
29/30 Apr.	Last Whitley op (except OTU)
30/31 May	First '1,000-bomber' op (1,050 aircraft)—Cologne
	First use of OTU on bomb raid
31 May	Mosquito first op with Bomber Command (No 105 Sqn)—Cologne
1/2 Jun.	1,000-bomber op (956 aircraft)—Essen
25/26 Jun.	1,000-bomber op (1,006 aircraft)—Bremen
	Last op by Manchester and Whitley (except minelaying)
11 Aug.	Pathfinder Force formed
17 Aug.	First attack over Europe by US 8th Air Force (VIII Bomber Command)
17/18 Aug.	Last Blenheim op by Bomber Command (No 18 Sqn)
18/19 Aug.	First Pathfinder op—Flensburg
19 Aug.	Dieppe Raid
10/11 Sept.	First use of 'Pink Pansies'—Düsseldorf
14/15 Sept.	Last Bomber Command Hampden op (No 408 Sqn)—Wilhelmshaven
17 Oct.	1,700-mile round trip to Le Creusot (Schneider factory), longest sortie to date
22/23 Oct.	First raid on Italy by 100+ aircraft—Genoa

24 Oct.	Daylight op by 88 Lancasters to Milan
3 Nov.	First Ventura op (21 Sqn)—Hengelo
21 Nov.	Directive: joint campaign against ball-bearing plants
28/29 Nov.	First use of 8,000lb bomb—Turin
28/29 Nov.	VC to F/S Middleton of 149 Sqn—Turin
6 Dec.	Attack on Philips factory, Eindhoven
20/21 Dec.	First operational use of 'Oboe'—Lutterade
31 Dec.	Chief of Staff memo on Allied bombing policy, plan for force of 3,000 heavy bombers

1943

1 Jan.	No 6 (RCAF) Group formed
3/4 Jan	Operational debut by 6 Group—Essen
14 Jan.	Directive
16/17 Jan.	First use of TIs (250lb)—Berlin
25 Jan.	No 8 (PFF) Group formed
Jan.	Casablanca Conference: 'to destroy German military, industrial and economic system'
30/31 Jan.	First operational use of H2S—Hamburg
4 Feb.	Casablanca Directive
3 Mar.	Nine Mosquitoes attack Knaben molybdenum mine, Norway
5/6 Mar.	Battle of Ruhr starts—Essen
12 Apr.	Eaker Plan for combined RAF/USAAF offensive
3 May	VC to S/L Trent of 487 Sqn—Amsterdam
May	Washington Conference
16/17 May	Op 'Chastise', the Dams Raid; VC to W/C Gibson of 617 Sqn
31 May	Last ops by No 2 Group as part of Bomber Command
1 Jun.	No 2 Group transferred to AEAF
10 Jun.	Directive for 'Pointblank'—German industry
14/15 Jun.	First use of 'Serrate'—Oberhausen
19/20 Jun.	First operational use of 'Monica'
20 Jun.	First use of Master Bomber technique by No 5 Group
20/21 Jun.	First 'Shuttle' op: 60 Lancasters attack Friedrichshafen, then land in N. Africa
30 Jun.	500+ heavy bombers available
9/10 Jul.	End of Battle of Ruhr—Gelsenkirchen.
24 Jul.	3 Aug.—Battle of Hamburg (Operation 'Gomorrah')
24/25 Jul.	First operational use of 'Window'
August	Quebec Conference/'Quadrant'. Confirmed 'Pointblank' directive
12/13 Aug.	VC to F/Sgt Aaron of 218 Sqn—Turin
16/17 Aug.	Last attack on Italy—Turin
17/18 Aug.	Attack on research centre at Peenemünde (Operation 'Hydra')
15/16 Sept.	First use of 12,000lb 'Tallboy'—Dortmund–Ems Canal
September	'Bullseye' missions introduced
22/23 Sept.	First use of 'spoof' target technique
7/8 Oct.	First operational use of 'Gee-H'—Aachen. First operational use of ABC—Stuttgart.
8/9 Oct.	Last Bomber Command bombing op with Wellington—Hannover
22/23 Oct.	First operational use of 'Corona'—Kassel
3/4 Nov.	VC to F/L Reid of 61 Sqn—Düsseldorf. First attack with 'G-H'—Düsseldorf
8 Nov.	No 100 (Special Duties) Group formed
Nov.	Cairo Conference/'Sextant'

18/19 Nov.	Battle of Berlin starts
30 Nov/1 Dec.	First op by No 100 Group—192 Sqn
16/17 Dec.	First 'Serrate' op—141 Sqn

1944

14 Jan.	Directive: attack cities producing fighter aircraft or components
23/24 Jan.	Start of 'Big Week', offensive against German aircraft manufacturing
28 Jan.	Reinforced directive by giving priority list of targets
4 Mar.	Directive: attack six French marshalling yards by day.
6/7 Mar.	Start pre-invasion bombing—Trappes
24/25 Mar.	Battle of Berlin ends
25 Mar.	Transportation Plan accepted for 'Overlord' support
30/31 Mar.	Last 'Pointblank' op, Nuremberg; VC to P/O Barton of 578 Sqn
14 Apr.	Operational control of Bomber Command passed to SHAEF
17 Apr.	Supreme Commander co-directive: prime aim to destroy German air combat strength
26/27 Apr.	VC to Sgt Jackson of 106 Sqn—Schweinfurt
12/13 May	First sea-mining by Mosquito—Kiel Canal.
6 Jun.	D-Day
12 Jun.	Commence Operation 'Crossbow' against V-1 sites
12/13 Jun.	VC to P/O Mynarski of 419 Sqn—Cambrai
14 Jun.	Daylight bombing raids by Bomber Command resume
16/17 Jun.	First op against V-weapon sites ('Noball')
7 Jul.	Heavy bombers used to area-bomb troops near Caen
27 Aug.	First major daylight raid on Germany—Homberg
8 Sept.	Last bombing op by Stirling—Le Havre
8 Sept.	VC to W/C Cheshire announced
14 Sept.	Operational Control of Bomber Command reverts to Air Staff
23/24 Sept.	Dortmund–Ems Canal breached
25 Sept.	Directive: oil and transport plan confirmed
13 Oct.	Revised directive: allowed attacks on Ruhr targets
1 Nov.	Directive
12 Nov.	*Tirpitz* destroyed by Nos 9 and 617 Sqns
14 Dec.	German Ardennes offensive starts
23 Dec.	Directive
23 Dec.	VC to S/L Palmer of 109 Sqn—Cologne

1945

1 Jan.	VC to F/S Thompson of 9 Sqn—Dortmund–Ems Canal
15 Jan.	Directive: oil and transport still primary but also resurgent German air force
7 Feb.	Directive
13/14 Feb.	Attack on Dresden, part of 'Thunderclap'
23/24 Feb.	VC to Capt Swales of 582 Sqn—Pforzheim
12 Mar.	Largest Bomber Command attack to date, 1,107 aircraft to Dortmund
14 Mar.	First operational use of 22,000lb 'Grand Slam'—Bielefeld Viaduct
16 Apr.	Directive, and area bombing halted
26 Apr.	Start Operation 'Exodus'—repatriation of PoWs.
29 Apr.	Start of Operation 'Manna'—food-dropping in Holland
2/3 May	Last Bomber Command op, naval targets in Kiel area
8 May	Victory in Europe (VE Day)

APPENDIX B: COMMAND POSITIONS

AOC-IN-C BOMBER COMMAND

ACM Sir Edgar Ludlow-Hewitt	12.9.37 – 2.4.40
AVM C. F. Portal	– 5.10.40
AM Sir Richard E. Peirse	– 8.1.42
AVM J. E. Baldwin	– 22.2.42 (acting AOC)
AVM A. T. Harris	– 15.9.45

GROUP COMMANDERS

No 1 Group

AVM A. C. Wright	3.9.39 – 27.6.40
A/C J. J. Breen	– 27.11.40
AVM R. D. Oxland	– 24.2.43

AVM E. A. B. Rice	– 5.2.45
AVM R. S. Blucke	– end

No 2 Group

AVM C. T. Maclean	16.5.38 – 17.4.40
AVM J. M. Robb	– 12.2.41
AVM D. F. Stevenson	– 17.12.41
AVM A. Lees	– 29.12.42
AVM J. H. D'Albiac	– May 43 (transfer to TAF)

No 3 Group

AVM J. E. A. Baldwin	29.8.39 – 14.9.42
AVM R. A. Cochrane	– 27.2.43
AVM R. Harrison	– end

No 4 Group
(A/C A. T. Harris   12.6.37 – 25.5.38)
AVM A. Coningham   3.7.39 – 26.7.41
AVM C. R. Carr   – 12.2.45
AVM J. R. Whitley   – end

No 5 Group
AVM A. T. Harris   11.9.39 – 22.11.40
AVM N. H. Bottomley   – 12.5.41
AVM J. C. Slessor   – 25.4.42
AVM W. A. Coryton   – 28.2.43
AVM R. A. Cochrane   – 16.1.45
AVM H. A. Constantine   – end

No 6 (RCAF) Group
AVM G. E. Brookes   25.10.42 – 29.2.44
AVM C. M. McEwen   – end

No 8 (Pathfinder) Group
AVM D. C. T. Bennett*   13.1.43 – end

No 100 (Bomber Support) Group
AVM E. B. Addison   23.11.43 – end

*A/C Bennett had been in command of the Pathfinder Force since inception and pre-Group status

APPENDIX C: ORDER OF BATTLE, MARCH 1937

Squadron	Aircraft	Location
No 1 Group		
15 Sqn	Hind	Abingdon
18 Sqn	Hind	Upper Heyford
21 Sqn	Hind	Lympne
34 Sqn	Hind	Lympne
40 Sqn	Hind	Abingdon
57 Sqn	Hind	Upper Heyford
90 Sqn	Hind	Bicester
101 Sqn	Overstrand	Bicester
108 Sqn	Hind	Farnborough
218 Sqn	Hind	Upper Heyford
226 Sqn	Audax	Upper Heyford
No 2 Group		
12 Sqn	Hind	Andover
35 Sqn	Gordon	Worthy Down
44 Sqn	Hind	Andover
49 Sqn	Hind	Worthy Down
52 Sqn	Hind	Upwood
63 Sqn	Hind	Upwood
83 Sqn	Hind	Turnhouse
98 Sqn	Hind	Hucknall
103 Sqn	Hind	Andover
104 Sqn	Hind	Hucknall
107 Sqn	Hind	Old Sarum
142 Sqn	Hind	Andover
207 Sqn	Gordon	Worthy Down
502 Sqn	Hind	Abbotsinch
605 Sqn	Hart	Castle Bromwich

No 3 Group		
7 Sqn	Heyford	Finningley
9 Sqn	Heyford	Scampton
10 Sqn	Heyford	Dishforth
38 Sqn	Hendon	Mildenhall
51 Sqn	Virginia/Anson	Driffield
58 Sqn	Virginia	Boscombe Down
61 Sqn	Anson	Hemswell
75 Sqn	Virginia/Anson	Driffield
78 Sqn	Heyford	Dishforth
97 Sqn	Heyford	Leconfield
99 Sqn	Heyford	Mildenhall
102 Sqn	Heyford	Finningley
114 Sqn	Hind	Wyton
139 Sqn	Hind	Wyton
144 Sqn	Anson	Hemswell
166 Sqn	Heyford	Leconfield
214 Sqn	Harrow	Scampton
215 Sqn	Anson	Driffield
No 6 Group		
500 Sqn	Hind	Manston
501 Sqn	Hart	Filton
502 Sqn	Hind	Aldergrove
503 Sqn	Hart	Waddington
504 Sqn	Wallace	Hucknall
603 Sqn	Hart	Turnhouse
609 Sqn	Hart	Yeadon
610 Sqn	Hart	Hooton Park
611 Sqn	Hart	Speke

Total: 53 Squadrons

APPENDIX D: ORDER OF BATTLE, 31 AUGUST 1939

Squadron	Aircraft Type	Location
No 1 Group		
12 Sqn	Battle	Bicester
15 Sqn	Battle	Abingdon
35 Sqn	Battle	Cranfield
40 Sqn	Battle	Abingdon
52 Sqn	Battle	Upwood
63 Sqn	Battle	Watton
88 Sqn	Battle	Boscombe Down
98 Sqn	Battle	Hucknall
103 Sqn	Battle	Benson
105 Sqn	Battle	Harwell
142 Sqn	Battle	Bicester
150 Sqn	Battle	Benson
207 Sqn	Battle	Cranfield
218 Sqn	Battle	Boscombe Down
226 Sqn	Battle	Harwell
No 2 Group		
18 Sqn	Blenheim	Upper Heyford
57 Sqn	Blenheim	Upper Heyford
82 Sqn	Blenheim	Watton

104 Sqn	Blenheim	Bassingbourn
108 Sqn	Blenheim	Bassingbourn
114 Sqn	Blenheim	Wyton
139 Sqn	Blenheim	Wyton
No 3 Group		
9 Sqn	Wellington	Honington
37 Sqn	Wellington	Feltwell
38 Sqn	Wellington	Marham
75 Sqn	Wellington	Stradishall
99 Sqn	Wellington	Mildenhall
115 Sqn	Wellington	Marham
148 Sqn	Wellington	Stradishall
149 Sqn	Wellington	Mildenhall
214 Sqn	Wellington	Feltwell
215 Sqn	Wellington	Honington
No 4 Group		
10 Sqn	Whitley	Dishforth
51 Sqn	Whitley	Linton-on-Ouse
58 Sqn	Whitley	Linton-on-Ouse
77 Sqn	Whitley	Driffield

78 Sqn	Whitley	Dishforth	83 Sqn	Hampden	Scampton
97 Sqn	Whitley	Leconfield	106 Sqn	Hampden	Cottesmore
102 Sqn	Whitley	Driffield	144 Sqn	Hampden	Hemswell
166 Sqn	Whitley	Leconfield	185 Sqn	Hampden	Cottesmore

No 5 Group

No 6 Group (operationally attached to No 2 Group)

7 Sqn	Hampden	Finningley	21 Sqn	Blenheim	Watton
44 Sqn	Hampden	Waddington	90 Sqn	Blenheim	West Raynham
49 Sqn	Hampden	Scampton	101 Sqn	Blenheim	West Raynham
50 Sqn	Hampden	Waddington	107 Sqn	Blenheim	Wattisham
61 Sqn	Hampden	Hemswell	110 Sqn	Blenheim	Wattisham
76 Sqn	Hampden	Finningley			

Total: 55 Squadrons

APPENDIX E: ORDER OF BATTLE, 14 NOVEMBER 1940

Squadron	Aircraft Type	Location
No 1 Group		
12 Sqn	Wellington	Binbrook
103 Sqn	Wellington	Newton
142 Sqn	Wellington	Binbrook
150 Sqn	Wellington	Newton
300 Sqn (Polish)	Wellington	Swinderby
301 Sqn (Polish)	Wellington	Swinderby
304 Sqn (Polish)	Wellington	Syerston
305 Sqn (Polish)	Wellington	Syerston
No 2 Group		
18 Sqn	Blenheim	West Raynham
21 Sqn	Blenheim	Watton
82 Sqn	Blenheim	Watton
101 Sqn	Blenheim	West Raynham
105 Sqn	Blenheim	Swanton Morley
107 Sqn	Blenheim	Wattisham
110 Sqn	Blenheim	Wattisham
114 Sqn	Blenheim	Horsham St Faith
139 Sqn	Blenheim	Horsham St Faith
No 3 Group		
7 Sqn	Stirling	Oakington
9 Sqn	Wellington	Feltwell
15 Sqn	Wellington	Wyton
40 Sqn	Wellington	Wyton
57 Sqn	Wellington	Wyton
75 Sqn (NZ)	Wellington	Feltwell
99 Sqn	Wellington	Mildenhall
115 Sqn	Wellington	Marham
149 Sqn	Wellington	Mildenhall
214 Sqn	Wellington	Stradishall
218 Sqn	Wellington	Oakington
311 Sqn (Czech)	Wellington	Honington
No 4 Group		
10 Sqn	Whitley	Leeming
35 Sqn	Halifax	Leeming
51 Sqn	Whitley	Dishforth
58 Sqn	Whitley	Linton-on-Ouse
77 Sqn	Whitley	Topcliffe
78 Sqn	Whitley	Dishforth
102 Sqn	Whitley	Linton-on-Ouse
No 5 Group		
44 Sqn	Hampden	Waddington
49 Sqn	Hampden	Scampton
50 Sqn	Hampden	Lindholme
61 Sqn	Hampden	Hemswell
83 Sqn	Hampden	Scampton
106 Sqn	Hampden	Finningley
144 Sqn	Hampden	Hemswell
207 Sqn	Manchester	Waddington
271 Sqn	(various transport)	Doncaster

Total: 45 Squadrons

Notes:
1. Fifteen squadrons at half strength during re-equipment and thus not operational.
2. Two squadrons non-operational—No 106 (Reserve) and No 271 (Transport).
3. No 3 Group had just lost Nos 37 and 38 Squadrons as reinforcement to Middle East.

APPENDIX F: ORDER OF BATTLE, FEBRUARY 1942

Squadron	Aircraft Type	Location
No 1 Group		
12 Sqn	Wellington	Binbrook
103 Sqn	Wellington	Elsham Wolds
142 Sqn	Wellington	Grimsby
150 Sqn	Wellington	Snaith
300 Sqn (Polish)	Wellington	Hemswell
301 Sqn (Polish)	Wellington	Hemswell
304 Sqn (Polish)	Wellington	Lindholme
305 Sqn (Polish)	Wellington	Lindholme
460 Sqn (RAAF)	Wellington	Breighton
No 2 Group		
21 Sqn	Blenheim	Walton
18 Sqn	Blenheim	Wattisham
82 Sqn	Blenheim	Bodney
88 Sqn	Boston	Swanton Morley/ Attlebridge
105 Sqn	Blenheim/Mosquito	Horsham St Faith
107 Sqn	Blenheim/Mosquito	Gt Massingham
110 Sqn	Blenheim	Wattisham
114 Sqn	Blenheim	West Raynham
226 Sqn	Boston	Swanton Morley
No 3 Group		
7 Sqn	Stirling	Oakington
9 Sqn	Wellington	Honington
15 Sqn	Stirling	Wyton
57 Sqn	Wellington	Feltwell
75 Sqn (NZ)	Wellington	Feltwell
101 Sqn	Wellington	Bourn
115 Sqn	Wellington	Marham
149 Sqn	Stirling	Mildenhall
156 Sqn	Wellington	Alconbury
214 Sqn	Wellington	Stradishall/Honington
218 Sqn	Wellington/Stirling	Marham
311 Sqn (Czech)	Wellington	East Wretham
419 Sqn (RCAF)	Wellington	Mildenhall

No 4 Group

10 Sqn	Halifax	Leeming
35 Sqn	Halifax	Linton-on-Ouse
51 Sqn	Whitley	Andover
58 Sqn	Whitley	Linton
76 Sqn	Halifax	Middleton St George
77 Sqn	Whitley	Leeming
78 Sqn	Whitley	Croft
102 Sqn	Whitley/Halifax	Dalton
138 Sqn (SD)	Whitley/Halifax	Newmarket
158 Sqn	Wellington	Driffield
405 Sqn (RCAF)	Wellington	Pocklington

No 5 Group

44 Sqn	Lancaster	Waddington

49 Sqn	Hampden	Scampton
50 Sqn	Hampden	Skellingthorpe
61 Sqn	Manchester	Woolfax Lodge
83 Sqn	Manchester	Scampton
97 Sqn	Lancaster	Coningsby
106 Sqn	Hampden	Coningsby
144 Sqn	Hampden	North Luffenham
207 Sqn	Manchester	Bottesford
408 Sqn (RCAF)	Hampden	Balderton
420 Sqn (RCAF)	Hampden	Waddington
455 Sqn (RCAF)	Hampden	Skellingthorpe

Total: 54 Squadrons

APPENDIX G: ORDER OF BATTLE, FEBRUARY 1943

Squadron	Aircraft Type	Location
No 1 Group		
12 Sqn	Lancaster	Wickenby
100 Sqn	Lancaster	Grimsby
101 Sqn	Lancaster	Holme
103 Sqn	Lancaster	Elsham Wooods
166 Sqn	Wellington	Kirmington
199 Sqn	Wellington	Ingham
300 Sqn (Polish)	Wellington	Hemswell
301 Sqn (Polish)	Wellington	Hemswell
305 Sqn (Polish)	Wellington	Hemswell
460 Sqn (RAAF)	Lancaster	Breighton
No 2 Group		
21 Sqn	Ventura	Methwold
88 Sqn	Boston	Oulton
98 Sqn	Mitchell	Foulsham
105 Sqn	Mosquito	Marham
107 Sqn	Boston	Gt Massingham
139 Sqn	Mosquito/ Blenheim	Marham
180 Sqn	Mitchell	Foulsham
226 Sqn	Boston	Swanton Morley
464 Sqn (RAAF)	Ventura	Feltwell
487 Sqn (RNZAF)	Ventura	Feltwell
No 3 Group		
15 Sqn	Stirling	Bourn
75 Sqn (NZ)	Stirling	Newmarket
90 Sqn	Stirling	Ridgewell
115 Sqn	Stirling	East Wretham
138 Sqn (SD)	Halifax	Tempsford
149 Sqn	Stirling	Lakenheath
161 Sqn (SD)	Halifax/Havoc/ Lysander	Tempsford
192 (SD)	Wellington/Halifax	Gransden Lodge
214 Sqn	Stirling	Chedburgh
218 Sqn	Stirling	Downham Market
No 4 Group		
10 Sqn	Halifax	Melbourne
51 Sqn	Halifax/Whitley	Snaith
76 Sqn	Halifax	Linton-on-Ouse
77 Sqn	Halifax	Elvington
78 Sqn	Halifax	Linton-on-Ouse
102 Sqn	Halifax	Pocklington
158 Sqn	Halifax	Rufforth
196 Sqn	Wellington	Leconfield
429 Sqn (RCAF)	Wellington	East Moor
431 Sqn (RCAF)	Wellington	Burn
466 Sqn (RCAF)	Wellington	Leconfield
No 5 Group		
9 Sqn	Lancaster	Waddington
44 Sqn	Lancaster	Waddington
49 Sqn	Lancaster	Fiskerton
50 Sqn	Lancaster	Skellingthorpe

57 Sqn	Lancaster	Scampton
61 Sqn	Lancaster	Syerston
97 Sqn	Lancaster	Woodhall Spa
106 Sqn	Lancaster	Syerston
207 Sqn	Lancaster	Langar
467 Sqn (RAAF)	Lancaster	Bottesford
No 6 Group		
405 Sqn (RCAF)	Halifax	Beaulieu
408 Sqn (RCAF)	Halifax	Leeming
419 Sqn (RCAF)	Halifax	Middleton St George
420 Sqn (RCAF)	Wellington	Middleton St George
424 Sqn (RCAF)	Wellington	Topcliffe
425 Sqn (RCAF)	Wellington	Dishforth
426 Sqn (RCAF)	Wellington	Dishforth
427 Sqn (RCAF)	Wellington	Croft
428 Sqn (RCAF)	Wellington	Dalton
No 8 Group		
7 Sqn	Stirling	Oakington
35 Sqn	Halifax	Graveley
83 Sqn	Lancaster	Wyton
109 Sqn	Mosquito	Wyton
156 Sqn	Lancaster	Warboys

Total: 63 Squadrons

Operational Training Units

No 91 Group		
10 OTU	Anson/Whitley	Abingdon
15 OTU	Wellington	Harwell
19 OTU	Whitley	Kinloss
20 OTU	Wellington	Lossiemouth
21 OTU	Anson/Wellington	Moreton-in-the-Marsh
22 OTU	Wellington	Wellesbourne Mountford
23 OTU	Wellington	Pershore
24 OTU	Anson/Whitley	Honeybourne
No 92 Group		
11 OTU	Wellington	Westcott
12 OTU	Wellington	Chipping Warden
13 OTU	Blenheim/Anson	Bicester
14 OTU	Wellington	Cottesmore
16 OTU	Wellington	Upper Heyford
17 OTU	Blenheim/Anson	Upwood
26 OTU	Wellington	Wing
29 OTU	Wellington	North Luffenham
No 93 Group		
18 OTU	Wellington	Bramcote
25 OTU	(disbanding)	Finningley
27 OTU	Wellington	Lichfield
28 OTU	Wellington	Wymeswold
30 OTU	Wellington	Hixon
81 OTU	Whitley	Whitchurch Heath

APPENDIX H: ORDER OF BATTLE, BATTLE OF BERLIN (NOVEMBER 1943)

Squadron	Aircraft Type	Location
No 1 Group		
12 Sqn	Lancaster	Wickenby
100 Sqn	Lancaster	Grimsby
101 Sqn	Lancaster	Ludford Magna
103 Sqn	Lancaster	Elsham Wolds
166 Sqn	Lancaster	Kirmington
460 Sqn (RAAF)	Lancaster	Binbrook
550 Sqn	Lancaster	Grimsby/Nth Killingholme
576 Sqn	Lancaster	Elsham Wolds
625 Sqn	Lancaster	Kelstern
626 Sqn	Lancaster	Wickenby
No 3 Group		
15 Sqn	Stirling	Mildenhall
75 Sqn (NZ)	Stirling	Mepal
90 Sqn	Stirling	Wratting Common
115 Sqn	Lancaster	Little Snoring
149 Sqn	Stirling	Lakenheath
196 Sqn	Stirling	Witchford
199 Sqn	Stirling	Lakenheath
214 Sqn	Stirling	Chedburgh
218 Sqn	Stirling	Downham Market
514 Sqn	Lancaster	Foulsham
620 Sqn	Stirling	Chedburgh
622 Sqn	Stirling/Lancaster	Mildenhall
623 Sqn	Lancaster	Downham Market
No 4 Group		
10 Sqn	Halifax	Melbourne
51 Sqn	Halifax	Snaith
76 Sqn	Halifax	Holme-on-Spalding Moor
77 Sqn	Halifax	Elvington
78 Sqn	Halifax	Breighton
102 Sqn	Halifax	Pocklington
158 Sqn	Halifax	Lissett
466 Sqn (RCAF)	Halifax	Leconfield
578 Sqn	Halifax	Burn
640 Sqn	Halifax	Leconfield
No 5 Group		
9 Sqn	Lancaster	Bardney
44 Sqn	Lancaster	Dunholme Lodge
49 Sqn	Lancaster	Fiskerton
50 Sqn	Lancaster	Skellingthorpe
57 Sqn	Lancaster	Scampton
61 Sqn	Lancaster	Syerston/Skellingthorpe
106 Sqn	Lancaster	Syerston
207 Sqn	Lancaster	Langar
463 Sqn (RAAF)	Lancaster	Waddington
467 Sqn (RAAF)	Lancaster	Waddington
619 Sqn	Lancaster	Woodhall Spa
630 Sqn	Lancaster	East Kirkby
No 6 Group		
408 Sqn (RCAF)	Lancaster	Linton-on-Ouse
419 Sqn (RCAF)	Halifax	Middleton St George
420 Sqn (RCAF)	Halifax	Tholthorpe
424 Sqn (RCAF)	Halifax	Skipton-on-Swale
425 Sqn (RCAF)	Halifax	Tholthorpe
426 Sqn (RCAF)	Lancaster	Linton-on-Ouse
427 Sqn (RCAF)	Halifax	Leeming
428 Sqn (RCAF)	Halifax	Middleton St George
429 Sqn (RCAF)	Halifax	Leeming
431 Sqn (RCAF)	Halifax	Tholthorpe
432 Sqn (RCAF)	Lancaster	Skipton-on-Swale
433 Sqn (RCAF)	Halifax	Skipton-on-Swale
434 Sqn (RCAF)	Halifax	Tholthorpe
No 8 Group		
7 Sqn	Lancaster	Oakington
35 Sqn	Halifax	Graveley
83 Sqn	Lancaster	Wyton
97 Sqn	Lancaster	Bourn
139 Sqn	Mosquito	Wyton
156 Sqn	Lancaster	Warboys
405 Sqn (RCAF)	Halifax	Gransden Lodge
627 Sqn	Mosquito	Oakington
635 Sqn	Lancaster	Downham Market
692 Sqn	Mosquito	Graveley

Total: 68 Squadrons

APPENDIX I: ORDER OF BATTLE, JANUARY 1945

Squadron	Aircraft Type	Location
No 1 Group		
12 Sqn	Lancaster	Wickenby
100 Sqn	Lancaster	Elsham Wolds
101 Sqn	Lancaster	Ludford Magna
103 Sqn	Lancaster	Elsham Wolds
150 Sqn	Lancaster	Hemswell
153 Sqn	Lancaster	Scampton
166 Sqn	Lancaster	Kirmington
170 Sqn	Lancaster	Hemswell
300 Sqn (Polish)	Lancaster	Binbrook
460 Sqn (RAAF)	Lancaster	Binbrook
550 Sqn	Lancaster	North Killingholme
576 Sqn	Lancaster	Fiskerton
625 Sqn	Lancaster	Kelstern
626 Sqn	Lancaster	Wickenby
No 3 Group		
15 Sqn	Lancaster	Mildenhall
75 Sqn (NZ)	Lancaster	Mepal
90 Sqn	Lancaster	Tuddenham
115 Sqn	Lancaster	Witchford
138 Sqn (SD)	Stirling/Hudson	Tempsford
149 Sqn	Lancaster	Methwold
161 Sqn (SD)	Stirling/Hudson	Tempsford
186 Sqn	Lancaster	Stradishall
195 Sqn	Lancaster	Wratting Common
218 Sqn	Lancaster	Chedburgh
514 Sqn	Lancaster	Waterbeach
622 Sqn	Lancaster	Mildenhall
No 4 Group		
10 Sqn	Halifax	Melbourne
51 Sqn	Halifax	Snaith
76 Sqn	Halifax	Holme-on-Spalding Moor
77 Sqn	Halifax	Full Sutton
78 Sqn	Halifax	Breighton
102 Sqn	Halifax	Pocklington
158 Sqn	Halifax	Lisset
346 (French)	Halifax	Elvington
347 (French)	Halifax	Elvington
462 Sqn (RAAF)	Halifax	Foulsham
466 Sqn (RAAF)	Halifax	Driffield
578 Sqn	Halifax	Burn
640 Sqn	Halifax	Leconfield
No 5 Group		
9 Sqn	Lancaster	Bardney
44 Sqn	Lancaster	Spilsby
49 Sqn	Lancaster	Fulbeck
50 Sqn	Lancaster	Skellingthorpe
57 Sqn	Lancaster	East Kirby
61 Sqn	Lancaster	Skellingthorpe
83 Sqn	Lancaster	Coningsby
97 Sqn	Lancaster	Coningsby
106 Sqn	Lancaster	Metheringham

189 Sqn	Lancaster	Fulbeck		35 Sqn	Lancaster	Graveley
207 Sqn	Lancaster	Spilsby		105 Sqn	Mosquito	Bourn
227 Sqn	Lancaster	Bardney		109 Sqn	Mosquito	Woodhall Spa
463 Sqn (RAAF)	Lancaster	Waddington		128 Sqn	Mosquito	Wyton
467 Sqn (RAAF)	Lancaster	Waddington		139 Sqn	Mosquito	Upwood
617 Sqn	Lancaster	Woodhall Spa		142 Sqn	Mosquito	Gransden Lodge
619 Sqn	Lancaster	Strubby		156 Sqn	Mosquito	Upwood
627 Sqn	Mosquito	Woodhall Spa		405 Sqn (RCAF)	Lancaster	Gransden Lodge
630 Sqn	Lancaster	East Kirkby		571 Sqn	Mosquito	Oakington
				582 Sqn	Lancaster	Little Staughton

No 6 Group

408 Sqn (RCAF)	Halifax	Linton-on-Ouse		608 Sqn	Mosquito	Downham Market
415 Sqn (RCAF)	Halifax	East Moor		692 Sqn	Mosquito	Graveley
419 Sqn (RCAF)	Halifax	Middleton St George		1409 (Met) Flt	Mosquito	
420 Sqn (RCAF)	Halifax	Tholthorpe				
424 Sqn (RCAF)	Halifax	Skipton-on-Swale		*No 100 (Bomber Support) Group*		
425 Sqn (RCAF)	Halifax	Tholthorpe		23 Sqn	Mosquito	Little Snoring
426 Sqn (RCAF)	Halifax	Linton-on-Ouse		85 Sqn	Mosquito	Swannington
427 Sqn (RCAF)	Halifax	Leeming		141 Sqn	Mosquito	West Raynham
428 Sqn (RCAF)	Halifax	Middleton St George		157 Sqn	Mosquito	Swannington
429 Sqn (RCAF)	Halifax	Leeming		169 Sqn	Mosquito	Great Massingham
431 Sqn (RCAF)	Halifax	Croft		171 Sqn	Halifax	North Creake
432 Sqn (RCAF)	Halifax	East Moor		192 Sqn	Halifax/Mosquito	Foulsham
433 Sqn (RCAF)	Halifax	Skipton-on-Swale		199 Sqn	Halifax	North Creake
434 Sqn (RCAF)	Halifax	Croft		214 Sqn	Fortress	Oulton
				239 Sqn	Mosquito	West Raynham
No 8 Group				515 Sqn	Mosquito	Little Snoring
7 Sqn	Lancaster	Oakington				

Total: 95 Sqns + 1 Met Flt

APPENDIX J: THE VICTORIA CROSS

Britain's highest military decoration for valour, the Victorian Cross, was awarded on just nineteen occasions to aircrew of Bomber Command. So many heroic deeds were carried out by the Command's members throughout the war, yet why did one act bring the award of a VC but another similar act pass seemingly unnoticed? In the words of Bill Reid, VC: 'I was lucky enough to get my aircraft back to England, and the story of what happened that night was told in full. I often wonder how many other crews went through what we did that night but failed to return. Had they have done, then I am sure that there would have been many more gallantry awards.' Bill Reid's point is valid. Bomber Command suffered so many casualties that there must have been no end of 'unsung heroes'.

Recommendations for individual awards were generally made by the Station Commander of the unit and passed up the chain of command before final approval by the Commander-in-Chief. The recommendation consisted of a narrative including details of the individual, number of operations flown and operational hours, and which award was recommended. It was often the case that an individual was recommended for a higher award than he would eventually receive. In some cases, a VC would be recommended but a 'lesser' gallantry award received. This could have been for several reasons. It may have been considered that the individual had not performed quite the 'outstanding courage or devotion to duty' required for the highest award, or it may have been considered that one area of operations should not be thought of more favourably than another. Sadly, many individuals rewarded for their gallantry in action never lived to see their award. Many awards were posthumous and several, although aware of their award, never lived long enough to receive it. Brief details of the awards of the Victoria Cross to members of Bomber Command are given below.

Flight Lieutenant Rod Learoyd, VC (No 49 Squadron)
Learoyd was the captain of Hampden P4403 detailed to attack the Dortmund–Ems Canal on the night of 12/13 August 1940. The last to attack, his aircraft was hit by shells and machine-gun fire. Despite this, he held the aircraft steady to complete the attack. With a ruptured hydraulic system, he nursed the bomber home. His attack against a well-alerted and heavily defended target had probably been the most hazardous of the operation. For his outstanding bravery and skill in pressing home his attack, Rod Learoyd was awarded the VC.

Sergeant John Hannah, VC (No 83 Squadron)
Hannah was the wireless operator/air gunner of Hampden P1355 detailed to attack the port of Antwerp on the night of 15/16 September 1940. Over the target, his aircraft was hit in the bomb bay. The fuselage

was enveloped in fire, causing unbearable heat and damage. All around him, ammunition started exploding and the second air gunner and navigator baled out. Hannah extinguished the fire and, eventually satisfied that the fire was out, he crawled forward to report the damage. When the captain saw him he was shocked. Hannah's face and hands were burned black, his eyes badly swollen and the remains of his flying clothing charred. Back at base, the extent of his horrific injuries were realized and he was rushed to hospital. Soon after came the announcement of the VC to Hannah. Aged just 18, he was the youngest airman ever to receive the award.

Wing Commander Hughie Edwards, VC, DFC (No 105 Squadron)
Edwards was captain of Blenheim V6028 chosen to lead a daylight raid on Bremen on 4 July 1941. Flying at chimney height he carried out a most determined attack. His aircraft was hit some 20 times during the raid. He eventually landed back at base, the last of the surviving aircraft to return. Soon after came the announcement of the VC to Edwards. 'He showed outstanding courage, determination and leadership during the operation. He knew that casualties would be severe and that his own personal chances of return, as leader of the raid, were extremely slender. Such dauntless courage in the face of such odds deserves the highest award and is in direct keeping with the great traditions of the Royal Air Force.'

Sergeant Jimmy Ward, VC (No 75 [NZ] Squadron)
Ward was the second pilot of Wellington L7818 detailed to attack Munster on the night of 7/8 July 1941. On the way home, his aircraft was attacked by a fighter resulting in the starboard wing catching fire. He clipped on his parachute, tied a rope around his waist, picked up some canvas and climbed out through the astro-dome. Having climbed onto the wing, he slowly pulled himself towards the fire. He stuffed the canvas into a gaping hole through which fuel was spilling onto the fire and held it there until forced to let it go. He could do no more and slowly, with difficulty, climbed back into the fuselage. The aircraft made a safe landing and, soon after, it was announced that the young New Zealander had been awarded the VC.

Squadron Leader John Nettleton, VC (No 44 Squadron)
Nettleton was the captain of Lancaster R5508 chosen to lead a daylight raid on Augsburg on 17 April 1942. His formation was engaged by enemy fighters. One by one, the aircraft of his formation were shot down until in the end his and one other Lancaster remained. Almost defenceless, he held his two remaining aircraft on course to Augsburg. Although fired at from point-blank range, they dropped their bombs on the target. The second aircraft was then shot down by flak. Nettleton's

Leslie Manser.

machine was the only one of the six to return. On 28 April it was announced that John Nettleton had been awarded the VC. 'He dispalyed unflinching determination as well as leadership and valour of the highest order.'

Flying Officer Leslie Manser, VC (No 50 Squadron)

Manser was the captain of Manchester L7301 detailed to attack Cologne on the night of 30/31 May 1942. Over the target, his aircraft was hit by flak and the port engine caught fire. On just one engine, the Manchester began to lose height and Manser ordered the crew to bale out. One of the crew handed him his parachute, but Manser waved it away saying that he could only hold the aircraft steady for a few more seconds. As the crew descended they saw the aircraft, still carrying their gallant captain, plunge to earth. Apart from one taken prisoner, the remainder of the crew evaded capture and returned to Britain. Then the full story was told and it was announced that Leslie Manser had been posthumously awarded the VC.

Pilot Officer Ron Middleton, VC (No 149 Squadron)

Middleton was the captain of Stirling BF372 detailed to attack Turin on the night of 28/29 November 1942. Over the target, his aircraft was hit by ground fire, wounding him, shattering his windscreen and making him temporarily unconscious. Regaining consciousness, he recovered control of the aircraft and set course for the long journey home. Growing weaker through the loss of blood and desperately short of fuel, he nursed the bomber slowly back to England. Having run out of fuel, he held the aircraft steady long enough for his crew to bale out. The Stirling, with the gallant Australian still on board, crashed into the Channel. Soon after, came the announcement of a posthumous VC to Ron Middleton.

Squadron Leader Leonard Trent, VC (No 487 Squadron, RNZAF)

Trent was the captain of Ventura AJ209 chosen to lead a daylight raid against Amsterdam on 3 May 1943. As his force of eleven Venturas reached the coast, they were met by enemy fighters. The result was devastating. Only Trent and one other Ventura reached the target. Concentrating solely on attacking the target, Trent released his bombs. His aircraft was immediately hit and began to spin. He ordered his crew to bale out and then the aircraft blew up, throwing Trent clear. Amazingly, he survived and was taken prisoner. Following his repatriation, the full story of the raid was told. Finally, on 1 March 1946, it was announced that Leonard Trent had been awarded the VC for his determined leadership of the raid.

Wing Commander Guy Gibson, VC, DSO and Bar, DFC and Bar (No 617 Squadron)

Gibson was the captain of Lancaster ED932 detailed to lead a raid against the Ruhr dams on the night of 16/17 May 1943. Under his inspiring leadership, the squadron executed one of the most devastating attacks of the war. Gibson made the initial attack on the Möhne Dam. Descending to within a few feet of the water, taking the full brunt of the defences, he delivered his attack with great accuracy. Afterwards, he circled very low, drawing enemy fire on himself to leave as free a run as possible for the following attacking aircraft. He then led the remainder of his force to the Eder Dam where, with complete disregard for his own safety, he repeated his tactics. Soon after, he was awarded the VC. 'Throughout his operational career, prolonged exceptionally at his own request, he has shown leadership, determination and valour of the highest order.'

Flight Sergeant Arthur Aaron, VC, DFM (No 218 Squadron)

Aaron was the captain of Stirling EF452 detailed to attack Turin on the night of 12/13 August 1943. Approaching the target, his aircraft was shot at by a Stirling of the same squadron. Aaron was wounded in the face and his right arm was severed. The windscreen and instrument panel were shattered and the hydraulics failed. Jettisoning the bombs, the crew headed from North Africa and safety. Desperately weak through the loss of blood and unable to speak, Aaron communicated with the crew through a series of written messages. For four hours the Stirling continued to safety. Desperately short of fuel, Aaron recovered enough to make a forced landing at Bone airfield. A few hours later, Arthur Aaron died of his wounds. Soon after, it was announced that he had been posthumously awarded the VC.

Flight Lieutenant Bill Reid, VC (No 61 Squadron)

Reid was the captain of Lancaster LM360 detailed to attack Düsseldorf on the night of 3/4 November 1943. After crossing the Dutch coast, his windscreen was shattered by fire from a Bf 110, wounding Reid. The rear turret was damaged and the communications system and compasses were put out of action. Soon after, the Lancaster was attacked by a Focke-Wulf Fw 190, the navigator killed and the wireless operator fatally injured. The mid-upper turret was hit and the oxygen system put out of action. Reid, again wounded, refused to be turned from his objective and reached Düsseldorf. Steering by the Pole Star, he set course for home. Growing weak from the loss of blood, he eventually made a safe landing. Reid made a full recovery and soon after came the announcement that he had been awarded the VC. 'Wounded in two attacks, without oxygen, his navigator dead, his wireless operator fatally wounded, his aircraft crippled and defenceless, he showed superb courage and leadership in penetrating into enemy territory to attack one of the most strongly defended targets in Germany. His tenacity and devotion to duty were beyond praise.'

Pilot Officer Cyril Barton, VC (No 578 Squadron)

Barton was the captain of Halifax LK797 detailed to attack Nuremberg on the night of 30/31 March 1944. Near the target, two night fighters attacked. The starboard-inner engine caught fire and the rear turret, radio and intercomm were knocked out. He then discovered that three of his crew had baled out. Unsure of exactly where he was, he continued to his target, released his bombs and turned for home. Having left the enemy coast behind, he continued north. Desperately short of fuel, he eventually coasted in. Knowing that a crash-landing was imminent, he managed to hold the Halifax in a glide long enough until the aircraft came to earth. The three crew members in the rear fuselage were taken to hospital. Barton was pulled out of the wreckage alive but died on the way to hospital. On 27 June, it was announced that Barton had been posthumously awarded the VC.

Sergeant Norman Jackson, VC (No 106 Squadron)

Jackson was the flight engineer in Lancaster ME699 detailed to attack Schweinfurt on the night of 26/27 April 1944. His aircraft was attacked by a fighter. A fire started in the starboard wing. Although wounded, he took an extinguisher and clipped on his parachute. He climbed out of the cockpit and along the top of the fuselage to the wing. Before he left the fuselage, his parachute opened and the canopy spilled into the cockpit. He slipped and, falling from the fuselage, grasped an air intake on the wing. By now, the fire had spread rapidly. His face, hands and clothing were severely burnt. Unable to hold on, he was swept through the flames and over the edge of the wing, dragging his parachute, only partly inflated and burning in several places, behind him. The captain then gave the order to bale out. Amazingly, Jackson survived although his injuries left him in a pitiful state. He was eventually taken prisoner. When the crew members were repatriated, the full story was told,

Guy Gibson.

the fuselage and starboard wing. Yet he pressed on gallantly to the target, marking and bombing it accurately. The port inner engined then failed and the starboard wing became a mass of flames. Bazalgette fought bravely to bring his aircraft and crew to safety. With two wounded, he ordered the others to bale out. He remained at the controls and attempted the almost hopeless task of landing the blazing aircraft in a last effort to save his colleagues. With superb skill, he brought the aircraft down. It then exploded and this gallant officer and his two comrades perished. The four survivors of the crew were hidden by the locals until liberated by the Allies. Following their return to England, the full story was told, followed by the announcement of the posthumous award of the VC to Bazalgette. 'His heroic sacrifice marked the climax of a long career of operations. His courage and devotion to duty were beyond praise.'

Wing Commander Leonard Cheshire, VC, DSO and two Bars, DFC
The only VC awarded for an extended period of operations went to Leonard Cheshire. At the age of 25, he was the youngest Group Captain in the RAF, having been awarded the DSO and two Bars and DFC. In September 1943 he reverted to Wing Commander to command No 617 Squadron. In July 1944 he flew his 100th 'op' and was immediately rested. On 8 September 1944 came the announcement of the award of the VC to Cheshire. 'In four years of fighting against the bitterest opposition he has maintained a record of outstanding personal achievement, which has established for Cheshire a reputation second to none.'

Squadron Leader Robert Palmer, VC, DFC and Bar (No 109 Squadron)
Palmer was captain of Lancaster PB371 detailed as Master Bomber to attack Cologne on 23 December 1944, his 111th 'op'. His aircraft came under heavy flak, two engines were set on fire and there were flames and smoke in the nose and bomb bay. Enemy fighters now attacked in force. Determined to complete the run and provide an accurate and easily seen aiming point, he kept the damaged aircraft on a straight course. He made a perfect approach and his bombs hit the target. His aircraft was seen spiralling to earth in flames. Only one of the crew escaped the aircraft, and soon after came the announcement of the posthumous award of the VC to Palmer. 'His record of prolonged and heroic endeavour is beyond praise.'

Flight Sergeant George Thompson, VC (No 9 Squadron)
Thompson was the wireless operator/air gunner of Lancaster PD377 detailed to attack the Dortmund–Ems Canal on 1 January 1945. Over the target, a shell hit the aircraft. Fire broke out and smoke filled the fuselage. He saw that the gunner was unconscious in the blazing mid-upper turret. He went into the fire and exploding ammunition, pulled the gunner from his turret and carried him away. With his bare hands, he extinguished the gunner's burning clothing, himself sustaining serious burns on his face, hands and legs. He then noticed that the rear turret was also on fire. Despite his injuries, he went to the rear of the fuselage where he found the rear gunner with his clothing alight, overcome by flames and fumes. A second time, he braved the flames. With difficulty he carried the helpless gunner clear. Again, he used his bare hands, already burnt, to beat out flames on his comrade's clothing. The aircraft crash-landed and broke up. Sadly, the mid-upper gunner died. The rear gunner, although badly burned, made a full recovery and owes his life to the courage of George Thompson. Thompson began to recover from his horrific injuries, but caught pneumonia and finally died. Soon after, came the announcement that George Thompson had been posthumously awarded the VC. 'He hazarded his own life to save the lives of others. Young in years and experience, his actions were those of a veteran.'

Captain Edwin Swales, VC, DFC (No 582 Squadron)
Swales was captain of Lancaster PB538 detailed as Master Bomber for a raid on Pforzheim on the night of 23/24 February 1945. Over the target, a fighter attacked, putting one engine and his rear guns out of action. The fighter closed and fired again, a second engine being put out of action. Almost defenceless, Swales stayed over the target issuing instructions until satisfied that the attack had achieved its purpose. His aircraft severely damaged, he then set course for home. The aircraft became more difficult to control and was losing height. Realizing the desperate situation he ordered his crew to bale out, holding the aircraft steady. Hardly had the last jumped when the aircraft plunged to earth. Swales was found dead at the controls. This sacrifice of the gallant South African was rewarded by the posthumous award of the VC. 'Intrepid in the attack, courageous in the face of danger, he did his duty to the last, giving his life that his comrades might live.'

followed by the award of the VC to Jackson. 'His attempt to extinguish the fire and save the aircraft and crew was an act of outstanding gallantry. By his willingness to face the dangers he set an example of self-sacrifice which will ever be remembered.'

Pilot Officer Andrew Mynarski, VC (No 419 Squadron, RCAF)
Mynarski was in the mid-upper turret of Lancaster KB726 detailed to attack Cambrai on the night of 12/13 June 1944. Attacked by a fighter, both port engines failed and fire broke out between the mid-upper and rear turrets. The captain ordered the crew to bale out. Mynarski went towards the escape hatch. He saw the rear gunner still in his turret and unable to leave it. He made his way through the flames to reach the rear gunner. His parachute and clothing were set on fire and all his efforts to free the gunner were in vain. Eventually, the rear gunner indicated that he should try to save his own life. Mynarski reluctantly went back through the flames to the escape hatch. He turned towards the trapped gunner, stood to attention in his flaming clothing and saluted before he jumped out of the aircraft, his parachute and clothing on fire. He was found by the French, but was so severely burnt that he died from his injuries. Amazingly, the rear gunner was thrown clear still inside his turret. The remaining crew also survived and, following repatriation, the last moments of the gallant Canadian's life were told and the announcement made of a posthumous award of the VC to Mynarski. 'With outstanding courage and disregard for his own safety, he went to the rescue. Accepting the danger, he lost his life by a conspicuous act of heroism which called for valour of the highest order.'

Squadron Leader Ian Bazalgette, VC, DFC (No 635 Squadron)
Bazalgette was captain of Lancaster ND811 detailed as Master Bomber to attack Trossy St Maximin on 4 August 1944. His aircraft was hit by flak; both starboard engines were put out of action and fires broke out in

OTHER DECORATIONS

Awarded only to commissioned officers, the Distinguished Service Order was established to reward individual instances of meritorious or distinguished service in war. It proved to be quite a scarce award to the RAF as only some 870 DSOs were awarded, with 62 first bars, eight second bars and just two third bars. One of the two third-bar awards was to Wing Commander 'Willie' Tait, already mentioned for his leadership during Operation 'Paravane'.

The most common gallantry award for the war to officers was the Distinguished Flying Cross, awarded for 'an act, or acts, of valour performed while flying in active operations against the enemy'. Yet every DFC must be taken on its own merit. For members of Bomber Command, to complete a tour of operations was a test of strength and character, coupled with skill and determination, followed by a lot of luck. To go back deep into enemy territory, night after night, against formidable opposition and defences deserves to be rewarded. Altogether, over 20,000 awards of the DFC were made to the RAF with 1,550 first bars and 42 second bars. Awards were either immediate or non-immediate with, typically, a specific act of courage rewarded by an immediate award, while a non-immediate award would be made for a period of courage and devotion to duty.

Second to the VC, the highest gallantry award to the non-commissioned aircrew was the Conspicuous Gallantry Medal, instituted in January 1943. Only 102 CGMs were awarded during the war. One award was to Flight Sergeant David Moriarty of No 75 Squadron. His citation reads: 'In June 1944, this airman was captain of an aircraft detailed to attack an objective in northern France. While over the target, his aircraft was hit by an anti-aircraft shell which exploded in the cockpit. Moriarty was severely injured about the face, being completely blinded in one eye; he also sustained a nasty scalp wound. He insisted on remaining at the controls and, in spite of his distress, he succeeded in flying the aircraft home. This airman displayed courage, fortitude and determination of a high order.'

The Distinguished Flying Medal was awarded to non-commissioned aircrew as an equivalent award to the DFC. However, far fewer DFMs were awarded than DFCs as only some 6,600 awards were made to the RAF, with 60 first bars and just one second bar. The reason for this vast difference in numbers awarded is open to discussion. Some might suggest that favouritism was shown to the officers and that the other ranks 'missed out'. A more sensible suggestion is that many members of Bomber Command were commissioned towards the end of their first tour, or during their second tour, and subsequently rewarded for their courage, making them eligible for the DFC as opposed to the DFM. Sergeant James Mallan of 467 Squadron, RAAF, was awarded the DFM in 1943. His citation reads: 'This airman has participated in 21 successful sorties against some of the most heavily defended targets in Germany. In September 1943, he was the rear gunner of an aircraft detailed to attack Mannheim. His aircraft was attacked by an enemy fighter. Coolly and skilfully, Mallan fought the attacker and, finally, the enemy aircraft burst into flames. This airman has invariably displayed coolness and courage in the face of the enemy.'

For the majority of Bomber Command crews there were no gallantry awards. Many flew a number of operational sorties without specific reward. Several campaign stars and medals were awarded after the war; those awarded to members of Bomber Command were generally:

1. *1939/45 Star*: For operations against the enemy provided that two months' service had been completed in an operational unit. Non-aircrew personnel had to complete six months' service in an area of an operational command between the dates 3 September 1939 and 2 September 1945.

2. *Air Crew Europe Star*: Awarded for operational flying from UK bases over Europe between 3 September 1939 and 5 June 1944. The time qualification was two months as aircrew and the recipient must have previously qualified for the 1939/45 Star.

3. *France and Germany Star*: For Bomber Command personnel, this star was awarded for any operations flown over Europe between 6 June 1944 and 8 May 1945. For non-aircrew personnel the Star was awarded for service in France, Belgium, Holland or Germany between D-Day and

Air Crew Europe Star.

the German surrender. The France and Germany Star was not awarded in addition to the Air Crew Europe Star. Those who qualified for both were awarded the star for which they qualified first and received a bar for the second.

4. *Defence Medal*: Generally awarded for service in non-operational areas subject to air attack, or closely threatened, provided such service lasted for three or more years. It was also for service overseas, provided that service lasted for one year, except in territories threatened by the enemy or bomb attacks, in which case it was six months.

5. *War Medal*: Awarded to all personnel of the Armed Forces wherever they served during the war. Operational or non-operational service counted provided that it was cf 28 days' or more duration. For anyone who was awarded a Mention in Despatches during the war, an oakleaf was worn on the ribbon.

Finally, it must be said that the gallantry awards to the aircrew must also represent the hours of dedication from the groundcrew, men and women alike, which 'made the whole thing possible'. Certainly, most of the effort by the many left behind on the ground, waiting for the returning crews, would have gone unrewarded. Satisfaction at having 'done their bit' was the only reward. Whether an individual was rewarded or not, there was never any doubt about the effort put in by all members of Bomber Command in getting the job well done.